LANDMINES
AND
HUMAN SECURITY

SUNY series in Global Politics
James N. Rosenau, editor

LANDMINES
AND
HUMAN SECURITY

International Politics and War's Hidden Legacy

Edited by
RICHARD A. MATTHEW,
BRYAN MCDONALD,
and
KENNETH R. RUTHERFORD

Forewords by
Her Majesty Queen Noor
The Honorable Lloyd Axworthy
Lady Heather Mills McCartney and Sir Paul McCartney
Senator Patrick Leahy

State University of New York Press

Color photo, by Regina Karasch/The Lutheran World Federation, taken in northwest Cambodia. Villagers were forced to return to their land, even before it was cleared, in order to avoid losing their land rights.

Published by
State University of New York Press, Albany

For information, address State University of New York Press,
90 State Street, Suite 700, Albany, NY 12207

Production by Marilyn P. Semerad
Marketing by Anne M. Valentine

Library of Congress Cataloging-in-Publication Data

Landmines and human security : international politics and war's hidden legacy / edited
     by Richard A. Matthew, Bryan McDonald, & Kenneth R. Rutherford.
         p. cm.—(SUNY series in global politics)
     Includes bibliographical references and index.
     ISBN 0-7914-6309-5 (alk. paper)
         1. Land mines (International law). 2. Arms control—International cooperation.
     3. Land mine victims. I. Matthew, Richard Anthony. II. McDonald, Bryan.
     III. Rutherford, Ken, 1962– IV. Series.

JZ5645.L37 2004
327.1'743—dc22

                                                                                2004041676

                    10 9 8 7 6 5 4 3 2 1

We dedicate this volume to landmine victims everywhere

Contents

PART III
RELATED ISSUES: DEMINING AND VICTIM ASSISTANCE

PART IV
IMPLICATIONS OF THE MINE BAN MOVEMENT

Foreword

HER MAJESTY QUEEN NOOR

It is a peculiarly modern paradox that the era of globalization should also be one of extremes. Twenty-first century civilization can, on one hand, claim unprecedented capabilities, yet, on the other, still face seemingly insurmountable global challenges. Today, virtually every sphere of human endeavor—science, transportation, communication, medicine, and education, to mention just a few—reflects an incredibly sophisticated repertoire of skills, technologies, and resources. But the enormity of our problems is equally evident in the violence, insecurity, poverty, disease, and environmental degradation that afflict our world. The same technologies that should be bringing us together are revealing all the more clearly the extent of the divides between us. Sadly, it is all too easy to become frustrated by the difficulties involved in bringing these tremendous abilities to bear on our pressing social and humanitarian needs.

One of the most promising strategies for resolving this paradox is through issue-oriented coalitions—inclusive, global networks bringing together individuals and groups from the private and the public realms of many countries. Through this strategy we have seen dramatic achievements in areas as diverse as human rights advocacy, health education, disease control, disaster relief, and environmental protection. Perhaps, however, the most inspiring and powerful example is the International Campaign to Ban Landmines (ICBL).

Antipersonnel landmines became a routine part of military arsenals in the second half of the twentieth century. Within a few decades, tens of millions of mines had been laid. They were rarely removed when hostilities ended, and thus landmines became one of the most horrifying legacies of modern war, a man-made epidemic. Antipersonnel mines have an average life span of fifty to one hundred years, meaning that mines left behind after World War II are still killing children today. By the early 1990s, landmines were claiming 26,000 innocent victims a year, mostly children and women in developing countries. Designed to maim for life, they terrified whole communities; made fields, roads, and water sources inaccessible; and left many victims permanently disfigured and unable to care for themselves.

In 1991, several prominent groups, including Asia Watch, Physicians for Human Rights, the Vietnam Veterans of America Foundation, and Medico International, decided to join forces to organize and coordinate a global mine ban movement. Members of these groups had witnessed the devastation of mines firsthand; in some cases, they themselves were survivors. They committed to work together until the problem was solved.

Their story, which soon came to include the stories of hundreds of groups and individuals around the world, is recounted in this volume. It is not only inspiring, but instructive. It demonstrates that motivated groups, acting together and making use of the vast technological resources that exist, can tackle a problem of enormous proportions with truly remarkable speed and effectiveness. As a result of the ICBL's efforts, an international treaty was signed in 1997 by over 130 countries. Today, the production and use of mines has been sharply curtailed, demining has made huge tracts of land accessible again, the annual number of victims has fallen dramatically, and many mine victims around the world are receiving various forms of support. Challenges remain, but there are good reasons to believe they will be met, and that one day we will have a mine-free world.

The authors of this book are dedicated individuals who have played significant roles in the mine ban and humanitarian demining activities of the past dozen years. Their personal perspectives are complemented by the views of journalists and scholars who have considered this case in the larger context of its implications—both positive and negative—for contemporary world politics. The result is a comprehensive and balanced investigation into a truly fascinating case of transnational coalition building.

For many years I have dedicated my time to a range of humanitarian and environmental causes, searching for the most effective ways to use all the resources at our disposal to solve the most urgent human problems. As early as the 1970s I had become deeply concerned about the deadly legacy of landmines infesting the ground of Jordan—where prophets had walked in ancient days, modern-day pilgrims could not tread without fear, and even the most basic uses of the land had become circumscribed with danger. In 1998, I became more formally involved with the landmines movement as a member of the advisory board of the

ICBL, and patron of the Landmine Survivors Network. In July of that year I was pleased to host the first Middle East conference on landmine injury and rehabilitation, "Surviving the Scourge of Landmines," in Amman, Jordan, and in October it was my privilege to announce at the United Nations the fortieth ratification of the Ottawa Mine Ban Treaty. The treaty entered into force on March 1, 1999, becoming binding international law. By the sixth anniversary of its launch in December 2003 the total number of countries ratifying or supporting the treaty stood at 150.

In my visits to regions throughout the world, in countries as diverse as Cambodia and Vietnam; Colombia; Bosnia, Kosovo, and Croatia; Lebanon, Egypt, and Jordan; and Pakistan and Afghanistan, I have seen even more vividly the devastation these weapons wreak on individual lives. But I have also seen the progress that has been made. The modern paradox is not intractable to those willing to work together for a common end. This dramatic account of the mine ban movement, which arose with unparalleled speed to touch so many lives, is both a model study in effective coalition activism and a moving story that will inspire anyone who seeks to make our world a more humane, just, and safe place for all who share it.

Foreword

THE HONORABLE LLOYD AXWORTHY

After a long and difficult effort, combining many different governments, groups, and individuals from around the globe, the treaty banning landmines was brought into existence. It was a time of hope. It meant a commitment to stop the slaughter of many innocent people and to help repair the damage and despair that many surviving victims faced as well as a willingness to begin cleaning up the killing fields.

So much of the credibility of the Ottawa Treaty and what it stands for is based on progress and accomplishment in keeping the flame alive—that means maintaining a drive toward universality, continuing to aid victims, destroy stockpiles, extract the mines from the ground and name and shame those who continue to flaunt the provisions and use landmines as a weapon of war. I would also say that it means a critical update of what needs to be improved, changed, altered, and revised to make the treaty a live, growing document relevant to its times and realities. One of the great features of the Ottawa process was a willingness to dare, to take chances, to show that the traditional diplomatic refrain copied from J. Alfred Prufrock—"do I dare to eat a peach"—was not the watchword. This means a serious need to see how the treaty can be improved, its mandate extended into A Landmine Treaty Part Two.

This means coming to grips with issues like the use of cluster bombs. Cluster bombs are intended to explode once they hit the ground, however, not all do. Similar to landmines, *The Economist* in November

2001 stated that cluster bombs "may kill, maim and make land inaccessible long after fighting has stopped."

The treaty must also begin to incorporate into its provisions the responsibility of nonstate actors and hold them accountable for their actions. Opposition groups are reported to have used antipersonnel mines in at least fourteen countries in the 2001–2002 reporting period. I have recently seen how devious and destructive the device of booby-trapping people in the camps of northern Uganda can be, where the weapons are used as a tool of revenge and intimidation—by the way, it doesn't get much media attention but there is a nasty war going on there. One consideration for our legal friends is how to apply the principle of legal accountability to individuals. Can the use of landmines become an offense under the International Criminal Court?

But the legacy and the meaning of the Ottawa Process go way beyond the banning of weapons and providing aid to victims. It spawned a new politics, new partnerships, new ways of thinking about the international environment. It was the forerunner of a clear notion of global citizenship. It challenged conventional notions of sovereignty and set in motion a form of coalition politics at the global level that could be used to shift power and political relationships. It was an inclusive process, universal, meaning that it didn't divide the globe into those who are for and those who are against.

The march began, not with governments and entrenched bureaucrats, but with citizens groups. They were the ones who eventually yanked officials out of their comfortable chairs and forced them into stride. The techniques and tools used by pro-ban campaigners were not conventional by any means. Focusing on the humanitarian impact of what was hitherto strictly seen as a disarmament issue, helped give the antipersonnel landmines (APL) ban campaign the emotional force that it needed.

The Ottawa Process had a significant impact on Canadians. Given certain geopolitical and economic realities, Canadians are often reluctant to embrace a foreign policy path independent of the 800-pound gorilla next door. Yet, the APL ban taught us that policy convergence with the United States was not inevitable nor was it necessarily crucial in order to have an influence on global policy. If anything, the Ottawa Treaty experience taught Canadians about their inherent capacity to play a leadership role. This capacity is strengthened by following what we call a "human security approach," putting the protection of individuals at the center of our foreign policy.

As one of the pioneers of the human security approach, Canadians have an interest in its survival. Whether it endures as a competing vision of global order or whether it withers away into the dustbin of history depends on maintaining the political inventiveness that has motivated and sustained the landmine movement.

What we must realize is what is at stake here. The present disdain for collaborative efforts that dominates the counterterrorism campaign has taken its toll on a number of global initiatives (for example, the International Criminal Court, Kyoto, and the Anti-Ballistic Missile Treaty). The United States has chosen to remain outside the APL ban. This decision among others has struck a blow to collaborative efforts in a number of areas and we cannot expect that the Ottawa Treaty is immune from such a setback. How do we get around that? Instead of focusing our efforts on improving the Ottawa Treaty, we should recall what got us to the Ottawa Treaty in the first place: the Ottawa Process. It must be remembered that human security is not only an outcome, it is a process. In fact, it is the human security process that enables a human security outcome. The Ottawa Process was an unconventional, bottom-up approach to diplomacy, instead of the classic top-down, undemocratic approach that typifies so much of today's decision making. So while improvements to the Ottawa Treaty, via an Ottawa Treaty II, would be a welcome action, to argue for it would be slightly misplaced.

In essence, what we really should be arguing for is an Ottawa Process II. That would be a clear signal that there is a will to continue working toward a global security order based on cooperative, democratic principles. I trust this book will help set a course in that direction.

Foreword

LADY HEATHER MILLS MCCARTNEY AND SIR PAUL MCCARTNEY

Domingas's face was calm, even a little wistful, as she told us about her life. She stepped on a mine in 1992. Abandoned by her husband after her injury and no longer able to farm her own field, she still suffers from grief and shock.

The legacy of landmines is an extremely serious issue that we can all do something about, if we are successful in awakening people's consciousness about the horrors of landmines and the unspeakable human suffering caused by these indiscriminate weapons of war. We can go a long way to right the wrongs that have already been perpetrated. We are committed to achieving this goal and believe not only that it can be done but that it will be done. For people around the world, shocked by the savagery of landmines, the International Campaign to Ban Landmines (ICBL), and the thousands of nongovernmental organizations that constitute its membership, plays an indispensable role in highlighting the humanitarian, moral, and economic issues related to the global landmine crisis. The campaign has brought the landmine issue to a broad range of people around the world. In particular, it has forged a permanent and mutually beneficial link between mine ban advocates and landmine survivors. Working together, the ICBL has produced a precedent-setting and widely inspiring international treaty on landmines: the Mine Ban Treaty. This treaty has ensured that the enormous challenge of assisting survivors remains a fundamental objective of the world community—as important as demining and banning the production, stockpiling, trade, transfer, and use of mines.

The emphasis on survivors is crucial. The horrifying reality of landmines, which are designed to maim rather than kill, is that they inflict their greatest damage on the planet's most vulnerable and innocent people. Year after year, mines have taken their highest toll on those women and children forced by poverty to use paths, fields, and waterways before they have been cleared. These people live each day on the front lines of an invisible war. They face constant fear as they struggle to survive, they suffer disproportionately to all other groups, and, far too often, they face the trauma of grave injury, penniless and alone.

The tendency to retreat from those whose bodies have suffered great harm is an unforgivable prejudice that affronts every moral code on the planet. Yet this prejudice, born of fear and ignorance, is evident throughout the world. In consequence, many landmine survivors find themselves deprived of employment and support, if not openly shunned by their own communities. The Mine Ban Treaty calls the world's attention to these innocent victims, and it demands that efforts be made to economically and socially reintegrate them back into society. The challenge is enormous, but with the signing of the treaty, over 140 countries have committed themselves to respond to it.

Landmines and Human Security brings together the diverse insights and experiences of nongovernmental leaders, politicians, civil servants, academics, and landmine survivors to tell the story of the ICBL, to assess its impact, to reflect on its lessons, and to remind us of the challenges that remain in addressing the global landmine crisis. We are pleased to contribute to this important volume as part of our commitment to help empower those who have been disabled by fate and prejudice.

Foreword

SENATOR PATRICK LEAHY

A dozen years ago, I visited a field hospital in Central America where I met my first survivor of a landmine, a young Honduran boy who had lost a leg from a mine on a jungle path. That boy was not only an innocent civilian, he had no idea what the war was about. But it made no difference because his life was changed forever in a country where physical labor was the only means of survival that he or his family knew.

Not long after, as I learned more about the enormity of the mine problem and the number of victims around the world, I could only ask what possible justification there could be for a weapon that indiscriminately kills and horribly maims civilians, often years after a war ends. Fortunately, I was not the only person asking that question. In 1991, I met Bobby Muller, head of the Vietnam Veterans of America Foundation, which runs programs by and for mine victims in Vietnam, Cambodia, and parts of Africa. Bobby convinced me to introduce legislation to halt U.S. exports of mines, which eventually led other countries to take similar steps, culminating in a global treaty banning antipersonnel mines signed in Ottawa in December 1997.

It was in 1993, when I chaired the first hearing in the Congress on the mine problem, that I had the good fortune to meet Ken Rutherford. Ken testified at that hearing, and it was among the most moving experiences of my Senate career. He described in graphic detail losing his leg in Somalia, and his realization that unlike the many Somali mine victims, he could radio for help and be quickly flown to safety. That began Ken's personal crusade on behalf of mine victims everywhere, which led to the creation of the Landmine Survivors Network, a nonprofit organization created by landmine survivors for landmine survivors, that is devoted to advocating for the rights and needs of mine victims.

In those early days of the campaign against mines, former President Bill Clinton announced that his administration would lead an international effort to ban the weapon. But the Pentagon refused, arguing that mines are necessary for the protection of U.S. troops, particularly in the defense of South Korea. While mines, like any weapon, have some military utility, 150 nations (at last count), including every NATO member except the United States and Turkey and every Western Hemisphere nation except the United States and Cuba, have concluded that the military utility of antipersonnel mines is outweighed by the immense humanitarian harm they cause. Moreover, many combat veterans speak of being blown up by their own mines, which impeded their mobility in the heat of battle.

The international campaign to ban landmines, which began as a mere trickle, turned into a flood of organizations and governments joining together in support of a ban. It was an unprecedented and remarkable process that I felt privileged to be part of. The trade in mines has virtually ended, and production and use are a fraction of what they were a decade ago. But our work is far from over. The United States, Russia, China, and several other major powers have yet to sign the treaty, and mines are still being used in internal conflicts in places like Angola, Chechnya, and Afghanistan. There is a great deal of work to be done to clear the unexploded mines and care for the victims.

The world today faces many threats that do not recognize international borders, and terrorism, AIDS, and the traffic in women and children are examples that require new forms of multilateral cooperation. Each of these poses unique challenges, but there are common threads. *Landmines and Human Security* is an important book for anyone who seeks to understand, and perhaps become involved in, these and other pressing issues. People who have taken part in the campaign against landmines, and others who have studied this process and its results, have come together in this volume to provide an account of what took place, an objective assessment of the treaty's impact, and a thoughtful discussion of the broader implications of this historic effort. There are important lessons to be learned, and *Landmines and Human Security* gives us the tools to apply these lessons as we move forward, both to universalize the Ottawa Treaty and to meet other challenges in today's dangerous and complex world.

Acknowledgments

The editors would like to thank the Focused Research Group on International Environmental Cooperation, the Global Environmental Change and Human Security Project, and the Center for Global Peace and Conflict Studies for funding the 2000 workshop at which this volume was first conceived, and the Center for Unconventional Security Affairs for supporting the preparation of this volume. All four entities are located at the University of California–Irvine. We would also like to thank Kate Merkel-Hess for her assistance in preparing the text of the volume.

We are grateful for the thoughtful and supportive comments and suggestions of the external reviewers, and for the patience and advice of Michael Rinella, our editor at State University of New York Press.

The contributors to this volume, many of whom have remarkably demanding schedules and careers that are not dependent on research and publication, have been exceptional in remaining enthusiastic and responsive for over two years as we slowly have brought this volume to completion.

We thank Her Majesty Queen Noor, the Honorable Lloyd Axworthy, Lady Heather Mills McCartney and Sir Paul McCartney, and Senator Patrick Leahy for their thoughtful and moving forewords to this volume.

Part I

The Global
Landmine Crisis

1

Human Security and the Mine Ban Movement I: Introduction

Richard A. Matthew

The Age of Global Issues

FOR MOST OF HUMAN HISTORY, THE EARTH'S PARTS HAVE APPEARED TO BE FAR more important than its whole. Since the first humans evolved some one to five million years ago, countless people have been born and educated in the same place in which they eventually would work, worship, raise families, and die. Most of them had no direct contact with the world beyond a fifty-mile radius of their birthplaces, and the indirect contacts that touched on their worlds were typically—although not always—diffuse and rare. While over the millennia there were massive movements of people from one region to another, the peopling of the planet was generally a slow and cumulative process, in that most individuals had little or no personal experience of dislocation or change. Indeed only a thousand years ago, small communities could plan enormous projects—such as the great cathedrals of medieval Europe and the towering temples of Southeast Asia—that would take centuries to complete, secure in the belief that their small villages and their descendants would always be available to continue the labor and, one day, to appreciate its hard-won fruit.

This situation began to change five hundred years ago when advances in maritime technologies made it possible to lose sight of the coastline, explore the vast domain of the oceans, visit new lands, and still have a reasonable chance of finding one's way back home months or years later. But it is only in the twentieth century that we can speak of the planet as a

3

shared home in ways that make sense to almost everyone. The emergence of a truly global village and the development of a sense of shared purpose and fate that stretches across borders and cultures are recent phenomena.

Technological innovation has played a special and essential role in enabling this remarkable transformation in perceptions of the planet and its inhabitants. The process is often called *globalization*, a term that embodies a wide range of values, beliefs, practices, and institutions that have been affected by new technologies.[1] Advances in communications make it possible to see and to speak to people anywhere in the world in more or less real time. New transportation systems rush food, medical supplies, tourists, and militaries across thousands of miles in a matter of hours. Medical breakthroughs can be shared instantaneously; funds can be gathered and sent anywhere in seconds; scientific information can be placed in databases immediately available to everyone who has access to a computer. The political leaders of countries can, and do, meet on a regular basis to discuss issues of common concern. Businesses explore new opportunities, form partnerships, and move skills and capital around the globe in ways that were unimaginable just decades ago.

The various technology-driven processes that are bringing the world together in so many ways have also laid the groundwork for new political activities by uncovering problems that are global in magnitude and that require multilateral cooperation to address them effectively. The global agenda that has emerged in the age of globalization, and which would have been unthinkable in the not-too-distant past, is now widely familiar.[2] It involves, for example, multilateral efforts to control weapons of mass destruction, fight poverty, eradicate infectious diseases, stop terrorism, promote human rights, help refugees, advance the status of women, and protect the environment. The roots of these problems vary. What is common is that, first, they transcend national borders and are relevant in some way to everyone on the planet; and, second, they often require extensive, if not universal, cooperation in order to be resolved.

The global agenda poses a considerable challenge to people around the world. Responsibility for a given problem, such as biodiversity loss or terrorism, often is distributed unequally from one country to the next.[3] The same may be true of the social and other impacts of a given problem, and also of the resources needed to address it. What does one do if country X unintentionally and disproportionately causes a global problem that is felt most acutely in country Y, and only country Z has the effective means to resolve it? It can be very difficult to persuade the various parties to work together, especially if they are unequal in power; if they disagree in their analyses of the problem's causes, effects, and solution; and if they have as their primary political goal advancing the interests, especially short-term ones, of the people they represent over the interests of all others.

The United Nations and many other regional and ad hoc forums exist to bring state leaders together to discuss items on the global agenda. This political process, however, can be undermined, slowed, or diluted by particular objectives and tangential areas of disagreement. Fortunately, many global problems have been adopted in recent years by transnational networks or coalitions of concerned groups and individuals who are dedicated to gathering information about a given problem, educating the public about it, identifying solutions to it, and mobilizing the support and resources needed to implement the solutions. Thus, while global problems can appear to be enormous problems inevitably destined to become worse and worse over time, and people are rightly frustrated by the difficulties involved in bringing the vast resources and skills of the world to bear on these problems, there are grounds for cautious optimism. And these grounds are growing. According to the scholar James Rosenau:

> The transformation [taking place in contemporary world politics] is marked by a bifurcation in which the state-centric system now coexists with an equally powerful, though more decentralized, multicentric system. Although these two worlds of world politics have overlapping elements and concerns, their norms, structures, and processes tend to be mutually exclusive, thus giving rise to a set of global arrangements that are new and possibly enduring, as well as extremely complex and dynamic.[4]

In this volume, a diverse group of authors describes, analyzes, and evaluates what has arguably been the single most successful transnational coalition so far: the International Campaign to Ban Landmines (ICBL).[5] The insights of activists, scholars, government officials, and journalists, most of whom have had extensive experience with some aspect of the mine ban movement, as well as the commentaries of landmine victims themselves, have been gathered to tell a dramatic and inspiring story.[6] It is a story that is fascinating in its own right. It is a story that is instructive for those tackling other global issues. And it is a story that makes an important contribution to our understanding of the profound changes taking place today in the international system.[7]

In the following pages I provide a brief preview of this story, discuss the objectives and structure of the volume, and summarize its contents.

The Transnational Mine Ban Movement

The movement to ban antipersonnel landmines (APLs) is rooted in concerns raised by the International Red Cross in the 1950s,[8] but these concerns were quite marginal to the global agenda until the 1990s, when members of nongovernmental organizations (NGOs) working in mine-infested countries became aware of the toll APLs were taking on civilian populations, and began to suffer casualties themselves. In 1991, Asia Watch (AW) and Physicians for Human Rights (PHR) published *A Coward's War: Landmines in Cambodia*, and appealed to the world to ban these destructive weapons that tended to do so much of their damage after hostilities had ended. Throughout the world, tens of millions of landmines (a commonly cited estimate was over 100 million) had been left behind by the troops that had placed them.[9] Hidden along roads and paths, in fields and pastures, and even in schools and hospitals, APLs could sit silently for many years before exploding under the pressure of a child's footstep or beneath the hands of a woman pulling vegetables from a garden.

Infuriated by the world's apparent lack of concern for some 26,000 civilian victims a year, the Vietnam Veterans of America Foundation (VVAF) decided in 1991 to unite with Medico International to coordinate a global mine ban movement. Both groups had extensive experience working in mine-infested states, and their members were aware of the great humanitarian costs APLs extracted. Within a year, they were joined by the French NGO Handicap International, Human Rights Watch-USA, Britain's Mines Advisory Group, and the PHR, together forming the ICBL.

The high-profile membership of the ICBL immediately gave it a fair amount of political leverage. In response to its first attempts to apply pressure on political leaders, the European Union asked its members to ratify the 1980 Convention on Conventional Weapons (CCW), which included a protocol designed to limit the use of landmines and agree to a voluntary five-year ban on mine exports. That same year, 1992, President George H. W. Bush signed the Leahy–Evans moratorium on landmine exports. Senator Patrick Leahy had worked with the VVAF in designing this piece of legislation.

At this time, the ICBL developed a two-prong strategy for attaining its ultimate goal of a global mine ban. It would focus on building a transnational coalition of NGOs that would (a) educate publics, mobilize domestic support, and apply pressure on national governments and other relevant parties, and (b) urge governments to work toward a complete ban through the existing Convention on Conventional Weapons. Because the United States was not a signatory to the CCW, attention for (b) was focused through Handicap International on the French government. In early 1993, President François Mitterand was presented with a petition, containing over 22,000 signatures, demanding an end to the "coward's war." A week later, in Cambodia, Mitterand called for a review of the CCW, noted France's voluntary abstention from exporting mines, and urged other nations to follow suit. In December, the UN General Assembly, at the request of the French ambassador, agreed to convene a CCW review meeting the following year.

The other track of ICBL's master strategy was pursued with equal vigor. In May 1993, fifty representatives from forty NGOs met in London at the ICBL's first NGO International Conference on Landmines, where agreement was reached to intensify efforts to mobilize public concern and support. Accordingly, Human Rights Watch-USA and Physicians for Human Rights produced *Landmines: A Deadly Legacy*. Public interest grew, and soon Bofors, a Swedish company, announced that, for moral reasons, it would no longer produce landmines. A pathway to the business community had been established, and the NGO movement was starting to affect behavior.

A second NGO International Conference on Landmines was held in Geneva in May, 1994. At the conference's keynote session, VVAF President Bobby Mueller argued that the ICBL

> must go beyond the structures of government. . . . We must build public awareness of what landmines are doing around the world directly. Only by building such awareness are we going to get the additional movement forward that this campaign critically needs. . . . If we continue the path of courting the military, if we continue the path of courting the political figures on an insiders-game basis, we will lose. We have to up the ante. We've got to take it public.[10]

Over the next eighteen months, commitment to the vision of a mine-free world grew: UNICEF, UNCHR (UN Commission on Human Rights), and the Vatican expressed support for a total mine ban; Mines Action Canada held its first meeting in Ottawa and began to apply pressure to the Canadian government to emulate the forward-looking policies of European middle powers; a report from the UN secretary-general concluded that a total ban would be the most effective approach to dealing with the problem; a large number of NGO Web sites were posted; and President Clinton, in a speech to the United Nations that raised hopes around the world, called for all countries to work toward the elimination of antipersonnel landmines.[11]

Unfortunately, the first CCW Review Conference, held in Vienna in September 1995, dampened NGO enthusiasm considerably. It became clear to the small group of NGO representatives attending the meetings that government officials had no mandate to work toward a mine ban, and were very quickly negotiating themselves into a procedural gridlock. Immediately the ICBL adjusted its strategy to place pressure on the governments of sympathetic countries while intensifying the mobilization of public support. Its members hoped that countries like Canada, France, and Sweden would form a bloc that would push the CCW review in a more positive direction. When this strategy failed in subsequent review meetings, the ICBL began to consider ways of working toward a ban outside existing mechanisms for arms control negotiations.

In April 1996, the ICBL organized a meeting with representatives from fourteen pro-ban states at the Quaker United Nations Office in Geneva. At this meeting, the Canadian representative, Robert Lawson, suggested that Canada might host a conference of pro-ban states outside the CCW framework. Enthusiastically supported by the ICBL, the conference was held that October in Ottawa, and proved to be a turning point in the campaign. Canadian Foreign Affairs Minister Lloyd Axworthy proposed working outside the UN system, with the NGO mine ban community, toward the goal of signing a convention banning APLs by the end of 1997.

Throughout the remainder of the year and into 1997, the ICBL organized meetings around the world to mobilize support, educate the public, and apply pressure to governments. The public space was flooded with statistics and images of mine victims; celebrities such as Princess Diana and Queen Noor lent their support to the campaign; and then, in October, the ICBL was awarded the Nobel Peace Prize, a high-profile acknowledgment of the humanitarian importance of its campaign.

Although the United States rejected the ICBL/Ottawa Process and expressed its commitment to working within the constraints of the CCW, and although other major and middle powers including China, Russia, Pakistan, and Iraq followed the American lead, the transnational political effort of the ICBL proved unstoppable. NGOs around the world had brought the issue to the public's attention. They had collected and published extensive data on the extent of the mine problem, and the high costs it forced onto individuals and societies. They had developed compelling moral, economic, and military arguments in support of a ban.[12] And they had shared in the creation of a vast transnational network that was successful in applying pressure to governments at every level and on every continent. On December 3, 1997, 121 countries signed the Convention on the Prohibition of the Use, Stockpiling, Production and Transfer of Anti-Personnel Mines and on Their Destruction—the Mine Ban Treaty—at a ceremony in Ottawa attended by four hundred ICBL representatives.[13]

The effects of the Mine Ban Treaty (MBT) have been as dramatic as the transnational process that produced it. According to a report prepared in December 2000 by Canada's Mine Action Team, established in the Department of Foreign Affairs and International Trade, the MBT is working as desired.[14] Canada has focused considerable effort on the implementation phase of the treaty, developing *An Agenda for Mine Action* immediately following the signing ceremony. According to statistics presented in this report, which are based on a global assessment effort, global production of APLs has declined enormously since 1997, and for the first time in three decades more mines are being cleared than are being laid. Extensive tracts of heavily mined areas in Nicaragua, Cambodia, Afghanistan, and Jordan, countries that had seemingly irreversible problems five years ago, have been cleared and declared safe for human use.[15] Thirty-three of thirty-four countries known to have been APL producers have taken official steps to end the production and transfer of mines. By 1999, casualty rates had declined tremendously in mine-infested countries: for example, by 89 percent in Bosnia, 45 percent in Mozambique, and 41 percent in Cambodia, from peaks experienced in the mid-1990s.

Although a number of major powers have refused to sign the ICBL, they appear, according to Robert Lawson, for the most part, to be acting in accordance with its regulations.[16] The country of greatest concern to many has been the United States, which once led the mine ban effort—at least according to its own rhetoric. In January 2001, President Clinton summarized the U.S. position as follows:

> Our goal has been to end the use of all anti-personnel landmines outside of Korea by 2003, and we have aimed to sign the Ottawa Convention by 2006 if suitable options can be found that will allow us to maintain the war-fighting capability and safety of our men and women in uniform.[17]

It will take some time to fully assess the impact of the MBT, and especially to assess the extent to which it has shaped behavior (versus, say, acknowledging and codifying changes already in progress). Preliminary assessments, however, are widely regarded as highly positive, and there is a conviction among NGO and government parties to the process that it would not have succeeded without the energetic, innovative, unrelenting, and transnational NGO effort.

Objectives and Structure of Volume

Is the mine ban movement an early indicator of the changing character of world politics? Can we expect more successes to arise through transnational politics, perhaps in areas such as counterterrorism, poverty alleviation, environmental rescue, preventing computer sabotage, and controlling illegal sales of small arms? What can we learn from the mine ban movement about the requirements for effective transnational efforts? To begin to answer these questions, we need a comprehensive, multiperspectival analysis of the mine ban movement. How did it happen? Was it exceptional? What lessons can be learned from it? What has its impact been? This volume is designed to answer the specific questions, and formulate some tentative answers to the more general ones.

Against this background, the volume has three explicit objectives. First, we seek to demonstrate the value of participatory research. We share a conviction that an authentic account of the mine ban movement can only emerge from bringing together the diverse perspectives and experiences of practitioners and observers who had been involved at every stage of the process. Chapters in this volume are written by those who founded and directed the ICBL; those who joined the coalition from both developed and developing countries; those who have been affected by the MBT—especially deminers and survivors; celebrities attracted to support this humanitarian cause; journalists and scholars who had studied the behavior of the ICBL as an important example of transnational politics; officials representing countries that support the MBT as well as countries that do not; individuals skeptical of the goals or actions of the ICBL; and military specialists familiar with the use and value of APLs in battlefield situations.

Second, we want to make a theoretical contribution to the academic literature on global civil society and transnational activism. In particular we are interested in using the case of the ICBL to assess the extent to which NGO networks can and do shape world politics, examine the processes through which this occurs, and consider ways in which these processes might be criticized.

Finally, we hope to offer practical lessons and insights to the NGO community. While many of the contributors do this, part 4 of this volume brings together these lessons in a very straightforward and compelling manner.

To realize these objectives, *Landmines and Human Security* is organized into four parts:[18]

- Part One, "The Global Landmine Crisis," provides an annotated chronology of the mine ban movement from 1991 to 1997, and a detailed description of the magnitude of the problem before and after the treaty, with special emphasis given to the challenges faced in the developing world.
- Part Two, "Perspectives on the Mine Ban Movement," brings together a diverse group of experts from the academic, governmental, and nongovernmental arenas in both the North and the South, each addressing the questions, What happened? Why? What is the significance of this phenomenon? How effective has it been? What do we learn from it? What remains to be done?
- Part Three, "Related Issues: Demining and Victim Assistance," provides supplementary analyses of specific aspects of this case in order to ensure that the reader has as complete an understanding of it as

possible. This section includes a critical view of the focus of the mine ban movement and an argument about the continuing military utility of APLs. In addition, the special case of the United States is examined in detail by several authors; experts comment on the technical and other requirements of effective demining and victim assistance; and an environmental specialist considers the extensive ecological effects of APLs, reminding us that this humanitarian challenge also has an environmentally destructive dimension to it.

- Part Four, "Implications of the Mine Ban Movement," responds directly to the specific and general questions raised in part 2 with commentaries by two leaders of the ICBL and a scholar who specializes in NGO coalitions and transnational politics.

Brief Summaries of Chapters

Landmines and Human Security begins with four forewords written by individuals who have committed their time and effort to supporting the mine ban movement. Her Majesty Queen Noor, the Honorable Lloyd Axworthy, Lady Heather Mills McCartney and Sir Paul McCartney, and Senator Patrick Leahy offer very personal statements about why they have supported the ICBL, and what, from their unique perspectives, the ICBL offers the world as a model for tackling global humanitarian issues. Their contributions also underscore an NGO strategy that has been facilitated by contemporary communications technologies, and that was used to great effect by the ICBL: generating interest and support in a cause by attracting highly regarded, celebrity spokespeople, whose presence extends across borders of all kinds.

The first section of the volume offers a detailed account of the mine ban process itself. In chapter 2, "The Global Landmine Crisis in the 1990s," Bryan McDonald offers a chronology and analysis of the main events and steps taken from the decision to form the ICBL in 1991 to the signing of the MBT in 1997. The structure of this chapter provides a framework for analyzing the mine ban process, aspects of which are examined in detail in subsequent chapters. The process is divided into four parts: identifying the problem and making a commitment to addressing it; developing a transnational organization with this purpose; framing the problem in order to attract broad public and governmental support; and writing, implementing, and monitoring the treaty itself.

Completing the first section of the volume, Leah Fraser draws on several sources to describe the impact the MBT has had on the developing world since 1997. In chapter 3, "Evaluating the Impacts of the Ottawa Treaty," Fraser notes that while there are many reasons to be encouraged by the treaty's effects, the world is still awash with landmines, the needs of victims remain costly and, in many areas, inadequately met, and a few countries continue to manufacture and use APLs.

The second section of the volume examines in great detail the impacts of the mine ban movement from the vantages of NGOs, states, and survivors in both the North and the South. Kenneth R. Rutherford, a landmine survivor who cofounded the Landmine Survivors Network and also wrote his PhD dissertation on the mine ban process, brings his insights as activist and scholar to bear on the issue of NGO involvement in chapter 4, "Nongovernmental Organizations and the Landmine Ban." Rutherford argues that NGOs led on this issue, and the success of the MBT has been largely due to NGO activity.

In chapter 5, "Clearing the Path to a Mine-Free World: Implementing the Ottawa Convention," Kerry Brinkert and Kevin Hamilton, who both worked for the Mine Action Team in Canada's Department of Foreign Affairs and International Trade, offer a detailed analysis of the diverse global activity that has been generated by the MBT, with a special focus on Canada. This line of inquiry is expanded in chapter 6, "Europe and the Ottawa Treaty: Compliance with Exceptions and Loopholes," written by scholars Paul Chamberlain and David Long. They examine how different countries in Europe have responded to the various provisions of the MBT, pointing out some of the exceptions and loopholes that have resulted in suboptimal outcomes. In spite of this, their overall assessment of the treaty's value is highly positive.

In chapter 7, "Perspective from a Mine-Affected Country: Mozambique," former Ambassador Carlos dos Santos writes about the impact the MBT has had in the Southern Hemisphere. According to dos Santos, the inclusive character of the ICBL allowed small, mine-infested countries like Mozambique to play a significant role in world politics—often for the first time. Instead of being relegated to the margins of discussion and negotiation, as so often happens in world affairs, they were welcomed into the center of activity, and their views and concerns were taken seriously. Not only has this led to significant progress in demining, mine awareness, and victim assistance in the developing world, but as countries in the South have come to realize the depth of multilateral commitment it has strengthened democratic practices, empowered NGOs and civil society, improved human security, and convinced many of the enormous value of international cooperation.

Finally, in chapter 8, "Victim Assistance: Landmine Survivors' Perspectives," Raquel Willerman discusses the impacts of the MBT from the perspective of landmine survivors. Landmines are a diabolical weapon, designed with the goal of disfiguring and maiming people for life. The victims of APLs may lose their livelihoods, be abandoned by their spouses and other family members, and find themselves shunned by their communities. Physical rehabilitation, psychological counseling, and job training are expensive and not always available when and where they are needed. The MBT is unique in its sustained focus on the needs of survivors, and Willerman argues that much has been learned about how to assist victims and reintegrate them into lives of dignity and productivity. At the same time, the needs of landmine victims continue to be great, often taxing local resources and making the maintenance of global assistance programs essential.

The third part of this volume brings together a diverse group of authors writing, sometimes enthusiastically and sometimes critically, about different aspects of the mine ban process. Michael J. Flynn begins this section with an incisive discussion of a rift in the ICBL between those focused on the ban and those focused on demining. In chapter 9, "Political Minefield," Flynn points out that there have been serious disagreements over priorities and suggests that these may have weakened the ICBL.

In chapter 10, "Tackling the Global Landmine Problem: The United States Perspective," Stacy Bernard Davis and Donald F. "Pat" Patierno describe in detail the U.S. position and the extensive humanitarian effort it has designed and funded over the past decade. Key figures in the Humanitarian Demining Program, Davis and Patierno provide a rare and highly informative look at what the United States is doing—rather than what it has failed to do. This chapter serves to remind us that even countries that fail to sign international treaties may act in ways that advance treaty objectives, as the United States has done. In this case, pressure applied by the NGO community—which has been remarkably active and ambitious in the United States—cannot be discounted insofar as shaping the behavior of the United States is concerned. Nor can the NGO movement be deemed a failure simply because it has not yet persuaded the United States to become a signatory of the MBT. The United States is a singular state at this point in world history, but it is not above sharing the world's concerns about the humanitarian crisis posed by abandoned fields of APLs and joining, on its terms, the struggle to respond to this crisis.

Mine clearance is a key provision of the MBT and it receives careful consideration in three chapters in this section. In chapter 11, "Demining: Enhancing the Process," Colin King, widely regarded as the world's leading expert on the technologies of demining, examines the nuts and bolts of optimizing the mine-clearing process. His extensive field experience undergirds a powerful account of the complicated real-world situations deminers face.

In chapter 12, "Public–Private Demining Partnerships: A Case Study of Afghanistan," Oren J. Schlein describes creative efforts to fund demining programs. As director of the United Nations Association of the USA

Adopt-A-Minefield program, Schlein has played a key role in a successful experiment to personalize demining activities and encourage private and public entities to provide financial support for clearing specific minefields around the world. Not only has this strategy brought together actors ranging from the U.S. government to anonymous individuals and grade school classes, it has raised enough funds to have a significant impact in mine-infested countries such as Afghanistan. Schlein's analysis of civil society working in close collaboration with government bodies is an excellent illustration of the depth and versatility of transnational politics.

Nay Htun, who works with the University for Peace in Costa Rica, rounds out this trio of chapters with a discussion of the need to address the high political, social, and economic costs that accrue when land is denied by APLs. In chapter 13, "Landmines Prolong Conflicts and Impede Socioeconomic Development," Htun argues that an integrated approach to demining is essential. By this he means that the funds and expertise for clearing mines must be accompanied by assistance for resettling people and for economic and social rehabilitation and recovery. The dramatic cases of Afghanistan, Cambodia, and Laos—three of the most heavily mined places on the planet—are used to clarify and illustrate the author's argument.

Part of the program Htun recommends is covered in the MBT provisions for victim assistance. In chapter 14, "The Victim Assistance Provision of the Mine Ban Treaty," Glenna L. Fak interprets these provisions, examines legal and other limitations on their implementation, and makes extensive recommendations for how to help victims most effectively. Fak describes a range of valuable activities that can be undertaken by states and NGOs.

The humanitarian focus of the ICBL was intentional and a key to its success. However, landmines have also inflicted great damage on the natural environment—an aspect of their destructiveness that is not widely known or studied. In chapter 15, "The Environmental Impacts of Landmines," Claudio Torres Nachón provides a richly detailed description and analysis of this aspect of the landmine problem. Torres, a key figure in the ICBL, presents the results of extensive research on this issue in Africa and the Americas, provides a lucid discussion of the legal basis for action on this front, and offers concrete recommendations on the steps that need to be taken.

Finally, one of the great dividing lines on this issue pertains to arguments over the military utility of landmines. While no one denies that APLs have been used effectively on the battlefield, mine ban advocates contend that the humanitarian costs greatly outweigh military benefits in any theater of conflict. From their perspective, alternatives to APLs are available for virtually every scenario one can imagine—effective alternatives that would be greatly preferable to APLs from both moral and economic perspectives. The militaries of the United States and other nonsignatory states have disputed these claims, suggesting that APLs play important and irreplaceable roles in efforts to maximize national security and provide soldiers with adequate protection on the battlefield.

In chapter 16, "A Necessary Evil?: Reexamining the Military Utility of Antipersonnel Landmines," Ted Gaulin explains why some fifty of the world's militaries have been reluctant to forego the use of landmines. A former U.S. Army officer with extensive combat experience, Gaulin describes in detail the military value of landmines, analyzes the limitations of alternatives, and concludes that APLs will retain their tactical utility in the years ahead.

In the final chapter of this section, "Are Landmines Still Needed to Defend South Korea?: A Mine Use Case Study," J. Antonio Ohe investigates the principal U.S. argument against signing the MBT. A master sergeant in the Army National Guard and a specialist in weapons of mass effect, Ohe draws on extensive military documentation to assess the role of APLs in defending South Korea. His conclusion is forceful and unqualified: APLs are not required in this case and their use may, in fact, be undesirable. From Ohe's perspective, the U.S. refusal to sign the MBT is due to institutional inertia and aversion to change rather than sound assessments of the military utility of APLs.

The volume concludes with a section on the broader implications of the mine ban movement for world politics. In chapter 18, "The Campaign to Ban Antipersonnel Landmines: Potential Lessons," Stephen Goose and Jody Williams draw on their unparalleled experience with this issue to suggest lessons that will be of great interest to participants in other transnational coalitions. Williams is the former coordinator and current international ambassador of the ICBL and also the corecipient of the 1997 Nobel Peace Prize. Goose is program director for the Arms Division of Human Rights Watch. Their chapter offers hard-won lessons in two areas: the first includes campaigning, coalition building, and organizing; the second refers to what they call the "new diplomacy" model. This model includes behavior structured outside the formal UN system with extensive NGO participation, key roles played by middle powers, a rejection of consensus rules, and geographic diversity. The lessons Goose and Williams share are the lucid and practical conclusions of years spent on the front lines of transnational politics. This brilliant chapter summarizes many of the claims made throughout the rest of the volume, and anchors the book to the real world as only the insights of highly experienced practitioner-observers could hope to do.

It is complemented by chapter 19, "The Campaign to Ban Antipersonnel Landmines and Global Civil Society." Written by Paul Wapner, a scholar whose award-winning work on global activism and transnational politics has been influential in the field of international relations, this chapter adds the dispassionate eye of a gifted academic to the volume. Wapner uses the case of the mine ban process to illuminate and defend the concept of global civil society. When the field of international relations emerged after World War I, it focused mainly on states and their foreign policies. Over the years, interest has grown in the activities of nonstate actors, but many remain skeptical about the significance of this dimension of world politics. Wapner argues that global civil society is a significant force in world affairs that is indeed global (rather than Western), civil (rather than self-interested), and societal (rather than unstructured). From his analytical perspective, the MBT is evidence of what global civil society can do in a world that is formally and legally organized into some 210 sovereign states. It is a case that rightly offers great hope for those who want to tackle other global challenges.[19]

The volume concludes with chapter 20, "Human Security and the Mine Ban Movement II: Conclusions." This chapter offers a brief evaluation of the book's success in achieving three objectives: encouraging participatory research, contributing to the academic literature on transnational politics, and drawing practical lessons from the mine ban case that might be used by political activists working on other transnational issues. Three "next steps" are suggested, based on this evaluation. The first is to apply a participatory methodology to other cases as we believe this provides valuable insight into contemporary global politics, and would generate a body of work that could be used to refine and revise existing theories. The second recommendation concerns the need to examine more carefully the implications of NGO-driven transnational politics for issues such as accountability. Transnational movements are able to mobilize enormous resources and shape policy that affects people worldwide. It is important that power generated and exercised in this way be accountable to the public it affects. A third and final recommendation is to ensure that the ICBL does not diminish at a time when great progress has been made, but much remains to be done. It seems that all too often NGOs bring considerable resources to bear on global problems, but are forced to withdraw before their work is done, because their funding depends on the shifting priorities of governments, foundations, and the public.

Conclusions

Landmines and Human Security is unique in bringing together the diverse perspectives of scholars, government officials, activists, and journalists from around the world to provide a comprehensive account of a very important example of successful transnational politics. Although the volume has a celebratory tone that reflects the views of many of the contributors, it also includes critical perspectives, counterarguments, and extensive discussions of the challenges that remain in this area. The editors believe that this inclusive, participatory approach to research and analysis is especially appropriate to the study of transnational activism. We feel that, taken as a whole, the volume is insightful, educational, balanced, and pioneering, and we invite readers to wander through its contents, secure in the knowledge that many years of hands-on field and research experience are represented in these pages.

Notes

1. I define globalization as a process driven largely by technological innovation (in the global context of expanding capitalism and democracy) that has empowered nonstate actors in ways that have no precedent during the modern age of the sovereign state. Globalization is characterized in large measure by an enormous increase in the speed, density, and character of cross-border transactions that states have not been able to regulate or manage (e.g, information flows and sales of goods and services via the Internet). Its impacts on fundamental human issues such as justice, security, welfare, and environmental quality have been mixed, and debate has raged over whether its negative effects will overwhelm its positive ones. Transnational processes can strengthen local communities fighting injustice or insecurity; they can also exploit communities and transform them into hubs for sex tourism or cheap labor. For a discussion of the negative effects, see Robert Kaplan, "The Coming Anarchy," *Atlantic Monthly* 273 (1994): 44–76; Benjamin Barber, *Jihad Versus McWorld* (New York: Times Books, 1995); and Samuel P. Huntington, *The Clash of Civilizations and the Remaking of World Order* (New York: Simon and Shuster, 1998). On the positive effects, see Paul Wapner, *Environmental Activism and World Civic Politics* (Albany: State University of New York, 1996); Francis Fukuyama, *The End of History and the Last Man* (New York: Avon, 1993); and Thomas L. Friedman, *The Lexus and the Olive Tree* (New York: Farrar, Straus and Giroux, 1999).

2. Perhaps the most influential and familiar recent attempt to formalize a global agenda is the World Commission on Environment and Development's *Our Common Future* (Oxford: Oxford University Press, 1987).

3. For a discussion, see Richard A. Matthew and George Shambaugh, "Sex, Drugs, and Heavy Metal: Transnational Threats and National Vulnerabilities," *Security Dialogue* 29, no. 2 (1998): 163–176.

4. James N. Rosenau, *Turbulence in World Politics: A Theory of Change and Continuity* (Princeton, NJ: Princeton University Press, 1990), 11.

5. Certainly the environmental and human rights movements have also been impressive. The mine ban movement is notable for the speed with which very concrete results have been achieved.

6. This participatory approach to scholarship brings together the knowledge, experience, and analytical skills of participants, observers, and participant-observers. The great diversity of perspectives provides wonderful insights into the mine ban movement, ranging from commentaries on the nuts and bolts of developing effective political strategies to dispassionate analyses of what this phenomenon tells us about the changing character of world politics. Writing styles, objectives, and standards for evidence vary among the contributors to this volume. We have not sought to impose an analytical framework that might rationalize the various contributions, however, because we feel that by accepting the validity of each voice we are able to tell a story that is both authentic and valuable.

7. An earlier, and very influential, version of this story is Maxwell J. Cameron, Robert J. Lawson, and Brian W. Tomlin, eds., *To Walk without Fear: The Global Movement to Ban Landmines* (Oxford: Oxford University Press, 1998).

8. Landmines first came into wide use during World War II.

9. Shawn Roberts and Jody Williams, *After the Gun's Fall Silent: The Enduring Legacy of Landmines* (Washington, DC: Vietnam Veterans Foundation of America, 1995), 3.

10. Robert Mueller, "The International Campaign to Ban Landmines: Where Do We Go from Here?" Keynote address, presented at the Second NGO International Conference on Landmines, May 9–11, 1999.

11. Under pressure from the Department of Defense, Clinton quickly retreated from his own call, claiming that American APLs were needed to protect U.S. soldiers, and noting that American mines were "smart" mines that deactivated automatically after a short period of time. For a discussion of the U.S. position, see Richard Matthew and Ken Rutherford, "Banning Landmines in the American Century," *International Journal of World Peace* 16, no. 2 (June 1999): 23–36.

12. These arguments are reviewed in detail in Matthew and Rutherford, "Banning Landmines"; and Richard Matthew and Ken Rutherford, "The Evolutionary Dynamics of the Movement to Ban Landmines," *Alternatives* 28, no. 1 (2003): 29–56.

13. Also referred to as the Ottawa Treaty.

14. Information in this paragraph is based on an unpublished report written in 2000 by Kerry Brinkert and Kevin Hamilton.

15. On recent trips to Cambodia (2000), Jordan (2000), and the Afghanistan border (1999), I have been able to observe a remarkable amount of activity related to mine education, mine clearing, and survivor assistance. For example,

travel to Siem Reap in Cambodia is possible today because of effective mine removal since 1997.

16. Based on personal communication, May 8, 2000.

17. The White House, "Final Statement on Landmines," January 19, 2001. Available on-line at: http://www.humptydumpty.net/in_the_press./asp.

18. The concept of human security received its most familiar definition in the United Nations Development Programme's (UNDP's) 1994 *Human Development Report*:

   security has far too long been interpreted narrowly: as security of territory . . . or as protection of national interests . . . or as global security from the threat of nuclear holocaust. . . . Forgotten were the legitimate concerns of ordinary people who sought security in their daily lives.

   The authors of the UNDP report suggest "human security" as a concept that can recover the earlier on-the-ground focus of the state's security practices.

   Human security can be said to have two main aspects. It means, first, safety from such chronic threats as hunger, disease and repression. And second, it means protection from sudden and hurtful disruptions in the patterns of daily life.

19. It should be noted that the editors had intended to include resource materials in this volume. However, these materials were left out of the final version of the volume due to space considerations. As such we have made these resources available online. These resources include the full text of the Mine Ban Treaty as well as an extensive listing of bibliographic and other resources on landmines complied by Julia Gelfand, the applied sciences librarian at the University of California–Irvine. These resources may be found at http://www.cusa.uci.edu/landmines and human security.htm.

2

The Global Landmine
Crisis in the 1990s

Bryan McDonald

THE 1997 MINE BAN TREATY (MBT) WAS THE RESULT OF THE COORDINATED efforts of groups from many countries concerned about the impact of antipersonnel landmines. It represents a revolutionary moment in the development of global society. In December 1997, representatives of 121 nations signed the Convention on the Prohibition of the Use, Stockpiling, Production and Transfer of AntiPersonnel Mines and on Their Destruction.[1] This agreement was hailed by United Nations Secretary-General Kofi Annan as "a historic victory for the weak and vulnerable of our world."[2] Antilandmine activists worked for six years to not only attract the interest of the public, celebrities, and nongovernmental organizations (NGOs) but also to forge a partnership with governments officials worldwide. This partnership between nonstate actors and middle power states like Canada and Norway enabled antilandmine activists to move an issue that had been marginalized in global arms control negotiations to the front of the international political agenda and to develop an international agreement to outlaw landmines even without the backing of major world powers.[3]

Aside from the significance of contributing to efforts to address the global problem of landmines, the Mine Ban Treaty is significant for representing a new mode of action in international relations. States have historically faced a variety of options for their actions, including cooperation with other states, opposition to other states, and maintaining a position of neutrality or nonalignment. During the latter part of the twentieth century, global civil society emerged as a sector of interest groups that seeks to influence the behavior of states and alter the actions of citizens within states.[4] Operating in a discursive space opened by the end of the Cold War and a rethinking of notions of security, the rise of global civil society corresponded with an expansion of technologies like cell phones and the Internet that empower nonstate actors, such as nongovernmental organizations (NGOs), to have more influence on international politics. The Mine Ban Treaty represents a further evolution of the potential of global civil society to impact state behavior and create international law through the forging of strategic partnerships with states. These partnerships allow nonstate and state partners to work together to mobilize the support necessary to accomplish desired ends and provide benefits to both state and nonstate actors. In the case of the Mine Ban Treaty, the partnership provided nonstate actors with access to resources and the experience necessary to draft a promulgate and international treaty, while state actors like Canada gained the benefit of a coalition of groups that was mobilized, vocal, and global and thus able to gain international attention and prestige by taking leadership on an issue that major powers had not embraced.

By the beginning of the 1990s, the world community was coming to recognize it faced a problem related to landmines that seemed global and intractable.[5] Yet, by the end of the decade, a great deal of attention had been focused on the issue, an international agreement to ban the use of landmines had been negotiated, and a number of activities had been undertaken to end the use of landmines, clear impacted areas, and assist landmine victims. The purpose of this chapter is to provide an overview of the development of the political process that culminated in the 1997 Mine Ban Treaty through a review of the history of the movement to ban landmines. Subsequent chapters in this volume will discuss the specific origins of aspects of the movement to ban landmines and assess its effectiveness. After a brief general discussion of landmines, this chapter begins by considering early calls to limit or ban the use of landmines, moves on to discuss the formation of the International Campaign to Ban Landmines (ICBL), and finally explores the process that culminated in the 1997 Mine Ban Treaty. Finally, this chapter concludes with a few reflections on antilandmine activities since the 1997 treaty, which many see as only the first step on a long path to a world free of landmines.

Landmines and Their Uses

While some form of landmines has been in use for over one hundred years, landmines first saw extensive use during World War II (1939–1945).[6]

Despite being considered a cowardly or dastardly weapon by military theorists,[7] landmines became a favored tool of militaries during the twentieth century that have been used in almost every military conflict since the end of World War II. Use of landmines in the developing world increased dramatically during the 1960s, 1970s, and 1980s as mines became cheaper to produce and harder to detect. A significant aspect of the military threat of landmines is the difficulty in detecting landmines and mined areas. Landmines can be used to channel enemy forces into or away from certain areas, or simply to slow down attacking forces in order to provide defending forces additional time to bring other weapons to bear. Due to continued developments in technology and doctrine, the military utility of mines has increasingly been a subject of debate.[8] Despite ongoing debates about their military utility, landmines have been used in a number of conflicts because they are inexpensive and easy to emplace. Once established, a minefield does not need to be maintained and many types of landmines can remain operable for years or even decades. It is these same characteristics that make landmines a continuing threat to civilians both during fighting and after conflicts have ended.[9]

Landmines are often grouped into two broad categories, antitank and antipersonnel landmines, based on their intended use. Antitank mines are intended to destroy or immobilize vehicles. They are relatively large (often between twenty and thirty-five pounds.) and often require hundreds to thousands of pounds of pressure to trigger a detonation. In contrast, antipersonnel landmines are relatively small and can range from around three ounces to five or more pounds. Antipersonnel landmines are often used to protect emplaced antitank mines and prevent enemy soldiers from easily detecting and disarming antitank mines. Both antitank and antipersonnel landmines consist of an explosive and a detonator used to trigger an explosion. Some types of mines will have metal or ceramic cases intended to send out fragments when the mine explodes. Both types of landmines are intended to create additional problems by wounding personnel and disabling vehicles rather than killing or destroying them, as injured soldiers or damaged vehicles increase the logistical demands on a military force. Landmines are often set to detonate upon contact, but can also be configured to allow a certain number of contacts or a set amount of time to pass before detonation. Such features allow initial elements of a military force to pass well into a mined area before detonation of mines. However, this characteristic also means that a soldier or military vehicle could initially trigger a landmine but leave it awaiting contact from another person or vehicle, possibly civilian, before the landmine would actually detonate. This feature highlights one of the major problems presented by landmines: they are indiscriminate (or dumb) weapons.[10]

Unlike more recent or advanced weapons ("smart weapons") most mines are unable to choose their targets. The majority of mines are simple devices that explode when triggered, and are unable to distinguish a tank from a bus, or an enemy soldier trying to disarm a mine from a child investigating an oddly shaped object. The indiscriminate nature of landmines combined with the length of time a mine can remain operable means that landmines pose a threat both during conflicts and long after combat has been concluded.

Identifying the Problem and Setting Goals

The initial stages of the effort to ban landmines involved a variety of efforts that included recognition of the magnitude of the problem by governments, ineffective attempts to address the issue through existing arms control agreements, and growing concern from nongovernmental organizations who were attempting to address the needs of landmine victims and survivors. Despite some disagreements about the precise magnitude of the global landmine crisis, there is general agreement that it is a transnational problem that impacts many countries and many thousands of people. The U.S. State Department estimates that there are 60 to 70 million landmines worldwide, with an average of 2 to 5 million new landmines planted annually.[11] For each year of the 1990s, it is estimated that between 24,000 and 26,000 people were killed by landmines.[12] Efforts to limit the use of landmines have been underway since at least 1980 when seventy-six states participated in the United Nations Convention on Conventional Weapons (CCW). Protocol II of the CCW specifically addressed the use of landmines, and included provisions stating they should only be used against military objectives, that mine locations should be recorded, and that parties in a conflict should attempt to remove mines following the end of a conflict. The CCW was adopted in 1981, and entered into force in 1983. However, many who sought to limit the impacts of landmines felt the CCW was too soft, and moreover too dependent on suggestions rather than enforceable guidelines of how landmines should be used and disposed of following an end to hostilities. By the early 1990s, many who opposed the use of landmines began to seek other, more effective means of addressing the landmine problem.

The effort to ban landmines that culminated in the 1997 Mine Ban Treaty began in 1991 with actions by NGOs focusing on health issues in developing countries. During testimony before the United States Congress in January 1991, the Women's Commission for Refugee Women and Children called for a ban on landmines. This call was repeated in September when two NGOs, Asia Watch and Physicians for Humans Rights, jointly called for a ban on the use of landmines and released *The Coward's War*, a report on the impacts of landmines in Cambodia. In October, Cambodia's Prince Norodom Sihanouk called for a ban on the use of antipersonnel landmines during his address to the United Nations on the occasion of the signing of the Cambodian peace agreement. One of the most significant events of the effort to ban the use of landmines occurred when two NGOs, the Vietnam Veterans of America Foundation (VVAF) in Washington, DC, and Medico International in Frankfurt, Germany, met in November 1991 and agreed to undertake a joint effort to bring developed and developing world NGOs together in a coordinated effort to push for a landmine ban.

Citizen and NGO efforts in 1992 continued to raise public awareness about the existence and magnitude of the global landmine problem. In February, fourteen hundred Austrian citizens presented a petition to their government to ban the Austrian manufacture and use of landmines. In May, more NGOs signaled their support as Handicap International issued a French-language edition of *The Coward's War*, and, along with the British Mines Advisory Group and Physicians for Human Rights, issued a call to end the use of landmines. Coordinated efforts among NGOs commenced in October, when Handicap International, Human Rights Watch, Medico International, the Mines Advisory Group, Physicians for Human Rights, and the Vietnam Veterans Foundation of America met in New York, and agreed to cosponsor an NGO conference on landmines in London during 1993. Also in October, American President George H. W. Bush signed the Leahy–Evans landmine export moratorium into law. This law banned the export of landmines from the United States for a period of one year, and was the first action by a government to restrict the sale and distribution of landmines.

Activities supporting a ban on landmines continued to increase through the fall of 1992. Additional reports detailing the impacts of landmines were published by Middle East Watch and Physicians for Human Rights. Activity to address the problem of landmines within the UN architecture began in October when the UN Departments of Humanitarian Affairs and Peace–Keeping Operations sponsored a meeting with UN departments and NGOs to exchange information about mine clearance and possible legal controls over the use of mines. Also in October, the International Committee of the Red Cross (ICRC) made a statement to the United Nations suggesting that the CCW prohibitions be made applicable to "noninternational conflicts," like civil wars and antiguerilla operations. During the fall of 1992, German and Swedish NGOs also met and began to develop strategies and unified materials to address the landmines issue.

In December, the European Parliament called on member states to ratify the 1980 CCW, and asked for a five-year ban on the export of mines, as well as funds to support demining activities by training deminers and funding mine clearance.

Developing an Organization to Push for a Landmine Ban

During the mid-1990s, many NGOs interested in addressing the problem of landmines began to see value in working with other NGOs to develop coordinated action plans. These first meetings and events marked the beginning of transnational efforts to find and develop a unified solution to the problems related to landmines. The decision among NGOs to cooperate with each other foreshadowed future cooperative efforts with state partners. Throughout 1993 and 1994, a number of states began to voluntarily offer limits on the exports of mines. Antilandmine activists, however, continued to press for a total ban on landmines.

In February, Handicap International and the French Institute of International Relations cosponsored a symposium on landmines where the French Foreign Ministry announced that it had sent a letter to the secretary-general of the United Nations requesting a review of the 1980 CCW. Also that month, Handicap International presented French President François Mitterand with 22,000 signatures in support of its call to stop the use of landmines. President Mitterand responded by announcing France's "voluntary abstention" from the export of landmines. Between February and May, meetings focusing on the impacts of landmines were held in England, France, Austria, and Germany.

In May 1993, the first NGO International Conference on Landmines was held in London to discuss the creation of a campaign to ban landmines. At that meeting, the International Campaign to Ban Landmines was formed. Handicap International, Human Rights Watch, Medico International, the Mines Advisory Group, Physicians for Human Rights, and the Vietnam Veterans of America Foundation were selected to form the steering committee of the ICBL, and the VVAF was chosen to coordinate the campaign. The group decided to focus on the goal of a ban on the use, production, and trade of antipersonnel landmines because it was felt that until the production and use of landmines were halted it would be difficult to deal with issues of victim assistance, demining, and rehabilitation of mined areas.[13] Throughout the summer of 1993, American, British, and New Zealand NGOs met to coordinate work on mine ban campaigns in their countries.

The fall of 1993 saw a number of important events that provided increasing momentum for the effort to ban landmines. During the year, the Swedish company Bofors announced it would stop manufacturing landmines for moral reasons, and that it would also cease exporting materials to buyers who might produce their own mines. In September, the U.S. State Department issued a report on landmines entitled *Hidden Killers: The Global Problem with Uncleared Landmines.*[14] Also in September, UNICEF Geneva focused on landmines, and asked national UNICEF committees to seriously consider advocating for the end of production of landmines. In November, Human Rights Watch released their report *Landmines: A Deadly Legacy*, which explored the production and trade of landmines, mine clearance efforts, and aspects of international law related to landmines.[15] In December, the United Nations General Assembly took several steps to address landmine problems. First, it adopted resolutions calling for a review of the 1980 CCW, and a moratorium on the export of landmines. Finally, the General Assembly adopted a resolution on children and war that initiated research into ways to protect children from war and from indiscriminate weapons of war, especially landmines.

In January 1994, the International Committee for the Red Cross held a seminar with military experts from sixteen countries to study military uses of landmines and begin consideration of alternatives. Also that month, UNICEF Geneva continued to develop its work on landmines by hosting a two-day conference. At a press conference in February, the president of the ICRC identified a ban on antipersonnel landmines as the most effective solution to landmine issues. State campaigns against landmines increased during March and April as Belgian and Irish NGOs commenced their efforts in support for a landmine ban.

In May, the Steering Committee of the International Campaign to Ban Landmines convened the Second International Conference on Landmines in Geneva. The conference was attended by representatives from over seventy-five NGOs. Support for a ban grew during the summer of 1994 as UNICEF, the UN Commission on Human Rights, the Vatican Council on Justice and Peace, and the Swedish Parliament endorsed a worldwide landmine ban. In September, President Bill Clinton called for the "eventual elimination" of landmines, and then UN Secretary-General Boutros Boutros-Ghali submitted a report on mine clearance in support of efforts to establish a demining trust fund. In the report, Secretary-General Boutros-Ghali recommended that the "best and most effective" way to address landmine problems was through a total ban on the production, use, and transportation of landmines. Also in September, the first meeting of the Canadian landmine campaign took place, and Italian landmines activists met in Brescia, Italy, the headquarters of mine producer Valsella. The United States outlined its proposed landmine control program at a State Department briefing in

October. NGOs were disappointed with what they saw as a retreat from the previously stated goal of the eventual elimination of landmines. Throughout the year, Spain, South Africa, the Slovak Republic, Germany, the Netherlands, Great Britain, Russia, and the Czech Republic joined other states that had declared some sort of moratorium on the production or export of landmines.

In 1995, hopes that a revision to the CCW would result in a total ban faded, while increasingly coordinated NGO efforts to enact a worldwide ban on landmines gained momentum. In a release of the new edition of the U.S. report on landmines, *Hidden Killers*, U.S. Secretary of State Warren Christopher restated the goal of the eventual elimination of landmines. In February, the U.S. National Research Council and the National Academy of Sciences cosponsored an international seminar on mine detection equipment. In March, Belgium became the first country to pass a law banning the use, production, trade, or stockpiling of landmines. This ban also included any components or parts that could be used in landmines. Through 1995, NGO activity included the continuation of meetings and efforts to coordinate activities, as well as calls for a total ban from Pope John Paul II and Archbishop Desmond Tutu. States also took action as Ireland, Germany, and the European Union all passed laws limiting the production or use of landmines, while the European Parliament and countries such as South Africa began to consider moving from an export moratorium to a total ban. In July, the UN Department of Humanitarian Affairs sponsored the International Meeting on Mine Clearance in Geneva to raise money for its demining trust fund. In August, a bill introduced to the United States Senate by Senator Patrick Leahy (D-VT) imposing a one-year moratorium on the production of landmines in the United States was passed. In September, VVAF released *After the Guns Fall Silent*, a report about the socio-economic impacts of landmines.[16] Events were held in Germany, South Africa, Australia, and Ireland to raise awareness of the landmines issue prior to the opening of the CCW review conference.

Later in September, the CCW conference opened in Vienna with many NGOs participating, but only as official observers to the proceedings. Despite announcements by several countries that they had or would soon ban production and destroy stocks of landmines, the conference failed to reach a consensus on a ban, and adjourned pending two additional sessions to be held in 1996. In November, the ICRC, working with national Red Cross and Red Crescent societies, launched an international media campaign designed to mobilize public action and stigmatize the use of landmines; this effort was the first such media campaign ever undertaken by the ICRC.

Framing the Problem and Expanding Public Support

The failure of efforts within existing structures of international government and law to address the landmine issue prompted many ban supporters to seek alternative means to immediately address the landmine problem. Additionally, moving beyond existing arms control conventions allowed antilandmine activists to frame the issue as a humanitarian issue rather than have negotiations framed by questions of military necessity. In January 1996, the American amendment introduced by Senator Leahy was signed into law and placed a one-year moratorium, beginning in 1999, on the use of landmines except on recognized borders or demilitarized zones. That same month, a follow-on session to the CCW review was held in Geneva. During the CCW review meeting, the ICBL convened a meeting of states that supported a ban and urged them to work toward a framework that would allow an immediate rather than an eventual ban of landmines. In March, the U.S. Department of Defense announced an expedited review of its policy against the banning of landmines. Following the announcement, the VVAF sponsored two full-page ads in the *New York Times* calling on President Clinton to ban landmines. One of the ads was a letter to the president signed by General Norman Schwarzkopf (Ret.) and fourteen other high-ranking officers. During the spring and through the close of the CCW Review Conference in May, a number of states, including Angola, Bulgaria, Croatia, Fiji, France, Germany, Honduras, Luxembourg, Lichtenstein, and Portugal, announced support for a landmine ban or renounced the use of landmines. At the close of the conference, the ICBL announced that an amended CCW protocol would not make a significant contribution to addressing the global problem with landmines, and landmine activists and pro-ban states continued their consideration of alternative means to develop a landmine ban.

In May, President Clinton announced a new landmine policy that was criticized by antilandmine activists for including no framework or time frame to enact its stated goal of an eventual total ban on landmines. At the close of the May meeting of the G7, a communiqué was issued calling for a ban on landmines. In July, representatives from forty-eight states and more than twenty international organizations met at the International Conference on Mine Clearance Technology. In September, the six Central American presidents announced they would ban the use, production, and trade of landmines, thus making Central America the world's first Mine Free Zone. In October 1996, a conference to promote the pro-ban movement was held in Ottawa, Canada, and was attended by seventy-five governments. At the conference, Canadian Foreign Minister Lloyd Axworthy proposed signing a convention by the end of 1997 to make landmines

illegal. The conference resulted in a declaration by fifty governments recognizing the need for a ban on landmines, an agenda for actions necessary
to reach an immediate ban, and an announcement by Canada that it
would hold a treaty signing conference for a total ban in December 1997.

The next twelve months saw a great deal of activity as pro-ban
NGOs and supportive governments worked to develop a landmine ban
and mobilize the support necessary to enact it by the end of 1997. In February, 111 countries attended a preparatory session hosted by Austria to
discuss the development of a comprehensive landmine ban treaty. In the
early months of the year, South Africa and Mozambique announced they
would ban landmines. In May, the new British government came out in
support of the ICBL call to ban landmines. In June, Germany and France
joined Great Britain in support of an international landmine ban, and the
leaders of the G8 established the urgent need for an agreement on landmines. Also in June, Belgium hosted the second preparatory session for
the Ottawa Treaty and the Steering Committee of the ICBL was expanded to include the Kenyan and South African Campaigns to Ban
Landmines. In August, Princess Diana, one of the most visible and well-
known advocates of a total ban, was killed in France shortly after ac-
companying representatives of the Landmine Survivors Network on a
trip to meet landmine survivors in Bosnia. In September, representatives
of 121 countries met in Oslo and negotiated a comprehensive treaty to
ban landmines. A concurrent meeting attended by 130 NGOs developed
an action plan to ensure that the treaty would enter into force by the year
2000. On October 10, 1997, it was announced that the Nobel Peace Prize
had been awarded to the International Campaign to Ban Landmines and
Jody Williams, the ICBL's coordinator.[17] The Ottawa Process began in
October 1996 and was concluded in December 1997 at a conference to
sign the antipersonnel landmine ban treaty. At this conference, which was
attended by more than 400 representatives from various NGOs and 157
countries, the treaty was signed by 122 of the attending countries. The
treaty required that all signatories destroy stockpiles of landmines within
four years, and mandated the removal of landmines in the ground within
ten years. In December, the ICBL and Jody Williams were presented the
Nobel Peace Prize in Oslo, Norway.[18]

With the Mine Ban Treaty completed, efforts turned to securing
enough signatories to ratify the agreement. In February, landmine survivor
Chris Moon participated in the torch run at the opening ceremonies of the
Nagano Winter Olympic Games.[19] At a policy conference in May, the
United States revealed its "Demining 2010" program, and announced it
would work to sign the Mine Ban Treaty by 2006. By the summer of 1998,
thirty of the forty ratifications required for the treaty to enter into force had
been gathered, and international meetings to draw attention to and gain

support for the ban continued, including events in Ottawa, New York, Budapest, Geneva, Washington, Brussels, Moscow, Pretoria, Oslo, Amman, Khartoum, Karlsruhe, Ougadugo, and Bangkok.[20] In September, Burkina Faso became the fortieth country to ratify the Mine Ban Treaty, beginning a six-month waiting period until the treaty would become international law on March 1, 1999.

Moving toward a Landmine Free World

Since the establishment of the 1997 Mine Ban Treaty, antilandmine activists struggled to maintain the momentum to complete the goals of the movement. Since 1997, 150 countries have signed and 141 have ratified the Mine Ban Treaty while a number of activities have continued to keep public interest and awareness high. Landmine activists have continued to encourage ratification of the treaty, while also emphasizing other aspects necessary to address the global problem of landmines. Many NGOs have focused on demining programs or victim assistance programs. Efforts to educate people about the threat presented by landmines have included the use of DC Comics superheroes Wonder Woman and Superman. DC Comics has worked with UNICEF and officers of the U.S. Southern Command Mine Awareness Team stationed in Central America to produce a special-edition comic book in Spanish to teach children in Nicaragua, Honduras, and Costa Rica about the dangers of landmines. A number of benefit concerts have been held to raise money for demining and victim assistance.

This chapter demonstrates the startling speed by which the issue of landmines gained international attention and resulted in international action. The end of the decades-long conflict between the United States and the Soviet Union provided opportunities for the reconsideration of security priorities and the means used to achieve those priorities. Landmines, which had seemed a necessary weapon to use in the event of an invasion of western Europe by Warsaw Pact forces, took on a different appearance in the changing security landscape of the early 1990s. Many international relief organizations began to draw attention to the fact that landmines were not simply waiting in arsenals to be used in the event of war, but that millions of mines had been emplaced in over one hundred countries. These organizations began talking to each other, and developed a common approach to address the problem. The end of the Cold War also provided opportunities for middle powers such as Canada to embrace and pursue an issue of international concern despite a lack of interest in a landmine ban from the United States.[21] The interest of middle powers and NGOs was essential to the development of the 1997 Mine Ban

Treaty. Consideration of events in the five years since the signing of the treaty suggest that the landmine movement faces a continuing struggle to maintain public attention on an issue that is too often seen to have been addressed by the mere signing of the 1997 treaty. Antilandmine activists and their government and private sector partners work to continue demining efforts, victim assistance programs, and rehabilitation of mined areas and the people living in them. These continued efforts suggest the possibility is still bright for a world where both combatants and noncombatants are free from the threat of landmines.

Notes

1. This agreement is also referred to as the Mine Ban Treaty, Ottawa Convention, and Ottawa Treaty.

2. UN Secretary-General Kofi Annan, "Address to the Signing Ceremony of the Anti-personnel Mines Convention," Ottawa, Canada, December 3, 1997.

3. For more discussion on the changing role of middle powers in international relations, see Kenneth R. Rutherford, Stefan Brem, and Richard A. Matthew, *Reframing the Agenda: The Impact of NGO and Middle Power Cooperation in International Security Policy* (New York: Praeger, 2003).

4. Paul Wapner, *Environmental Activism and World Civic Politics* (Albany: State University of New York Press, 1996).

5. A number of publicly available chronologies were useful in developing this chapter: International Campaign to Ban Landmines, "Ban Movement Chronology," available online at http:www.icbl.org; Friends Committee on National Legislation "Chronology of U.S. Policy and International Mine Ban Treaty Events," available online at http://www.fcnl.org/issues/arm/sup/lan_chron.htm; Landmine Survivors Network, "Chronology," available online at http://www.landminesurvivors.org/heritage/chronology.php; and Professor Landmine's "Chronology of Events 1949–2001: Landmine Regulation and Elimination," available online at http://www.professorlandmine.com/chronology.html.

6. On the history and uses of landmines, see Mike Croll, *The History of Landmines* (Barnsley, UK: Pen and Sword Books, 1998); Rae McGrath, *Landmines and Unexploded Ordinance: A Resource Book* (London: Pluto Press, 2000); and Lydia Monin and Andrew Gallimore, *The Devil's Gardens: A History of Landmines* (London: Pilmoco, 2002).

7. Martin van Creveld, *Technology and War: From 2000BC to the Present* (New York: Free Press, 1989), 71.

8. For examples of this debate, see the chapters in this volume by J. Antonio Ohe and Ted Gaulin. See also Richard A. Matthew and Ted Gaulin, "Time to Sign

the Mine Ban Treaty," *Issues in Science and Technology* (Spring 2003): 69–73; and Dipankar Banerjee, "Military Utility," in *Stalking Terror: Landmines in Peace and in War* (Delhi: Wordsmiths, 2000).

9. Colin King, ed., *Jane's Mines and Mine Clearance* (Surrey, UK: Jane's Information Group, 1996).

10. Ibid.

11. United States Department of State, *Hidden Killers: The Global Landmine Crisis* (Washington, DC: U.S. Department of State, 1998), 16.

12. The lower figure is from International Committee for the Red Cross, *Landmines Must Be Stopped* (Geneva: ICRC, 1998), 16. The higher figure is from Maxwell A. Cameron, Robert J. Lawson, and Brian W. Tomlin, "To Walk without Fear," in *To Walk Without Fear: The Global Movement to Ban Landmines*, ed. Maxwell A. Cameron, Robert J. Lawson, and Brian W. Tomlin (Oxford: Oxford University Press, 1998), 2.

13. NGO Conference on Antipersonnel Mines, *Report of the Final Plenary Session*, London, May 26, 1993.

14. See note 11.

15. Physicians for Human Rights and Human Rights Watch, *Landmines: A Deadly Legacy* (New York: Human Rights Watch, 1993).

16. Shawn Roberts and Jody Williams, *After the Guns Fall Silent: The Enduring Legacy of Landmines* (Washington, DC: Vietnam Veterans of America Foundation, 1995).

17. Carey Goldberg, "Peace Prize Goes to Land-Mine Opponents," *New York Times*, October 11 1997, late. ed., A1.

18. Jody Williams and Stephen Goose, "The International Campaign to Ban Landmines," in Cameron, Lawson, and Tomlin, *To Walk without Fear* (See note 12), 20–47.

19. Jere Longman, "The XVIII Winter Games: A Display of Culture and Hope Opens Games," *New York Times*, February 7, 1998, late ed., A1.

20. Robert J. Lawson, Mark Gwozdecky, Jill Sinclair, and Ralph Lysyshyn, "The Ottawa Process and the International Movement to Ban Anti-Personnel Mines," in Cameron, Lawson, and Tomlin, *To Walk without Fear* (see note 12), 160–184.

21. Rutherford, Brem, and Matthew, *Reframing the Agenda*.

3

Evaluating the Impacts of
the Ottawa Treaty

LEAH FRASER

SINCE THE 1997 SIGNING OF THE MINE BAN TREATY (MBT), THERE HAS BEEN significant progress made in third world nations toward landmine clearance and victim assistance. To date, 150 nations have signed the treaty, and 141 have ratified. There remain forty-four nations (as of October 2003) who are nonsignatories. In 1999 alone, 168.41 square kilometers were cleared in seven of the largest mine clearing programs.[1] In June 2002, the HALO Trust, the world's largest private nonprofit humanitarian demining organization, announced the clearance of one million mines and bombs worldwide.[2] Five years have elapsed since the inception of this treaty, and it is important that we examine in detail the resulting progress that has taken place in the third world.

The previous chapter outlined the history of the MBT, its component parts, and areas of concern. The goal of this chapter is to examine changes made in light of the new state–nonstate strategic alliance and treaty. The goal is to see whether the increased attention paid to the issue of landmines transnationally has led to success regarding the three most critical provisions: ban on the use, stockpiling, and trade of landmines; demining; and victim assistance. Although change has been varied in these three areas, this chapter will assess what progress has been made to date.

Ban on the Use, Stockpiling, and Trade of Landmines

The victims of landmines are mainly civilians in the developing world. To date, eighty-eight states[3] have been affected, to various degrees, by landmines and unexploded ordnance (UXO).[4] In the nations littered with these weapons, there are nearly five hundred deaths or injuries per week—26,000 per year occur.[5] According to the *Landmine Monitor Report 2000*, reporting from March 1999 through May 2000, there were new landmine and UXO victims in seventy-one nations.[6] Table 3.1 provides a list of these nations.

Table 3.1 shows that most nations registering new landmine casualties are third world nations, especially those that are considered not free and have low United Nations Development Programme's (UNDP) Human Development Index (HDI) ratings. In fact, nearly every mine-affected nation in Africa scored low on the HDI. In all other regions, the nations scored low or medium on the HDI with only six of the seventy-one nations scoring a high in 1999. Nations with low HDI scores face the difficult task of providing for their landmine victims and implementing mine information campaigns with limited resources. Landmine Monitor found that thirty-nine of the seventy-one nations suffering mine casualties in 1999 were not currently engaged in armed conflict.[7] Some nations did face increased civil conflict in the period 1999–2000, however, which increased their casualty rates from previous years. These nations are Albania, Angola, Burundi, the Democratic Republic of the Congo, Chechnya, Ethiopia, Eritrea, Kosovo, Lebanon, Namibia, and the Philippines.[8]

In the 1990s, there was a visible shift in the global landmine situation. Table 3.2 highlights these differences over time through the nations identified as having the most extensive landmine problems.

In the *Landmine Monitor Report 2001*, Nicaragua reported that its landmine numbers were down to 70,769. Yet, no other nations had made their self-report available at the time of this report. Whether the source of mine victims was civil strife, mines left over from wars past, or both, the paucity of data makes it difficult to assess the exact extent of the problem in the third world.

As seen in table 3.2, the numbers of landmines in these most heavily mine-infested nations has declined, suggesting a promising trend. This success is due in part to two factors: advances in demining and better mine assessment capabilities. The issue of demining will be discussed in more detail in the following section. Yet, it is important to point out that our ability to make better quantitative assessments of landmines globally has allowed us to realize that previous estimates were too high. Changes in these assessments account for part of the declining trend in landmine numbers globally. Although there is improvement, there is still a real need to continue to demine and assist victims.

Table 3.1. Nations with New Mine and Unexploded Ordnance Victims from 1999–2000

Area	Nation	HDI Ranking	Freedom House Rating (2000)	Victims/ Year Range	Landmine Estimate (1998)
Africa	Angola	146 Low HDI	Not Free	High	6M–15M
	Burundi	160 Low HDI	Not Free	High	50,000
	Chad	155 Low HDI	Not Free	High	50,000–70,000
	Dijibouti	137 Low HDI	Partly Free	Low	
	DR Congo	142 Low HDI	Not Free	High	
	Eritrea	148 Low HDI	Not Free	High	1M
	Ethiopia	158 Low HDI	Partly Free	High	500,000
	Guinea-Bissau	156 Low HDI	Partly Free	Low	
	Kenya	123 Medium HDI	Not Free	Medium	
	Mauritania	139 Low HDI	Not Free	Low	10,000
	Mozambique	157 Low HDI	Partly Free	Medium	1M
	Namibia	111 Medium HDI	Free	High	50,000
	Niger	161 Low HDI	Partly Free	Low	
	Rwanda	152 Low HDI	Not Free	Medium	100,000–250,000
	Senegal	145 Low HDI	Partly Free	High	
	Sierra Leone	162 Low HDI	Partly Free	Low	
	Somalia		Not Free	High	1M
	Sudan	138 Low HDI	Not Free	High	1M
	Tanzania	140 Low HDI	Partly Free	Medium	

(continued)

Table 3.1. Nations with New Mine and Unexploded Ordnance Victims from 1999–2000 *(continued)*

Area	Nation	HDI Ranking	Freedom House Rating (2000)	Victims/ Year Range	Landmine Estimate (1998)
	Uganda	141 Low HDI	Partly Free	Medium	50,000
	Zambia	143 Low HDI	Partly Free	Low	100,000
	Zimbabwe	117 Medium HDI	Partly Free	Low	200,000–2.2M
	Somaliland			High	
Americas	Chile	39 High HDI	Free	Low	1,500
	Colombia	62 Medium HDI	Partly Free	High	60,000–80,000
	Ecuador	84 Medium HDI	Free	Low	85,000
	Nicaragua	106 Medium HDI	Partly Free	Medium	
	Peru	73 Medium HDI	Partly Free	Low	
Asia-Pacific	Afghanistan		Not Free	High	5M–7M
	Bangladesh	132 Low HDI	Partly Free	Medium	
	Burma		Not Free	High	
	Cambodia	121 Medium HDI	Not Free	High	4M–6M
	China	87 Medium HDI	Not Free	High	10M
	India	115 Medium HDI	Free	High	
	Korea, DPR		Not Free N		
	Korea, RO	27 High HDI	Free S	High	250,000
	Laos	131 Low HDI	Not Free	High	
	Nepal	129 Low HDI	Partly Free	High	
	Pakistan	127 Low HDI	Not Free		
	Philippines	70 Medium HDI	Free	High	
	Sri Lanka	81 Medium HDI	Partly Free	High	25,000
	Thailand	66 Medium HDI	Free	High	100,000

Region	Country	HDI rank	Freedom status	Level	Population
Europe/Central Asia	Vietnam	101 Medium HDI	Not Free	High	3.5M
	Albania	85 Medium HDI	Partly Free	Medium	
	Armenia	72 Medium HDI	Partly Free		100,000
	Azerbaijan	79 Medium HDI	Partly Free		
	Belarus	53 Medium HDI	Not Free		
	Bosnia and Herzegovina			Medium	600,000–1M
	Croatia	46 High HDI	Partly Free	Medium	400,000
	Cyprus	25 High HDI	Free		17,000
	Estonia	44 High HDI	Free		
	Georgia	76 Medium HDI	Partly Free	High	150,000
	Kyrgyzstan	92 Medium HDI	Partly Free		
	Latvia	50 Medium HDI	Free		
	Moldova	98 Medium HDI	Partly Free		
	Russia	55 Medium HDI	Partly Free	High	
	Tajikistan	103 Medium HDI	Not Free	High	100,000
	Turkey	82 Medium HDI	Partly Free		
	Ukraine	74 Medium HDI	Partly Free		1M
	Yugoslavia, FR		Partly Free	High	500,000
	Abkhazia		Not Free		
	Chechnya				
	Kosovo		Not Free	High	
	Nagorny-Karabakh		Not Free		
Middle East/North Africa	Algeria	100 Medium HDI	Not Free	Medium	22.5M
	Egypt	105 Medium HDI	Not Free		16M
	Iran	90 Medium HDI	Not Free	High	
	Iraq		Not Free	High	10M

(continued)

39

Table 3.1. Nations with New Mine and Unexploded Ordnance Victims from 1999–2000 (continued)

Area	Nation	HDI Ranking	Freedom House Rating (2000)	Victims/ Year Range	Landmine Estimate (1998)
	Israel	22 High HDI	Free		260,000
	Jordan	88 Medium HDI	Partly Free	Low	206,193
	Kuwait	43 High HDI	Partly Free		
	Libya	59 Medium HDI	Not Free		100,000
	Lebanon	65 Medium HDI	Not Free	High	8,795–35,000
	Oman	71 Medium HDI	Not Free		
	Syria	97 Medium HDI	Not Free		100,000
	Yemen	133 Low HDI	Not Free	Medium	100,000
Golan Heights					
Northern Iraq				High	10M
Palestine			Not Free		
Western Sahara			Not Free		

Notes: HDI = Human Development Index ratings of the United Nations Development Programme (UNDP). This table uses country data from the *Landmine Monitor Report 2000*, which is available at www.hrw.org/reports/2000/landmines. Italicized words are those areas not recognized internationally as states. Data for landmine estimates are from the U.S. State Department, *Hidden Killers 1998: The Global Landmine Crisis—Country Landmine Data*, which is available at www.state.gov. The data for victim estimates is from the ICBL Mine Action Working Group Intersessional Standing Committee on Mine Clearance, *Mine Awareness and Mine Action Technologies*, May 28, 2002, which is available at www.icbl.org. These ratings are measured as High (over 100 victims/year), Medium (15–100 new victims/year), and Low (less than 15 new victims/year). The Freedom House ratings are a measure of political and civil rights ranging from Free (1–2.5), Partly Free (3–5.5), and Not Free (5.5–7). For information on how the scale is created, see www.freedomhouse.org. HDI data are from 1999 and are found in the UNDP's *Human Development Report 2000*, which is available at www.undp.org. Blank spaces represent unavailable data.

Table 3.2 Trends in Landmine Presence, 1994–2001

Country	Hidden Killers (1994)	UN Landmine Database (1997)	Hidden Killers 1998 (Low–High Range)
Afghanistan	10M	10M	5M–7M
Angola	9M–20M	15M	6M–15M
Bosnia and Herzegovina		3M	600,000–1M
Cambodia	7M–9M	6M	4M–6M
Croatia	1M	3M	400,000
Eritrea	1M–2M	1M	1M
Iraq		10M	10M
Mozambique	> 1M	3M	1M
Namibia		50,000	50,000
Nicaragua	132,000	108,297	85,000
Somalia		1M	1M
Sudan		1M	1M

Sources: U.S. State Department, *Hidden Killers 1998.*

Demining

Although there are numerous activities involved in creating a mine-free world, demining relies heavily on first world technological advances. Demining an area allows economic and social development to take place in areas previously off-limits to citizens. Therefore, it is critically important to the less-developed nations. RONCO Consulting Corporation, TAMAR Consulting, and Mines Clearance International are the international groups most often mentioned when the particulars of demining are discussed. Yet, there are also an increasing number of nation-based groups getting involved in the demining project. The pervasiveness of domestic civil society groups throughout the developing world at the local level can be seen in many developing nations. For example, the Albania UXO and Mines Action Group is one such organization that is working within Albania to demine its own landscape. In the country of Angola, there is the Angolan National Institute for the Removal of Explosive Ordnance.[9] Despite this, recent reports suggest that the national implementation measures are less than substantial. Although article 9 of the treaty calls for each state party to "take all appropriate legal, administrative and other measures, including the imposition of penal sanctions, to prevent and suppress any activity prohibited" by the treaty, this report shows that only 31 of the 124 nations that have ratified the treaty have passed domestic laws.[10]

Although they remain a nonsignatory of the MBT, the financial contributions of the United States remain strong.[11] The United States also contributes by funding much-needed training and research. Landmine clearance is an expensive process. Landmines can cost as little as $3 to produce, yet as much as $1,000 to remove. The demining process relies on a combination of manual clearance teams, mechanical systems, and mine detection dogs. The U.S. military has trained over one-quarter of the world's humanitarian deminers.[12] The U.S. Humanitarian Demining Program works to clear mines in more than thirty countries and, since 1993, the program has spent nearly $400 million to fight the landmine problem. In fact, its Demining 2010 Initiative aims to end the civilian threat of landmines globally by 2010.[13]

Victim Assistance

Assistance to countries most affected by landmines comes from a combination of government and nongovernment organizations. Issues ranging from demining to victim assistance volunteer projects are taken up by groups around the world. Yet, there have been a few permanent institutions designed to provide support for victim assistance. The creation of Landmine Monitor in 1998 to provide extensive monitoring of the situation is a step toward victim assistance by disseminating information. There are also international and domestic nongovernment organizations providing wide-ranging support as well as third world governments that have set up particular laws to aid their landmine victims.

Landmine Monitor

Landmine Monitor has played a critical role in the process of landmine eradication. Established in 1998 by the International Committee to Ban Landmines (ICBL) as an organization promoting demining globally, it provides a global reporting network, an online database of landmine activity, and the creation of numerous country reports.[14] The maintenance of these streams of information requires the continual involvement of indigenous nongovernmental organizations (NGOs) to monitor and report on the landmine situation.

The *Third Annual Landmine Monitor Report* was released in September 2001. This offers hard evidence as to the success and failure of the Landmine Treaty. The 2001 Landmine Monitor meeting for the report was held in Washington, DC, in March 2001 with 112 researchers from around the globe. Among those groups represented were the Indian Institute for Peace, Disarmament and Environmental Protection; Mines Action of Southern Africa; the Kenya Coalition to Ban Landmines; the Croatian Mine Action Center; the Thailand Coalition to Ban Landmines; the Nicaraguan

Campaign to Ban Landmines; the Centre for Defense Studies; the University of Zimbabwe; and the Campana Colombiana Contra Minas.[15]

National Governments and Policies in the Third World

Progress toward a mine-free world cannot be discussed without an examination of the role that third world governments have had in the process. Whereas it is often suggested that international organizations are created when indigenous governments are nonresponsive to a particular crisis (landmines in this case), the case of the international movement to ban landmines proves quite different. Many of the third world nations battling the issue of landmines have created official government programs that work on demining and other aspects of the landmine crisis.[16] Although much progress has been made in involving third world governments in the process of mine clearing and rehabilitation, there remains room for work. In fact, of the four major recommendations for future success, the Cambodian Mine Action Center, a prominent third world landmine NGO based in Cambodia, notes, "[We] request [that] the relevant government ministries and institutions should expand their involvement and roles in mine action in Cambodia."[17]

Although mine action and clearance play critical roles in the movement to create a mine-free world, it is equally important that nations work to assist and fully reintegrate their landmine survivors into society. In July 1998, Her Majesty Queen Noor proposed a Bill of Rights for Landmine Survivors at the Landmine Survivor Network's First Middle East Conference on Landmine Injury and Rehabilitation in Amman, Jordan. This bill lists the human rights of landmine survivors, and the working group is currently reviewing national disability legislation and UN standards. The goal of this bill of rights is to ensure that national disability laws exist worldwide to assist landmine survivors.[18]

Landmine victims in third world nations can benefit from sympathetic equal opportunity laws and policies for the disabled. According to Human Rights Watch, only thirty-two of the seventy-one nations reporting landmine incidents for the period 1999–2000 have explicit legislation for disabled citizens.[19] Half of the nations in Africa alone have no type of legislation designed to protect the disabled.[20] Only South Africa, Uganda, and Mozambique have national disability laws in place.[21] In Mozambique, where there were still nearly one hundred mine victims reported in 1998 despite a heavy NGO presence, there is no special assistance to civilians affected by landmines.[22] Considering that most Mozambique citizens injured by landmines fall victim while farming their land (and are not military personnel who enjoy special legal status and state assistance when disabled by landmines), this is a tragedy. Mozambique does have disability laws on the books but national disability organizations suggest that these rights are rarely respected in practice.[23] In 1999, the Ministry of Coordination for Social Action began working on a national disability law that will offer rights and privileges to the physically and mentally disabled.[24]

In the Asia-Pacific region of the world, Cambodia, Pakistan, and the Philippines have coordinated bodies dealing with disability; yet, only half of the total nations there have explicit disability laws.[25] In Cambodia, where 1,249 casualties occurred in 1998, there is an attempt to strengthen disability laws. As of the *Landmine Monitor Report 1999*, Cambodia had created a Draft Law to Protect the Rights of Persons with Disabilities that has not yet been submitted to the National Assembly of Cambodia.[26] In the Middle East, no nations have a coordination committee on disability, although Egypt, Jordan, and Iraq have disability laws and Israel, Palestine, and Yemen currently are revising their existing disability laws and policies.[27] This type of legislation is crucial for the rehabilitation and reintegration of the citizens back into the community. However, even when these policies exist in third world nations, it is often difficult to implement them. This implementation is often left wholly to the civil society groups working on the ground with limited funds. The injured citizens have little access to the government to pressure their government into compliance.

Hospital care and rehabilitation are also pressing issues. Once the immediate medical needs of the victims are met with hospital care, these persons require further, more socially directed, assistance to get further rehabilitated and integrated into their society. This is where the need for physiotherapy, prosthetics, and psychological support are critical to the patient's proper recovery. Landmine Monitor and other victim assistance organizations have identified the following trends in the hospital care of third world victims. Not only is it a less-quantifiable benefit as is, for example, "number of mines cleared," but it is also more difficult to monitor and measure success. As a result, less funding is directed specifically at rehabilitation and reintegration of landmine victims into society. This results in long waiting lists for government-funded rehabilitation services that often require the patient to pay part of the cost.[28] When the government does offer rehabilitation services to its injured, psychological support is seldom included. Furthermore, government rehabilitation services are often available to military victims but not civilians, as is the case in the Middle East, Africa, and the Americas.[29] Because of the scarcity of government assistance in the area of rehabilitation and reintegration, the role of community-based rehabilitation programs and NGOs offering services and prosthetics is critical to the quality of life in these mine-affected communities.

A final issue in the complex process of rehabilitation of landmine victims is the process of social and economic reintegration. This is an area where the NGO community is often the only concerned party. Mine-affected countries often do not have the final stage of economic reintegration as a part of their victim assistance programs. Issues such as creating associations, skills and vocational training, and developing income generating projects, peer counseling and recreation activities are too often overlooked.[30] When these activities are implemented, like most aspects of health care and rehabilitation, they take place in the more urban areas even though most victims reside in the rural outskirts. In Africa, for example, there are reintegration activities reported in twelve countries; yet, these benefits are only widely accessible in Kenya and Namibia.[31] In the Americas, only El Salvador has implemented a free socioeconomic program for reintegration and in Europe, only three nations (Albania, Bosnia and Herzegovina, and Croatia) have implemented such activities.

According to the Human Rights Watch report *Landmine Casualties and Survivor Assistance*, Asia-Pacific has been the most successful region at the socioeconomic reintegration of its landmine victims. These nations rely heavily on NGO assistance, yet have managed to launch successful efforts in Afghanistan, Burma, Cambodia, India, Korea, Nepal, Pakistan, Sri Lanka, and Thailand. Many of these nations also offer landmine victims extensive benefits, grants, and pensions to help along the path to recovery.[32]

Conclusion

It is clear that the crisis of landmines in the third world has made some significant progress since the inception of the 1997 Landmine Convention. With the help of a large NGO presence and various degrees of state involvement, the lives of landmine victims are improving steadily. That is not to suggest that the work there is complete. Continued attention must be paid to educating the public in mine-affected nations about how to identify field markers and keep their communities and children safe during mine clearance projects.[33] There is still a need for the continued monitoring by projects such as Landmine Monitor. This provides not only clear, reliable documentation on the circumstances in mine-affected nations, but it also reminds those nations that their progress is important and is acknowledged by the international community. In addition to such monitoring activities, there is also a need for continued work with state lawmaking bodies to ensure that all landmine victims are given basic humanitarian disability benefits and access to health care. It is only when the landmine victims are provided with safe rehabilitation and health care that they may become fully reintegrated into their communities to participate fully in their socioeconomic well-being.

Notes

1. This area includes both antipersonal landmines and unexploded ordnance clearing. See Humanitarian Mine Action report (3), available at www.hrw. org/reports/2000/landmines.

2. Environmental News Service, "HALO Trust Celebrates Removing One Million Mines,"available at http://ens-news.com/ens/jun2002/2002-06-19-09.asp.

3. Of these eighty-eight, only thirty-three are state parties to the Mine Ban Treaty and eighteen are signatories.

4. Humanitarian Mine Action report (1), available at www.hrw.org/reports/ 2000/landmines.

5. *Landmines: A Global Scourge,* available at www.fas.org/asmp/campaigns/ landmines/lmhistory.htm.

6. *Landmine Monitor Report 2000,* available at http://www.hrw.org/reports/ landmines.

7. Ibid.

8. Ibid.

9. Further data on particular mechanical mine clearance and other demining operations can be found at www.sya.de/demin-en.htm.

10. *Human Rights Watch Report* prepared for the Fifth Meeting of the Intersessional Standing Committee on the General Status and Operation of the 1997 Mine Ban Treaty, Geneva, Switzerland, February 1, 2002.

11. For information on demining activities, see U.S. State Department, *Hidden Killers 1998: The Global Landmine Crisis,* available at www.state.gov.

12. U.S. State Department, *Landmines: A Hidden Global Threat,* available at www.state.gov.

13. Ibid.

14. Further information on the Landmine Monitor and its publications and data can be found on the ICBL Web site: www.icbl.org.

15. For the complete listing of attendants at the 2001 general meeting, see the Landmine Monitor 2001 research participant list at the ICBL Web site: www.icbl.org.

16. For an extensive listing of these mechanical mine clearance and other demining operations, see www.sya.de/demin-en.htm.

17. See the Cambodian Mine Action Center Web site: www.cmac.org (96).

18. For more information about the proposed bill of rights, please see International Campaign to Ban Landmines, *Landmine Monitor Report 1999,* May 1999 (p. 935). Available at http://www.icbl.org/lm/1999/.

19. Human Rights Watch, *Landmine Casualty and Survivor Assistance* (p. 4), available at www.hrw.org/reports/2000/landmines.

20. Ibid., 5.

21. Ibid.

22. *Landmine Monitor 1999*, 64.

23. Ibid.

24. Ibid.

25. *Landmine Casualties and Survivor Assistance.*

26. *Landmine Monitor 1999*, 408.

27. *Landmine Casualties and Survivor Assistance*, 5.

28. Ibid., 6.

29. Ibid., 5.

30. Ibid., 7.

31. Ibid.

32. Ibid.

33. For a critical discussion of mine awareness programs and the future benefits of emerging mine action teams, see Rae McGrath, *Landmines and Unexploded Ordnance: A Resource Book* (London: Pluto Press, 2000).

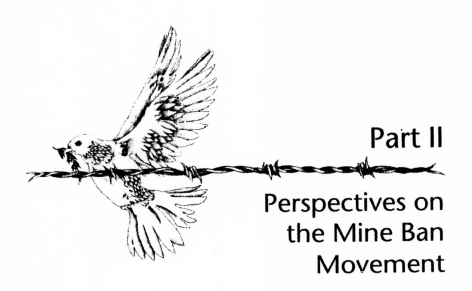

Part II

Perspectives on the Mine Ban Movement

4

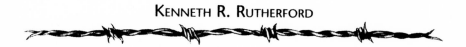

Nongovernmental Organizations and the Landmine Ban

Kenneth R. Rutherford

Mr. Chairman, we are firmly convinced, after considering the impact of landmines—primarily on the less developed countries of the world, those countries with the least resources to deal with the massive landmine contamination—that nothing short of a complete ban on the use, production, trade and stockpiling of the weapon will begin to address the global landmines epidemic.

—Robert (Bobby) Mueller

Nongovernmental organizations (NGOs) targeted banning landmines long before governments were ready to do so, proposed most of the precepts of a formal landmine ban treaty, and mobilized public pressure to force through a weapons prohibition. Virtually no one thought the convention was possible when the International Campaign to Ban Landmines (ICBL) was formed. The ICBL's success illustrates the difficulty in building transnational coalitions around a single issue. It is especially hard if the goal is to attain a nearly universal collection of NGOs from all states. Moreover, there are so many NGOs working on so many issues, with wide political ranging opinions and priorities, that any effort to create a unified coalition is bound to be difficult.[1]

While NGOs operating in mine-infested countries initiated and generated the ban issue, the ICBL formation was marked by an expansionist phase in which its principled beliefs were used to attract new members.

Even though realists will argue that cultural effects are epiphenomenal of the distribution of power, the socialization and advocacy network literature argues that cultural effects have great autonomy.[2] Chemical and nuclear weapons taboos, for example, were reinforced not by intensive verification measures, but instead by the responsible behavior of states upholding specific cultural norms.[3] Such an emerging norm is exactly what the ICBL hoped to achieve. This chapter examines the NGO role in the land-mine ban process. It focuses on the ICBL's founding, landmine expertise, expansion, grassroots activities, and use of data in educating and pres-suring states to ban landmines. It ends with a conclusion considering possible implications of the NGO role in banning landmines for other NGO involvement in international politics.

The Founding of the ICBL

The landmine issue was born when NGO experts in the landmine issue and/or in mine-infested states decided to cooperate to ban their use. NGO experts in the field identified landmines as a major obstacle to their work. These groups viewed landmines as exacerbating regional conflicts, hinder-ing postconflict reconstruction, seriously undermining infrastructure, and denying land to civilian use, thereby leading to extreme pressures on ex-isting land.[4] They also considered landmine use a violation of humanitar-ian legal principles. Landmines are indiscriminate weapons—they cannot target their victims. Landmines killed more than 24,000 people in each year of the 1990s,[5] which by itself may not be illegal, but a significant number of the victims are civilians. Moreover, landmine injuries cause un-necessary suffering, a key consideration of international humanitarian law. According to the U.S. State Department, between 59 and 69 million land-mines are currently deployed worldwide,[6] thereby making them "one of the most toxic and widespread pollution[s] facing mankind."[7]

These problems escaped public and government attention until the early 1990s, when the ICBL was launched by six NGOs in 1992. These NGOs believed that a comprehensive landmine ban provided the only re-alistic solution to the devastation caused by their use. In less than seven years, the ICBL grew to an organization encompassing more than one thousand NGOs in more than seventy states. More important, the ICBL effectively encouraged states, international organizations and other inter-national actors to address the landmine issue and alter their views of landmine use. The ICBL played the critical role in agenda setting and con-trolling the ban landmine issue, and moved the issue forward toward the eventual goal of a codified comprehensive ban, which was contained in the Mine Ban Treaty that was signed in December 1997.

Until the NGOs began advocating for a ban, many governments were unable or unwilling to address the devastating consequences of landmine use. For example, in the 1970s, governments participating in the states 1980 Convention on Conventional Weapons (CCW) negotiations attempted to restrict landmine use in order to protect civilian populations. These attempts resulted in the Landmines Protocol (officially known as Protocol II), which placed limitations on their use. By the early 1990s, it became evident to many NGOs working in mine-infested areas that the protocol was not working properly. Increasing civilian landmine casualties and land denial due to landmine infestation indicated that states and other international actors had disregarded the protocol and that the protocol was an inadequate response to the growing humanitarian crisis caused by landmines. Physicians for Human Rights and Human Rights Watch wrote in 1993 that "the complete failure of the Landmines Protocol to control landmine use, its [the protocol's] failure to conform to the requirements imposed by customary humanitarian law, and the extreme devastation that has resulted from mine warfare, supports a ban on the production, stockpiling, transfer and use of landmines."[8] It was also evident to the NGOs that governments opposed addressing the landmine issue in a multitude of national, regional, and international forums. In April 1996, the final CCW Review Conference in Geneva ended without significant moves toward a ban. In the same month, Canada, with the ICBL's support, announced that it would host a landmine strategy conference in Ottawa in October 1996. This conference, in turn, launched the "Ottawa Process," which entailed fourteen months of swiftly negotiating with NGOs and pro-ban states and eventually cumulated in the December 1997 signing of the convention.

NGO Expertise

In general, NGOs often are the first to notice relational breakdowns within countries.[9] Because of their knowledge of local landmine situations, ICBL members were able to react quickly and lobby governments to adjust their landmine policies. Oftentimes, the ICBL members' expertise was greater than that of the United Nations and the states. ICBL members, for example, were often the major sources of information for state delegations participating in the treaty-drafting conferences. Their credibility, garnered in field operations in mine-infested states, greatly contributed to influencing the debate, and provided states with detailed and specific information that directed the landmine discussion toward the humanitarian consequences of landmines. In particular, the ICBL's NGO epistemic community had expertise in two areas: operating in mine-infested states, and landmine use and effects. Each will be discussed briefly below.

The ICBL also had the significant advantage in being able to narrow its focus on the landmine issue to the exclusion of all others, which increased their value to governments participating in the landmine discussions. Several times, the ICBL's ability to focus on banning landmines saved the convention from becoming a noncomprehensive treaty with many loopholes. The ICBL landmine expertise proved a potent tool in keeping the Ottawa Process focused on a comprehensive ban, especially given the fact that one word could have made such a significant difference in treaty interpretation.

International attention to the landmine issue was initially brought by NGOs in the human rights and humanitarian fields, which were specifically affected by the issue. These organizations had expertise in working with mine-disabled populations and in mine-infested areas. Some also had experience with weapons issues that directly affected civilians and were questionable under current international humanitarian law (see table 4.1). The ICBL's first stage of formation stemmed from two humanitarian NGOs, the Vietnam Veterans of America Foundation (VVAF) and Medico International, which focused on assisting amputees with rehabilitation. Based in Washington, DC, the VVAF was founded by Robert (Bobby) Mueller, a Marine veteran paralyzed in combat in Vietnam, in part to focus on helping prevent the causes and alleviate the consequences of war.[10] The other founding NGO member, Medico International, was a German-based NGO that also focused on helping people with disabilities in developing states. Medico International's director Thomas Gebauer asserted that landmines should be banned in light of the tragic consequences wrought in Cambodia, Vietnam, El Salvador, and Kurdistan.[11]

To get states to recognize the landmine issue, NGO experts promoted statistics as systematic indicators to indicate that there was a problem. These statistics resonated with the media, the public, and policymakers because they were so outrageous that the problem could no longer be ignored. This strategy to garner attention is similar to the assumption that new issues need to encourage action by promoting systematic indicators, such as crises and disasters, or by feedback from ongoing programs.[12] Changes in these indicators usually highlight that there is a problem in the system because "[a] steady state is viewed as less problematic than changing figures."[13] Policymakers use these indicators to decide whether to address an issue, first, by assessing the magnitude of the problem, and, second, by becoming aware of changes in the problem.[14]

The prime indicator used by the ICBL was that landmines kill and maim more than 24,000 people per year, of whom an estimated 80 percent are civilian.[15] The claim was also made by international landmine experts that this carnage will not end anytime soon because there "may

Table 4.1. Founding ICBL Members and Their Expertise Areas

ICBL Founding Member	Landmine Expertise Area	Landmine-Infested State Area	Home State
Handicap International	Physical rehabilitation	Cambodia; Vietnam; Mozambique	France
Human Rights Watch	Human rights	Cambodia	United States
Medico International	Physical rehabilitation	Angola; El Salvador	Germany
Mines Advisory Group	Demining	Afghanistan; Cambodia; Kurdistan	United Kingdom
Physicians for Human Rights	Medical support and human rights	Bosnia; Cambodia	United States
Vietnam Veterans of America Foundation	Physical rehabilitation	Angola; Cambodia; Vietnam; El Salvador	United States

be 200 million landmines scattered in at least sixty-four countries,"[16] making them "one of the most toxic and widespread pollution[s] facing mankind."[17]

Moreover, the ICBL emphasized that for many civilian communities the nature of war had recently changed from targeting the professional military of the enemy to targeting its civilians. For example, a 1991 study of Cambodia's amputee population found that out of the country's "8.5 million inhabitants over 30,000 are amputees, and a further 5,000 or so amputees live in refugee camps along the Thai border."[18] A 1998–1999 study found that while Cambodia's populations had grown to 10 million people, "at least 24,410 survived mine injuries" and more than "14,500 have died as a result of landmines.[19]

Furthermore, according to UN demining expert Patrick Blagden, a fiftyfold increase in the world's mine-clearing capability is needed to "stabilize" the current situation.[20] Such an effort would require training 170,000 to 200,000 new mine clearers worldwide costing $1.02 billion to $1.2 billion per year.[21] He warned, however, that accidents happen at a rate of one out of every one thousand to two thousand mines destroyed: "A fifty fold increase in manual mines clearance would probably cause a death and injury toll among mine clearers of about 2,000 per year, a rate that in the long term may not be supportable."[22] A case in point is Kuwait. Within in the first week after the 1991 Gulf War ended, all five Kuwaiti mine-clearing experts were killed attempting to clear landmines.[23] This is in addition to the nearly one hundred international mine clearance experts killed since the end of the Gulf War conducting the same activity.[24]

Another strategy to help policymakers understand the landmine issue and encourage the media and public to get involved entailed comparing the effects of landmine use to more commonly despised and feared weapon systems: biological, chemical, and nuclear weapons. NGOs currently estimate that more people have been killed and maimed by landmines than biological, chemical, and nuclear weapons combined.[25]

Many of the NGO generated statistics, however, are inflated and, more significantly, regurgitated by the media and policymakers without proper fact checking and research. Some of the overinflated figures became so widely common that original sources and methodological data collection techniques were unknown, while "[s]ome land mine figures are repeated so often that they are now regarded as fact."[26] The more common inflated claims regard the number of currently deployed landmines, such as in Afghanistan where 35 million were initially estimated, but then later reduced to a lower number of ten million "as a conveniently round figure."[27] Even this figure is suspicious because it would have required that the Soviets deploy "3,000 mines per day, every day of the nine-year occupation, which, given the mountainous nature of the terrain and the style of conflict, was unrealistically high."[28] Another example of grossly inflated statistics regards the deployment of mines during the Gulf War. It was initially estimated, for example, that 9 million landmines were laid by Iraqi forces immediately preceding and during Operation Desert Storm.[29] A few years after the war, a survey showed only around 1.7 million mines had been emplaced.[30]

These statistics were promoted via the Internet and through conference mechanisms, such as speeches and prepared reports, and immediately picked up by the media, which, in turn, provided a source of information to the public and governments. As recently as September 1999, CNN was still quoting NGO figures that more than 40,000 landmines are being deployed each week,[31] while this figure has no factual basis and is no longer used by NGOs, especially the ICBL. Since CNN reports are broadcast around the world and are an important informational source for many people, the report is sure to be the source for more people learning about landmines. This is one example of how information and media technologies were used to prod the public and policymakers to pay attention to the landmine issue by highlighting dramatic statistics and disseminating information.[32]

Expansion of the ICBL

The ICBL-founding NGOs were able to persuade other NGOs not directly involved with the landmine issue to join the landmine ban movement under a common understanding that banning landmines was in their organizations' interest. The international relations scholar Ernst Haas observes that "[s]uccessful negotiations for institutionalizing collaboration depend on the congruence of interests as much as on changes in consensual knowledge."[33] This proved the case in securing the landmine ban. By showing that there was a congruence of interests among the NGO community, the ICBL NGO landmine experts were able to expand and broaden the campaign to NGOs not directly affected by landmines.

By its second year, the ICBL recognized that the campaign's success depended on broad public support that was still lacking. Eventually the platform developed into a vertical campaign with organizational structure and goals. While Medico International and VVAF decided in 1991 that landmines should be banned as a way of reducing civilian deaths after wars end and of preventing more people from losing limbs, the other founding NGOs did not join in the organized call until 1992.

The ICBL founders realized that they needed to create a broad-based international coalition in order to achieve a landmine ban. The message they centered on was the premise that landmine use was inhumane and not legally justifiable, as the humanitarian impact was more severe than its military utility. Specifically, the NGOs agreed that the campaign's core identity should be focused on a basic, simple advocacy for a ban on the use, production, and trade of antipersonnel landmines.[34] The ban goal was chosen over demining and mine victim assistance because the NGOs believed that the problems of mined areas and mine victims would not be resolved until the mine deployment was prevented and production was permanently stopped. By May 1994, they realized that any campaign's success is due to widespread public pressure, therefore ICBL leaders decided that a public awareness campaign should be developed and emphasized.[35] ICBL recruiting of nonexpert NGOs was best characterized as a transnational activist movement based on a uniform principle. As explained above, the uniform principle of a landmine ban was created by NGO experts. With respect to recruiting, scholars stress the influence of transnational NGO movements that are centered on principles and norms.[36] This study expands beyond the literature by providing a more intensive investigation of the NGO role in the landmines issue and the NGOs ability to generate international action and control the agenda. In other words, the epistemic community literature has limitations in explaining how the ICBL membership expanded to nonexpert NGOs. As the ICBL began to expand, the numbers of technical experts relative to the ICBL membership began to decline.

A majority of ICBL members neither worked in the major mine-infested states nor were affected directly by landmine use. Yet, they joined the campaign driven by the core belief that banning landmines was the right thing for governments to do. And they contributed not landmine expertise, but social power or moral authority. For example, NGOs grounded in religious beliefs joined after their leaders, such as Pope John II, issued letters in support of a landmine ban. While participant NGOs were labeled "utopian" and their landmine ban goal was branded as "impossible," the ICBL gathered support from prominent persons, such as UN Secretary-General Boutros Boutros-Ghali, and former U.S. Secretary of State Cyrus Vance.[37] Former President Jimmy Carter also stated his opposition to continued landmine use, while Princess Diana lent her public support in 1997.

What makes the ICBL's achievement of building a nearly universal coalition of more than one thousand NGOs is that it is logistically difficult and expensive. The Internet allowed the ICBL to reach out to NGOs across geographical space in an effort to broaden and expand its membership base to the South. Most important, the Internet allowed the ICBL to expand to southern states at a minimal cost. The low cost and easy use of the Internet enhanced the ICBL's political strategy to get as many states on board the ban to counter treaty opposition from the major powers, such as China, Russia, and the United States.

Moreover, since most of the mine-infested southern states, it would be symbolic as well as more effective for treaty implementation if the ICBL could get southern NGOs to join the campaign. Northern NGOs could help incorporate southern NGOs into the decision-making process, which, in turn, provided the southern NGOs from most of the world's most heavily mined areas with an inexpensive avenue to provide field data. Northern NGOs, in turn, disseminated it to governmental representatives, the media, and the public. This is important because it was very important to the campaign to show that it was not just a European and North American effort, but it was truly universal, especially since most mine-infested countries are in the South.

After the 1997 treaty signing, the ICBL, the Landmine Survivors Network, and several other northern-based organizations encouraged newly forming national landmine ban campaigns to use the Internet in order to stay in contact with the campaign. Funding for some of these technologies came from the Landmines Project at the Open Society Institute, which supported some communications costs for NGOs. Individual NGOs, such as the Mines Advisory Group (MAG), supported procurement of communications technologies by forming a small grants project funded by Comic Relief, which raises money every other year for African development projects. MAG gave some of these funds to ban landmine activists requesting "grants for the purpose of equipment purchase or email/modems or fax machines . . . or towards communications costs."[38]

Grassroots Activism

The ICBL expert NGOs used a range of techniques to recruit other NGOs to the fold and pressure governments to ban landmines. These techniques included massive publicity campaigns and protest demonstrations. According to the ICBL conference and grassroots organizer Liz Bernstein, "NGO lobbying entailed communicating to Government decision-makers and diplomats in various ways, such as personal conversations, writing, face-to-face meetings, and collecting and presenting petitions."[39] As a result, a major focus of ICBL activities became public activities. The ICBL organizers encouraged national ban landmine campaigns to take public action through public demonstrations and events, which should be culturally specific and planned by the local campaign. NGOs were encouraged to customize and tailor the ban landmine message to their own communities. In fact, one factor propelling the ICBL toward success was its vertical, decentralized, and informal organizational structure, which allowed national landmine ban campaigns to determine the best strategies for getting their own governments on board. The ICBL leaders believed that "[p]ressure tactics that worked in Germany or Belgium would not necessarily be effective in Mozambique or Afghanistan."[40]

Moreover, such a strategy empowered national campaigns to take the initiative, rather than wait for a decision to evolve through the consensus-based decision making of the ICBL Steering Committee. As one international relations scholar commented "localism is based on empowerment."[41] A major force in the ICBL's grassroots efforts was Liz Bernstein, who began her human rights work in Cambodia in the peace and conflict resolution issue area. She later said that locally inspired ban landmine events were most appropriate for the ICBL because no blueprint or formula existed for NGOs to persuade their respective governments to sign the treaty.[42]

A twofold interrelated goal applied to public events: first, they allowed the ICBL to reach its goals of state signing and ratification of the convention, and second, they allowed the ICBL to reach these goals earlier. The thrust of these events worked to push governmental decision makers to "go from their brain to their heart" and "help them see landmine victim pictures and the landmine issue in a different way."[43]

The ICBL's membership included those NGOs concerned with a wide range of issues, including arms control and disarmament, economic and social development, human rights, and refugee assistance. Most important was that these NGOs gave the ICBL permission to speak for them, which resulted in the ICBL's leaders being able to speak with a single, clear voice. Rather than a cacophony of varied voices calling for a ban, with differences in ban definitions, the ICBL was allowed to represent the broad coalition, which thereby created a unified presence at international conferences and for state representatives and the media. Eventually, a multitude of voices arose with a single viewpoint on a narrow issue.

The coming together of NGOs to work internationally on an issue amplifies their communication channels and influence. According to Margaret E. Keck and Kathryn Sikkink, NGOs use information as a means to lobby and pressure governments to behave according to certain standards. They argue that one reason for the cessation of human rights violations in Latin America was the work of human rights NGOs "who provided crucial information on human rights violations and lobbied governments international organizations to express concern, investigate, and bring pressure for change." More broadly, their thesis is that at the core of transnational NGO activity is the "production, exchange, and strategic use of information."[44] When NGOs capitalize on their expertise and are successful in their use of informational strategies, they can become "important sources of new ideas, norms, and identities in the international system."[45] By working as an advocacy network, these NGOs "contribute to changing perceptions that both state and societal actors may have of their identities, interests, and preferences to transforming their discursive positions, and ultimately to changing procedures, polices and behaviors."[46] Sikkink argues elsewhere that these movements also reveal how NGOs can persuade other actors of the salience and value of new norms.[47] The landmine case provides evidence confirming Keck and Sikkink's theses that international NGO coalitions can change state behavior.

Conclusion

Most major arms control and disarmament treaties negotiated militarily were initiated by major powers. Unlike all previous international arms control agreements, the landmine ban is not a result of hegemonic influence, as evidenced by the absence of major states among state signatories.[48] The Mine Ban Treaty represents a significant change for the NGO role in arms control treaty negotiations. NGOs went beyond informing and moving international public opinion by educating and lobbying governments, who in turn were moved to view landmines differently—as a humanitarian threat rather than merely as a military weapons. The ICBL activities herald an international trend of NGOs moving into portions of international relations once dominated by governments. Perhaps the NGO role in banning landmines is evidence of how NGOs will be incorporated into future international negotiations and policymaking. If the past is prologue, the landmine campaign may auger how future international relations will be conducted. Should that be the case, NGO activities might well foster new sources of international norm creation, on the way to building a more civil international society.

The NGO role in banning landmines also provides a distinctive form of international politics that this chapter assesses: a collaborative process among NGOs. This form of international politics provides a process model that could be useful in current and future efforts to promote security and prohibitions and restrictions. For example, the NGO Coalition to Stop the Use of Child Soldiers is attempting to attach an optional protocol banning the recruitment and participation of child soldiers to the Convention on the Rights of the Child.[49] Another effort that evinces this distinctive form of world politics is the Global Campaign on Small Arms and Light Weapons.[50] The campaign is composed of NGOs and seeks to address the problems caused by the proliferation and misuse of small arms and light weapons. The "distinctive form of world politics" evidenced by the landmine campaign "provided the foundation" for this effort to alleviate the effects of "the widespread availability of light weapons."[51]

The ICBL success sheds light on a few conditions under which NGOs, especially working with states, can affect state behavior in an area traditionally at the heart of state sovereignty: security and weapons. It also provides a process model for current and future NGO–state collaborative efforts to alleviate the negative effects of certain weapons, especially those with a dubious military strategy or utility. Since the ban landmine norm originated from the substate level and not with major state powers, the rise of the landmine ban norm may help explain why particular issues take off.

Notes

The chapter opening quotation is from a statement made on May 13, 1994, before a subcommittee of the Committee on Appropriations of the U.S. Senate by

Robert (Bobby) Mueller, who is the executive director of the Vietnam Veterans of America Foundation and cofounder of the International Campaign to Ban Landmines, to Senator Patrick J. Leahy, who was the chairperson of The Global Landmine Crisis hearing.

1. According to the Union of International Associations, there are 38,243 international NGOs working around the world and in a wide range of issue areas. See their *Yearbook of International Organizations 1996–1997*, which is available at http://www.uia.org/uiastats/stybv196.htm.

2. Ronald L. Jepperson, Alexander Wendt, and Peter J. Katzenstein, "Norms, Identity, and Culture in National Security," in *The Culture of National Security: Norms and Identity in World Politics*, ed. Peter J. Katzenstein, 33–75 (New York: Columbia University Press, 1996).

3. Richard Price and Nina Tannenwald, "Norms and Deterrence: The Nuclear and Chemical Weapons Taboos," in Katzenstein, *The Culture of National Security*, 114–152.

4. U.S. Department of State, *1998 Hidden Killers: The Global Landmine Crisis* (Washington, DC: U.S. Department of State, 1998), 8–9, 11.

5. International Committee for the Red Cross, *Landmines Must Be Stopped* (Geneva: ICRC, 1998), 16.

6. U.S. Department of State, *1998 Hidden Killers*, 9.

7. U.S. Department of State, *1993 Hidden Killers: The Global Problem with Uncleared Landmines* (Washington, DC: U.S. Department of State, 1993), 2.

8. The Arms Project of Human Rights Watch and Physicians for Human Rights, *Deadly Legacy* (New York: Human Rights Watch, 1993), 263.

9. Judy Mayotte, "NGOs and Diplomacy," in *Multilateral Diplomacy and the United Nations Today*, ed. James P. Muldoon Jr., JoAnn Fagot Aviel, Richard Retiano, and Earl Sullivan (Boulder, CO: Westview, 1999), 167.

10. Susan Reed and Andrea Pawlyna, "A Marine's Reparation: Thanks to a Vietnam Vet, Cambodia Amputees Have New Legs and Jobs," *People*, December 11, 1995, 103.

11. Statement of Thomas Gebauer, director, Medico International, to the Oslo Landmines NGO-Forum, September 7–10, 1997, as quoted in the ICBL report "NGO Forum on Landmines" Oslo, Norway, September 7–10, 1997 (unnumbered pages).

12. John W. Kingdon, *Agendas, Alternatives, and Public Policies* (Glenview, IL: Scott, Foresman, 1984), 20–21.

13. Ibid., 96.

14. Ibid.

15. Gino Strada, "The Horror of Land Mines," *Scientific American* (May 1996): 42. It is also argued that most of the landmine victims are women and chil-

dren (see Donovan Webster, "One Leg, One Life at a Time," *New York Times Magazine*, January 23, 1994, 33).

16. Patrick M. Blagden, United Nations demining expert, estimates that there may be more than 200 million in "Summary of United Nations Demining," *Symposium on Anti-personnel Mines*, Montreux, 21–23, April 1993 (Geneva: ICRC), 117. The U.S. Department of State estimates that there are 80–110 antipersonnel mines in sixty-four countries; see their *Hidden Killers: The Global Landmine Crisis, 1994 Report to the U.S. Congress on the Problem with Uncleared Landmines and the United States Strategy for Debiting and Control*, Department of State Publication 10225, December 1994, v.

17. U.S. Department of State, *1993 Hidden Killers*, 2.

18. Eric Stover and Dan Charles, "The Killing Minefields of Cambodia," *New Scientist*, October 19, 1991, 27.

19. International Campaign to Ban Landmines, *Landmine Monitor Report 1999*, May 1999, 405. Available at http://www.icbl.org/lm/1999/.

20. Patrick Blagden, "The Use of Mines and the Impact of Technology," in *Clearing the Fields: Solutions to the Global Land Mines Crisis*, ed. Kevin M. Cahill, 112–123 (New York: Basic Books, 1995), 114.

21. Ibid., 114–115.

22. Ibid., 115.

23. Webster, "One Leg, One Life at a Time," 29.

24. Ibid.

25. *America's Defense Monitor*, PBS TV, Spring 1994.

26. Laurie H. Boulden, "A Mine Field, Statistically Speaking: The Dangers of Inflating the Problem," *Washington Post*, February 8, 1998, C2.

27. Mike Croll, *The History of Landmines* (Barnsley, UK: Pen and Sword Books, 1998), 131.

28. Ibid.

29. International Committee for the Red Cross, *Anti-personnel Landmines Friend or Foe? A Study of the Military Use and Effectiveness of Anti-personnel mines* (Geneva: ICRC, March 1996), 37.

30. ICBL, *Landmine Monitor Report 1999*, 15.

31. Bernard Shaw, CNN *World News Tonight*, September 6, 1999.

32. For further information on the role of information technologies in promoting the landmine ban and victim assistance, see Ken Rutherford, "Virtual Activism: Survivors and the Mine Ban Treaty," *Georgetown Journal of International Affairs* (Summer/Fall 2000): 37–43.

33. Ernst B. Haas, "Why Collaborate? Issue-Linkage and International Regimes," in *International Organization: A Reader*, ed. Friedrich Kratochwil and Edward D. Mansfield, 357–405 (New York: HarperCollins College Publishers, 1994), 369.

34. NGO Conference on Antipersonnel Mines, *Report of the Final Plenary Session*, London, May 26, 1993, 1.

35. Ibid., 3.

36. Margaret E. Keck and Kathryn Sikkink, *Activists Beyond Borders: Advocacy in International Politics* (Ithaca, NY: Cornell University Press, 1998).

37. NGO, *Report*, 1.

38. E-mail interview with Tim Carstairs, Mines Advisory Group, January 31, 2000.

39. Statement by Liz Bernstein, ICBL cocoordinator, to the Panel Presentation and Discussion "Campaigning: Launching National Campaigns, Using the Media, Public Awareness Raising, Coalition Building, and Direct Action," Regional Conference on Landmines, Budapest, Hungary, March 27, 1998. Report: *Regional Conference on Landmines, International Campaign to Ban Landmines*, Budapest, Hungary, March 26–28, 1998, p. 58.

40. James Bandler, "Laureate in a Minefield," *Boston Globe Magazine*, June 7, 1998, 28.

41. Paul Wapner, *Environmental Activism and World Civic Politics* (Albany: State University of New York Press, 1996), 115.

42. Bernstein, Statement, 58.

43. Statement of Dalma Foldes, ICBL resource coordinator, ICBL 2000 Landmine Monitor Researchers Meeting, Brussels, Belgium, January 30, 2000.

44. Keck and Sikkink, *Activists Beyond Borders*, vii–viii.

45. Ibid., x.

46. Ibid., 3.

47. Kathryn Sikkink, "Transnational Politics, International Relations Theory, and Human Rights: A New Model of International Politics is needed to Explain the Politics of Human Rights," *Political Science and Politics* (September 1998), 519.

48. Every major multilateral arms control agreement in the twentieth century has entailed major power participation in its creation, development, and implementation. See Ken Rutherford, "The Hague and Ottawa Conventions: A Model for Future Weapon Ban Regimes," *Nonproliferation Review* (Spring–Summer 1999): 36–50.

49. See the Coalition to Stop the Use of Child Soldiers Web site: www.childsoldiers.org.

50. See the Preparatory Committee for a Global Campaign on Small Arms and Light Weapons Web site: www.prepcom.org.

51. Liz Clegg, "NGOs Take Aim," *Bulletin of the Atomic Scientists* (January/ February 1999), 49.

5

Clearing the Path to a Mine-Free World: Implementing the Ottawa Convention

KERRY BRINKERT AND KEVIN HAMILTON

O N DECEMBER 3 AND 4, 1997, 121 STATES GATHERED IN OTTAWA TO SIGN the Convention on the Prohibition of the Use, Stockpiling, Production and Transfer of Anti-Personnel Mines and on Their Destruction (Ottawa Convention or Convention), signaling their intention to adhere to the Convention at a later date. The ceremony represented the culmination of the Ottawa Process, which had begun a mere fourteen months prior. In that short period, the Ottawa Process—characterized by close partnerships between governments and nongovernmental organizations (NGOs) and an emphasis on fast-track diplomacy—achieved what many observers thought impossible: an unequivocal ban on an entire class of conventional weaponry. The Ottawa Convention bans the production, use, and transfer of antipersonnel landmines (APLs), requires the destruction of stockpiled APLs and the clearance of mined areas, and calls on states in a position to do so to provide resources to assist landmine victims and to implement the Convention.

For NGOs, which had tirelessly raised awareness of the humanitarian cost of APLs, for diplomats who had worked hard to defy the normally slow pace of multilateral diplomacy, and for political leaders who in many instances took significant risks to advance the ban, this was a remarkable accomplishment. However, codification of an international agreement is not synonymous with implementation. The Ottawa Convention had provided a schedule for the eradication of APLs; but the ultimate gauge of its success would rest with the extent to which it truly lived up to its promise as an instrument that would put an end to the suffering and casualties caused by these weapons.

While some of the euphoria surrounding the ban may have worn off since 1997, the Convention remains one of the most important international humanitarian legal instruments ever developed. The Convention has been in force for more than four years and the States Parties to it have commenced their preparations for the Convention's First Review Conference. The natural question to ask at this point is whether the Convention is living up to its promise as a comprehensive framework for addressing the global landmine problem.

The purpose of this chapter is to document the manner in which the Convention is making a significant contribution in addressing the impact of APLs and preventing any further impact. Through the continuation of the cooperative relationship between states, NGOs, and international organizations (IOs), efforts to ensure the application of the Convention began as soon as the Convention was opened for signature. Many of these efforts were early examples of ensuring that the Convention's assistance and cooperation mechanisms would be more than simply words on paper. This effort has continued since the entry into force of the Convention through the decisions taken by the States Parties to establish flexible and dynamic implementation mechanisms to complement those already in the text of the Convention. In advance of the Convention's First Review Conference, the States Parties have used these implementation mechanisms to focus coherently on those matters most closely related to achieving the core humanitarian aims of the Convention. While it is often difficult to draw a causal relationship between this broad coherence and on-the-ground results, it is possible—given a range of positive indicators—to suggest that the Convention is making a difference in addressing the global landmine problem. Finally, this chapter will note that the activities undertaken to establish and implement the Convention may serve as a model for multilateral efforts to address other humanitarian problems or other international challenges.

Agenda for Mine Action

Canada had played a leading role in the establishment of the Convention, largely through the political will of its prime minister, Jean Chrétien, and the political gamble of its foreign minister, Lloyd Axworthy, in challenging the international community to negotiate a ban on APLs. Many have reflected on why Canada took such a lead on this issue, but it may be best summed up by Robert Lawson and his colleagues who have recorded that "while the Ottawa Process deployed many of the traditional skills and practices of Canadian multilateralism," the end of the Cold War "opened up new opportunities for middle powers to influence the course of international affairs."[1] Given its commitment to the establishment of the Convention, it was a natural that Canada would accept a sense of responsibility in ensuring that the Convention would in fact be implemented as a framework for addressing the global landmine problem. In particular, Canada—working closely with its partners from the Ottawa Process—was determined to ensure that the December 1997 Convention signing ceremony in Ottawa would be more than ceremonial.

In parallel to the signing ceremony, Canada organized a workshop titled "An Agenda for Mine Action" as a forum for all relevant actors to reflect on and draw lessons from the Ottawa Process with a view to implementing and universalizing the Convention. At the outset, Canada recognized the need to build on the momentum gained over the preceding months through a series of agenda-setting and regional support conferences. The Ottawa workshop represented the apex of these regional efforts, and it transferred the final text of the Convention—negotiated in Oslo three months earlier—into a binding, comprehensive commitment among nations to take concrete action aimed at eradicating APLs and addressing their negative effects on human security.

In his opening address at An Agenda for Mine Action, Lloyd Axworthy noted that the Convention had come into being because policymakers and ban advocates had recognized that diplomacy can work in new ways to bring about unprecedented progress and that full partnerships between states and NGOs can produce results that neither group could achieve on its own.[2] Canada hoped that these lessons would inspire the three-day forum, and produce a road map for the international community to move forward in a coherent and coordinated way to ensure the effective implementation of the Convention. The workshop dealt with matters such as propagating the messages of the abhorrent humanitarian cost of APLs and their questionable military utility, promoting the Convention within all relevant multilateral and regional forums, and building on the public awareness and political will generated by the Ottawa Process. Round-table sessions were designed to facilitate an understanding of the various Convention obligations and methods for acting on them. For example, the workshop highlighted the need to collect data in the field in order to comply with the Convention's reporting obligations; it initiated dialogue on the need to build capacities to monitor compliance with Convention obligations; and it raised issues regarding the need to mobilize large amounts of resources—an obligation of states "in a position to do so" under article 6 of the Convention—and the related need to effectively coordinate resources for mine action.

Perhaps most significantly, An Agenda for Mine Action focused the attention of the international community on tasks related to the achievement of the Convention's core humanitarian aims, including clearing mined areas, reducing casualties, and providing assistance to landmine survivors. With respect to mine clearance, the forum helped develop a common discourse around a "toolbox" approach to the problem: the need for an effective coordination and supervisory structure, data collection and information management, and a survey and detection capacity—complete with mine detection dogs, as well as manual and mechanical clearance assets. Promoting a common understanding of the principles underlying the approach to the problem was also a feature of victim assistance discussions. For instance, the event clearly identified that victim assistance is an ongoing obligation that involves not only medical care and rehabilitation, but also support for the social and economic reintegration of landmine survivors in their communities. Round-table discussions on mine risk education[3] not only noted the value of such programming in reducing casualties, but also pointed to the need to develop mine risk education in a manner consistent with the specific requirements of individuals in mine-affected communities.

In March 1998, Canada hosted another event that sought to push the mine action agenda forward. At the Mine Action Coordination Workshop state representatives and their nonstate partners again gathered in Ottawa, displaying the same level of urgency demonstrated during the Ottawa Process, to discuss specific means to achieve the Convention's objectives. Outcomes of the workshop included strategies for bolstering the mine action capacity of the United Nations, maximizing coordination among donors, and ensuring that necessary resources would be mobilized to assist states in meeting Convention obligations to provide information on mined areas and stockpiles requiring destruction. Recommendations resulted related to data standardization, the need for transparency and efficiency in data management, and the complementary relationships between the reporting obligations of the Convention and the types of impact data required to determine mine action priorities. Discussions were held on issues pertaining to mine action standards, including the development or refinement of training and demining standards and accreditation. In addition, the involvement in the workshop of those with experience in the field contributed to a major shift in focus of the mine action community from numbers-based assessment (i.e., crude estimates of the number of mines in the ground) to impact-based assessment (i.e., assessing the impact of mines on a specific population and working to reduce and eliminate that threat).

An Agenda for Mine Action, the Mine Action Coordination Workshop, and a third Canadian-hosted event, the December 1998 meeting titled "Developing a Vision for Global Mine Action," served as catalysts, or launching pads in some instances, for some of the most significant structures now in place to facilitate the implementation of the Convention. At An Agenda for Mine Action, the creation of the UN Mine Action Service was announced and since that time the service effectively has established itself as the focal point for mine action in the UN system, a provider of services such as assessment missions in mine-affected countries and a facilitator of dialogue between donors, mine action officials, and the United Nations. The Mine Action Coordination Workshop recommended that impact surveys and assessment missions be standardized as a means of identifying high-priority areas for mine action and proposed that a survey contact group convene for the purpose of developing these standards and processes. The result of these discussions has been that the Survey Action Centre has coordinated Landmine Impact Surveys, which provide vital standardized information to improve priority setting by donors and mine action agencies in the international effort to eliminate or control the threat of mines. As of March 2003, Landmine Impact Surveys had been completed in Cambodia, Chad, Kosovo, Mozambique, Thailand, and Yemen, and were underway or planned in eleven additional mine-affected countries. Related to the Mine Action Coordination Workshop, recommendations regarding standardized impact surveys was the suggestion that the United Nations commence with the development of a mine action information system that could be made available to all national mine action programs. Acting on this suggestion, the Geneva International Centre for Humanitarian Demining developed for the United Nations the cutting-edge Information Management System for Mine Action, which by 2003 had been made available to mine action programs operating in more than twenty countries. The Mine Action Coordination Workshop also highlighted the need for a civil-society-based global monitoring system to complement the transparency measures contained in the Ottawa Convention. These discussions led to the creation of the Landmine Monitor initiative, which was launched by the ICBL in June 1998 and which since that time has seen the ICBL publish 1,000-plus page annual reports on the implementation of the Convention and the overall pursuit of its aims. An addition, the 1998 Developing a Vision for Global Mine Action led to the United Nations establishing a comprehensive global portfolio of mine action funding opportunities and an innovative online database of donor contributions.

Implementation Mechanisms

By the time of the December 1998 Developing a Vision for Global Mine Action, almost three months had passed since the west African nation of

Burkina Faso had deposited its instrument of ratification with the United Nations—the fortieth country to do so. This action triggered a six-month countdown to the Convention's entry into force on March 1, 1999.[4] Two months after the Convention took effect, the States Parties set about to ensure the full operationalization of the implementation mechanisms contained in the text of the Convention.

Those who drafted the Convention had the foresight to incorporate into the text a trio of implementation mechanisms, with the centerpiece of these being article 6. This article contains a set of rights of each State Party to seek and receive assistance in the fulfilment of its Convention obligations and to request assistance in the elaboration of a national mine action plan. Article 6 also contains a set of responsibilities of States Parties to provide assistance—including assistance for demining, the destruction of stockpiled mines, and the care and rehabilitation of landmine victims. In essence, article 6 codified cooperation and made it clear that it will take partnership to ensure that the Convention lives up to its humanitarian promise. In addition, the article ensured that partnership would be defined broadly, to include partnership between the States Parties as well as with the UN system; international, regional, or national organizations or institutions; the International Committee of the Red Cross, the national Red Cross, and the Red Crescent societies; and NGOs.

Serving as an important forum for dialogue in the pursuit of the Convention's core humanitarian aims is another important Convention implementation mechanism: the annual meeting of the States Parties. Article 11 indicates that the States Parties shall meet annually until the Convention's First Review Conference to consider any matter regarding the application or implementation of the Convention. These meetings are specifically mandated to consider "international cooperation and assistance in accordance with Article 6." From the outset, meetings of the States Parties have alternated between countries affected by antipersonnel mines and Geneva. The meetings in mine-affected countries (i.e., Mozambique, Nicaragua, and Thailand) have served as poignant reminders to all of the Convention's importance in addressing real-life humanitarian problems.

The third implementation mechanism contained in the Convention is the provision in article 12 for review conferences. This mechanism provides a five-year period of reflection regarding cooperative efforts to fulfill the humanitarian aims of the Convention. In accordance with the provisions of article 12, the First Review Conference will be held in 2004.

Meetings of the States Parties, review conferences, and article 6 of the Convention are important, but they are simply words on paper unless brought to life through the Convention's unique spirit of cooperation. In this context, the States Parties at an early stage knew that more would be required to operationalize the cooperation and assistance provisions of the

Convention. At their first annual meeting in 1999, the States Parties created the innovative Intersessional Work Programme "to ensure the systematic, effective implementation of the Convention through a more regularized programme of work." Standing committees, as they are now known, were created to "engage a broad international community for the purpose of advancing the achievement of the humanitarian objectives of the Convention."[5] The Intersessional Work Programme's committee structure largely mirrors the humanitarian aims of the Convention in that distinct forums are dedicated to deliberations on cooperative means to assist victims, clear mined land and destroy stockpiled mines, and review the general status and operation of the Convention, including the status of efforts to mobilize resources for implementation. In keeping with the Convention's tradition of partnership between developed and developing countries, States Parties selected to serve as cochairs and corapporteurs of the Standing Committees are matched to ensure a balance between mine-affected and donor states and between different regions of the world.

In addition to having established the Intersessional Work Programme, in being pragmatic in addressing new needs as they have arisen, the States Parties in 2000 established a committee to coordinate matters related to the Intersessional Work Programme. The Coordinating Committee includes the Standing Committee's sixteen cochairs and corapporteurs and is chaired by the president of the most recent meeting of the States Parties.

In responding to additional identified needs, the States Parties in 2001 provided the Geneva International Centre for Humanitarian Demining with the mandate to furnish ongoing support to the States Parties through the Implementation Support Unit. The Implementation Support Unit provides independent professional advice and support to the presidents of meetings of the States Parties, the cochairs of the Standing Committees, and individual States Parties. It disseminates a range of information on the Convention to the States Parties and all other interested actors. In addition, on the basis of its mandate the Implementation Support Unit has established and maintains a documentation resource facility.

The practical-minded approach of the States Parties has even gone one step beyond their formal agreements to establish various implementation mechanisms as a third category of mechanisms has emerged to assist in implementing the Convention. These are mechanisms that have emerged on an informal basis. To promote widespread international participation in the work of the Convention—to a degree rarely seen with similar instruments—a group of States Parties has established a delegate sponsorship program. On the basis of voluntary contributions from a group of donors, this program has ensured that over two hundred delegates each year are provided with financial support, thereby ensuring that voices from states like Chad, Mozambique, Angola, Honduras, Tajikistan, Cambodia, and Bosnia and Herzegovina can be heard as loudly as those from states like Canada, Germany, France, Norway, and the United Kingdom. Other informal mechanisms that have emerged include contact groups, voluntary associations of States Parties and non-state partners that meet regularly to discuss cooperative means to promote the universal acceptance of the Convention, the exchange of information in accordance with the Convention's reporting requirements, and the mobilization of resources.

Coherent Action and Active Progress

The September 2002 Fourth Meeting of the States Parties featured the agreement by the States Parties that stepped-up action will be required to ensure the fulfillment of the Convention's core humanitarian aims. By that time it was clear that a great deal had been accomplished in implementing the Convention and promoting its universal acceptance. However, it was also clear that in advance of the Convention's First Review Conference in 2004 additional efforts would be required to ensure that the Convention lives up to its humanitarian promise.

With a view to focusing the collective efforts of the States Parties and their partners, the Fourth Meeting of the States Parties warmly welcomed the *President's Action Programme*. This document sought to ensure that efforts would focus on the core humanitarian aims of the Convention: clearing mined areas, destroying stocks, assisting survivors, and universalizing the ban on APLs. In addition, it proposed a concrete set of supportive actions that could be taken in the period leading up to the Fifth Meeting of the States Parties in 2003.

In essence, the effort of the States Parties to focus coherently on the core objectives of the Convention has produced a better sense of how progress should be measured. Quite simply, progress will be indicated by assessments such as how many states have joined the Convention and the impact of their joining on reduced global production and transfer of APLs; how many stockpiled APLs have been destroyed and the extent to which States Parties have adhered to stockpile destruction deadlines; the extent to which progress has been made in clearing mined areas, not only in terms of the area cleared but also in terms of how mine-affected States Parties have taken ownership over their landmine problems; the extent to which efforts have been undertaken to provide for the care and rehabilitation of landmine survivors; and the amount and sustainability of resources generated for mine action.

With respect to the level of acceptance of the Convention and its impact on matters such as the production and transfer of APLs, it is significant to note that by March 1, 2003, the fourth anniversary of the entry into force of the Convention, 131 states had agreed to be formally bound by the Convention, including almost every state in the Americas, Sub-Saharan Africa, and Europe, as well as forty-five mine-affected countries. This level of acceptance means that thirty-four of the fifty-five countries that the NGO community considers to have been producers of APLs legally have accepted that they shall never do so again. An additional seven states that have yet to join the Convention also have ended their production of these weapons. As well, the trade in APLs has all but disappeared. *Janes Mines and Mine Clearance 2000–2001* noted that there has been a "virtual absence of mines—legitimate or otherwise—at arms shows and military equipment exhibitions this year. The stigmatization process has clearly had a major impact: even non-signatories to the (Convention) seem to feel the need to appear politically correct."[6]

The March 1, 2003, fourth anniversary of the Convention's entry into force, in coinciding with the Convention's first deadline for the destruction of stockpiled APLs, also served to highlight one of the Convention's major early achievements: the fact that fifty-five States Parties by that date collectively had destroyed almost 30 million landmines. One of the ICBL's most experienced campaigners, Susan B. Walker, a veteran of humanitarian assistance operations along the heavily mined Thai–Cambodian border, was effusive at a news conference marking this achievement: "At a time when there is a great deal of pessimism surrounding multilateral affairs, this Convention serves as a beacon of hope that citizens and their governments, working in partnership, can make a difference." Walker continued, noting that "the actions taken by States Parties to destroy almost 30 million mines means these weapons will never threaten to take life or limb of an innocent civilian, or affect the socio-economic development of some of the world's poorest countries." The celebration over the number of mines destroyed was matched by an extremely high compliance rate. Ambassador Jean Lint of Belgium, the president of the Fourth Meeting of the States Parties, noted on February 27, 2003, that every State Party but one with a March 1 deadline for destruction had indicated that it no longer would possess stockpiles by that date.[7]

The first deadline for some States Parties to clear mined land does not occur until March 1, 2009—six years after the first deadline for stockpile destruction. Nevertheless, major strides already have been made. Leading the way has been Costa Rica, which in December 2002 became the first State Party that had reported mined areas to indicate that it had completed clearance of these areas in accordance with the provisions of the Convention.[8] In addition, incredible advances have been made by the remaining forty-four mine-affected States Parties to reduce the size of areas thought to be hazardous by confirming that suspect areas are indeed safe from mines, to clear mined areas, and to return this land to communities for productive use. In 2002, Croatia, for example, reported that an area greater than 42 million square meters had been handed over to community use in 2001. For its part, Cambodia has reported that 166 million square meters was cleared from 1992 to 2001. In addition, Nicaragua— the most-mine-affected country in the Americas—reported that more than 2.5 million square meters of land had been cleared in 2001 for agriculture and grazing.[9]

As encouraging is the extent to which the mine-affected States Parties to the Convention have taken ownership over their national situations. This is an absolute necessity because, ultimately, the responsibility for clearing mined areas lies with the state that has accepted the obligation to do so. Some examples of this progress include Mozambique, which has used the findings of its Landmine Impact Survey to develop a five-year national mine action plan that takes into account the Convention's ten-year time frame for mine clearance while embedding mine action into Mozambique's national poverty reduction strategy.[10] Similarly, Bosnia and Herzegovina has taken command of its national landmine problem by incorporating a comprehensive mine action sector strategy into its draft poverty reduction strategy paper.[11]

The concept of states taking responsibility for the impact of landmines within their own borders is central to the Convention's humanitarian imperative to provide for the care and rehabilitation of landmine survivors. Actions taken by the mine-affected States Parties to the Convention in accordance with their responsibilities are having a real impact. Casualty rates in some of the most affected countries have steadily dropped. In Cambodia, for example, recorded casualties have declined every year since the beginning of the Ottawa Process—from a high of 4,151 in 1996 to 813 in 2001. Chad saw casualty numbers drop from 148 in 1999 to 10 in 2001.[12] At the global level, a leading NGO in the delivery of assistance to victims, Handicap International, recorded 7,728 new victims in 2001, down from at least 8,700 recorded in 2000.[13] While it is encouraging to note decreasing numbers of new casualties, the fact remains that the cumulative number of survivors continues to increase. It is impossible to know for certain how many landmine survivors there are in the world. It is likely, though, that hundreds of thousands of landmine victims have been added to the ranks of those disabled, psychologically scarred, and socially and economically marginalized in some of the world's poorest countries.

Unlike for mine clearance and stockpile destruction, for victim assistance the Convention contains no time-bound, concrete task. Determining measures of progress, therefore, falls to each individual State Party that has citizens who have fallen victim to landmines and hence require care and assistance. This element of national ownership is even more important given that measures of progress and the pace of expected progress is different for each individual State Party, depending on its level of development. To facilitate a bottom-up process of mine-affected States Parties articulating these measures of progress, the Colombian and French cochairs of the Standing Committee on Victim Assistance and Socio-Economic Reintegration opened up the space in 2003 for each State Party in need to express what its current situation is, what it desires it to be, what its plan is to get there, and what its priorities are for assistance. As of March 2003, over one-quarter of these States had taken advantage of this opportunity, thereby suggesting that in the time remaining before the 2004 Review Conference all mine-affected States Parties could indicate how progress will be defined in the care and rehabilitation of landmine survivors.

Whether it be victim assistance, mine clearance, or the destruction of stockpiled mines, what drives progress are two important ingredients: will and resources. In terms of political will, it is heartening to see that a survey of activities in 2002 indicates that in several countries there is an ongoing high-level commitment to ensuring the Convention lives up to its promise. In June of 2002 the foreign ministers of Chile and Peru issued a communiqué in which they reaffirmed their dedication to eradicate antipersonnel mines. The same month Switzerland's defense minister underscored that country's commitment to the Convention at Switzerland's national exposition. In July 2002, the foreign ministers of the thirteen member states of the Human Security Network indicated their desire to redouble efforts to universalize the Convention and to eliminate antipersonnel mines. A month later, the vice ministers from Guatemala, Honduras, El Salvador, Nicaragua, Costa Rica, Colombia, Ecuador, and Peru issued the Llamado de Managua—or Managua Call—reaffirming their governments' commitment to implement the Convention and calling on those who have not yet joined the Convention to do so. In September 2002, Norway's international development minister stated Norway's intention "to maintain the same level of (financial) support in the comings years" as in the past.[14] And three months later—on the eve of the fifth anniversary of the historic Convention signing ceremony in Ottawa—Canada's Minister of Foreign Affairs Lloyd Axworthy announced a C$72 million renewal of Canadian funding to mine action.

The financial commitments made by Canada and Norway—five years after the euphoria of the establishment of the Convention—are indicative of how funding support for the implementation of the Convention has been sustained many years beyond the landmine issue's peak in public awareness. In a study released by Norway in February 2003, it was noted that more than US$1.32 billion had been generated since the year of the Convention's establishment for the pursuit of its humanitarian aims. The same study noted that thirty-seven States Parties had delivered on commitments to provide assistance to mine-affected States Parties. As significant, though, was the study's mention that thirteen mine-affected States Parties had themselves allocated more than US$167 million in national resources since 1997 to address their own landmine problems. Clearly, both donors and those States Parties affected by landmines have taken full ownership over the implementation of the Convention and have not relented in their commitment to achieve the Convention's aims.[15]

The Lessons of Ottawa, The Lessons for Ottawa

The record of implementation of the Ottawa Convention suggests that some of the defining characteristics of the Ottawa Process have been sustained years after the December 1997 signing ceremony in Ottawa. States have continued to work in close partnership with NGOs and IOs. The States Parties have been pragmatic in developing new implementation mechanisms as needs have arisen. As well, in advance of the Convention's First Review Conference, the States Parties have applied a very practical-minded and business-like approach used during the Ottawa Process to focus even more intensively on those matters most closely related to achieving the core humanitarian aims of the Convention. Clearly, these efforts are paying off in terms of the Convention making a difference in addressing the global landmine problem.

Because the Convention works well is precisely why it is often seen, and should be seen, as a model for multilateral efforts to address other humanitarian problems or other international challenges. In fact, those active in efforts to address the humanitarian impact of the proliferation of small arms and light weapons and in promoting the establishment of an international criminal court have attempted to some degree to apply many of the Ottawa Convention's lessons. Without doubt, there are some lessons that are transferable. Nevertheless, the landmines issue remains somewhat unique, perhaps due to the unwavering focus of NGOs, IOs, diplomats, and political leaders—the same set of actors that made the Convention possible in the first place—on keeping their eye on the ultimate prize: conclusively ending the suffering caused by APLs. But because this prize still remains on the horizon, it is important to consider not only how the lessons of Ottawa can be applied to other issues but also how these lessons can be recycled to be applied back to the ongoing implementation of the Convention itself. The role of partnerships, flexibility, pragmatism, and innovation undoubtedly will remain extremely relevant in ensuring the ongoing movement toward, the fulfillment of the Convention's humanitarian promise. In addition, a continued emphasis on state responsibility and ownership undoubtedly will ensure the sustainability of this effort.

Notes

1. Robert J. Lawson, Mark Gwozdecky, Jill Sinclair, and Ralph Lysyshyn, "The Ottawa Process and the International Movement to Ban Anti-Personnel Mines," in *To Walk without Fear: The Global Movement to Ban Landmines*, ed. Maxwell A. Cameron, Robert J. Lawson, and Brian W. Tomlin, (Oxford: Oxford University Press, 1998): 160–184.

2. Lloyd Axworthy, *An Address by the Honourable Lloyd Axworthy, Minister of Foreign Affairs, to the Opening of the Mine Action Forum*, Ottawa, Canada, December 2, 1997.

3. At the time, what is now known as "mine risk education" was referred to as "mine awareness."

4. Article 17 of the Convention states that "(the) Convention shall enter into force on the first day of the sixth month after the month in which the 40th instrument of ratification, acceptance, approval or accession has been deposited." Burkina Faso submitted their ratification on September 18, 1998, with five additional states submitting theirs later the same month. Therefore, when the Convention entered into force on March 1, 1999, it did so for all those States—forty-five in total—that had ratified or acceded to it by the end of September 1998. The full text of the Mine Ban Treaty can be found online at http://www.icbl.org/.

5. United Nations, *Final Report of the First Meeting of the States Parties to the Convention on the Prohibition of the Use, Stockpiling, Production and Transfer of Anti-Personnel Mines and on Their Destruction*, May 1999. Available at http://www.mines.gc.ca/VII/VII_B_I-en.asp.

6. *Janes Mines and Mine Clearance 2000–2001*, 5th ed., quoted in International Campaign to Ban Landmines, *Landmine Monitor, Executive Summary 2001* (New York: Human Rights Watch, August 2001), 13.

7. United Nations, *4th Anniversary of Landmines Treaty Coincides with its First Deadline: Almost 30 Million Mines Destroyed*, Press Release issued February 27, 2003.

8. Permanent Mission of Costa Rica to the United Nations and Other International Organizations in Geneva, *Statement Delivered by Deputy Ambassador Nora Ruiz de Angulo to the Fourth Meeting of the States Parties to the Convention on Certain Conventional Weapons' Amended Protocol II*, December 11, 2002.

9. Information on progress in demining was obtained from article 7 transparency reports that each States Party is required to submit to the United Nations secretary-general no later than April 30 each year.

10. Instituto Nacional de Desminagem, *The Five-Year National Mine Action Plan 2002–2006*, (Lourenço Marques: República de Moçambique Ministério dos Negócios Estrangeiros e Cooperação, November 19, 2001).

11. Bosnia and Herzegovina, *Development Strategy BiH–PRSP: Draft for Public Discussion*, 2002. (Note: Poverty reduction strategy papers are designed to provide the basis for assistance from the World Bank and the International Monetary Fund as well as debt relief.)

12. International Campaign to Ban Landmines, *Landmine Monitor 2002* (New York: Human Rights Watch, 2002).

13. Handicap International, *Landmine Victim Assistance: World Report* (Lyon, France: Handicap International, 2001 and 2002).

14. H. F. Frafjord Johnson (Norwegian Minister of International Development), *Statement Delivered at the Conference, the Future of Humanitarian Mine Action*, Oslo, September 13, 2002.

15. Norway, *Resources to Achieve the Convention's Humanitarian Aims: A Preliminary Review*, a study presented to the Standing Committee on the General Status and Operation of the Convention, February 3, 2003.

6

Europe and the Ottawa Treaty: Compliance with Exceptions and Loopholes

PAUL CHAMBERLAIN AND DAVID LONG

THE OTTAWA TREATY BANNING ANTIPERSONNEL LANDMINES (ALSO KNOWN AS the Mine Ban Treaty) has been signed and ratified by all but a few European states. Some of these countries were significant former producers and users of antipersonnel landmines (APLs), a fact that reveals the considerable importance of Europe to the entire process. The role of smaller states in the Ottawa Process as agenda setters and facilitators has been well documented, and again in this regard European states such as Austria and Norway were crucial.[1] On March 1, 1999, the treaty entered into international law after Burkina Faso became the fortieth state to ratify it, and today over 140 countries are a party. However, the nonsignature of the United States and Russia has not only created cause for concern among European states but also produced tangible political and military dilemmas in which the matter of APLs converges with many wider issues in the context of the post–Cold War European security architecture.

This chapter examines the developments and patterns in the European response to the Ottawa Treaty. It serves as an update on the events since 1997 and a consideration of the actions of the signatory states in the specific areas laid down in the Ottawa Treaty. In addition, the motivations and underlying strategies of those states choosing to remain outside of the Ottawa Process are scrutinized with the intention of discerning a pattern of adherence and nonadherence to the treaty among European countries. This chapter also looks at the role of the European Commission, a role that is unique to the European context. Though the global movement, spearheaded by the International Campaign to Ban Landmines and the core group states, managed to achieve its goal of a treaty without exceptions and loopholes, the outlook in Europe is not universal or complete adherence. Thus, we analyze various discrepancies stemming from the function of the treaty, especially the question of signatory countries' attitudes toward "joint operations" with nonsignatories in which APLs may potentially be utilized. This problem has emerged most clearly in the European context within NATO, between European signatories, and the nonsignatory United States.

Compliance

Almost All of the European Union Complies

Twenty-seven European countries have ratified the Ottawa Treaty, including thirteen of the fifteen European Union (EU) member states. In addition, seven of the thirteen EU applicants are parties. The EU big three—France, Germany, and the United Kingdom—have each completed the destruction of their considerable stockpiles of APLs. As the major European powers in NATO as well, they have provided an example to Europe and the wider world of significant military powers determining the utility of APLs as a weapon to be outweighed by other (although not necessarily humanitarian) concerns. Here we will consider their actions since the signing of the Ottawa Treaty, as well as those of Belgium and Italy, both EU and NATO states that were significant producers of landmines before the Ottawa Treaty.

The French military completed destruction of its almost 1.1 million APLs in December 1999, and, after initial reluctance, has become a leading advocate of the Ottawa Treaty within the EU framework. It has also taken a noticeably strong line on some of the contentious issues emanating from the treaty, especially on joint operations and exports to nonsignatory states (discussed later). Within France, the government set up the Commission Nationale pour l'Elimination des Mines Anti-personnel (the National Commission for the Elimination of Anti-personnel Mines), which is charged with the task of coordinating French efforts (including nongovernmental Organizations) in monitoring compliance with the treaty and mine action aid. However, France is not a generous donor country, with a total contribution of only US$2.74 million in 1999, which includes its share of multilateral programs and its share of EU spending on the issue.[2]

It has spent US$19 million on research and development in mine clearance technology, a benefit to French industry but arguably rather less help in advancing humanitarian demining in affected countries to this point.

The position of Germany is always crucial in European politics, and especially so in an issue, such as landmines, with wide-ranging security ramifications. The future role of Germany in pressuring the Baltic states to sign the Ottawa Treaty, or offering Russia some form of concessions as reward for signing, may provide a litmus test for the position Germany may play in the post–Cold War European security landscape. Germany has contributed US$11.4 million in humanitarian mine aid in 1999, and another US$6.7 million to the EU fund.[3] This is not surprising given the important role Germany took in the early stages of the Ottawa Process, and the swift destruction of its APL stockpile within weeks of the treaty signing ceremony in December 1997. However, it remains a major developer of antitank mines.

The United Kingdom has played an important role in legitimizing the Ottawa Treaty. Given its historical role as a major European and global power, Britain has retained a seat at the high table of international politics and, along with France, exerts particular influence within the Eoropean Union and in transatlantic defense and security affairs more generally. Therefore, the support for the Ottawa Process shown by the Labour government from 1997 was crucial in the European context. However, since the heady early days of the Blair administration, in which the landmines issue was a relatively cost-free way of demonstrating Britain's new "ethical foreign policy," the British position has, in some areas, showed signs of reluctance. Of particular concern has been the wording of the 1998 Landmines Act (the domestic legislation enacting the Ottawa Treaty in British law) that has been the subject of criticism by several nongovernmental organizations (NGOs) for equivocating on the question of joint operations with nonsignatory states. The United Kingdom completed destruction of its stockpile of APLs in October 1999, and has maintained its support for the overarching goals of the treaty. The cessation of British production and exports of APLs was noteworthy given that the United Kingdom was a major former producer and is still one of the leading arms exporters in the world. An area in which Britain has provided a lead has been in mine action funding, contributing US$25.7 million in 1999.[4]

While not a great power in the manner of the United Kingdom and France, or a major global economic power like Germany, Italy's path in the campaign against landmines was an important and significant one. Its journey from being in the top three of the world's APL producers to a robust advocate of the antilandmine cause has been one of the more remarkable in Europe. Early domestic legislation and strong pressure from indigenous NGOs, as well as the drying up of key export markets contributed to this shift.[5] In February 1999, Italy launched the Comitato Nazionale per l'Azione Umanitaria Contro le Mine (National Committee for Humanitarian Mine Action), a permanent working group bringing together all the relevant domestic actors, both governmental and nongovernmental. However, Italy has been a laggard in destroying its sizable stockpile of APLs, and will likely be the last EU member state to complete this task (with the exception of Finland and Greece), the government estimating a date in late 2002. Its contribution of US$7.33 million during the period 1999–2000 in mine action funding places it near the top of EU donors.[6]

Belgium had also been a significant producer of APLs but in the early 1990s reversed its policy on the issue. It took an early role among the core group of states advocating a total ban, and, in 1995, was the first country in the world to adopt domestic legislation banning the production and export of APLs. The Belgian military destroyed its stockpiles by September 1997, and contributed US$2.3 million in 1999 to various mine action programs.[7] In addition, Belgium has been at the forefront of research and development in minefield clearance technologies and its location at the hub of EU activity has guaranteed its participation in community-wide mine action activities.

In summary, all EU member states are parties to the Ottawa Treaty, with the exception of Finland and Greece. Ten member states no longer hold stockpiles of APLs, other than a militarily insignificant number held for training purposes allowable under the treaty. In addition, several other European states outside of the European Union, such as Switzerland, Iceland, and Norway, have behaved in a similar manner to the EU states. Norway, of course, was one of the most important countries in the core group of states during the Ottawa Process. A general pattern of adherence to the Ottawa Treaty across the European Union is clear, displaying a commonality in interests rarely seen in defense matters.

The European Union Funds Victim Assistance and Demining

As a group, the European Union has been a strong supporter of the Ottawa Treaty and has the stated goal of "removing the scourge of landmines within the next 10 to 15 years at the latest."[8] In November 1997, only days before the Ottawa Convention was signed, the EU states agreed on a "Joint Action" on APLs. This urged all members to sign and adopt a common position on the issue to the outside world.[9] As we have seen, this has not been a total success, with two EU states still not parties to the treaty. The Joint Action also signaled an increase in EU contributions, and since then the European Union has become the largest single donor of mine action funding in the world, over EUR 100 million in 1999.[10] This has included a wide range of programs: the physical removal of mines from affected areas, minefield surveying and marking, training and education of local populations, landmine destruction, victim assistance, and research into more efficient demining technologies. The EU has funded such programs in Afghanistan, Angola, Bosnia, Cambodia, Croatia, northern Iraq, Kosovo, Laos, Lebanon, Mozambique, and, to a lesser extent, Central America, the former Soviet Union, Vietnam, and five other African states. However, the complexity of managing the funds from its member states, and the many differing programs and locations in which action is being taken, has served to undermine some EU activities in the area (see the section "The Balkans: Europe's Mine Victims").

A further analysis of EU mine action funding reveals a less rosy picture than they seek to portray. Of the EUR 30.3 million spent in 1999, EUR 13.5 million (45 percent) never left the European Union, instead it went into various research and development programs carried out by companies within the member states. These programs seek to improve the ease of both detecting and destroying APLs in the field. Most of this is coordinated through the European Commission's Joint Research Centre, based in Ispra, Italy. It has links with similar programs run by the United Nations and the U.S. State Department.

The latest initiatives by the European Union, under the Portuguese and Swedish presidencies in the period 2000–2001, have sought to assuage criticisms of the EU's mine action fundings. In an attempt to streamline EU actions, two regulations have been introduced. They set out the scope and objectives for EU mine action throughout the world and establish managerial procedures aimed at harmonizing the funding budget. By calling for a more centralized and coordinated approach, the new regulations also increase the role of the European Commission. In addition, a recent proposal has indicated a subtle change in emphasis for European mine action projects away from narrow, prescriptive solutions to the landmine problem toward a more holistic, development-oriented approach:

> Projects should be . . . wherever possible, integrated into the wider development or reconstruction framework of the country or region in question. . . . The aim should be for the project to be taken over, in due course, by the beneficiary government itself or by local society or NGOs in order to enhance local capacity and the sustainability of the project.[11]

The APL issue can also be used as a test case for the European Union as it seeks to develop a stronger common foreign and security policy. If the member states cannot agree on a common position on landmines, then the likelihood of reaching agreement on the bigger issues of international relations would appear slim.[12]

Exceptions

Impasse in the Eastern Baltic

While the Ottawa Treaty has been ratified and implemented consistently in the countries of western and northern Europe, it has been a conspicuous failure in one area of the continent—the states bordering the eastern part of the Baltic Sea. None of these states—inland, Russia, Estonia, Latvia, Lithuania, and Poland—are parties to the treaty. This distinct geographical configuration of nonadherence is not simply a function of opposing viewpoints on the question of the APL ban itself, but is a manifestation of the broader geopolitical concerns in the region. To understand how antipersonnel landmines fit into this equation, we must look at each country and analyze their perceptions and behavior vis-à-vis the Ottawa Treaty.

As the only EU member in the region, Finland is in a unique and influential position. As the only member state of the European Union not to sign the treaty, Finland has, in the past, been subject to the collective pressure of EU partners to a more restrictive policy on landmines. When holding the rolling presidency of the European Union in late 1999, Finland was placed in the rather embarrassing position of delivering a joint EU statement to the United Nations in favor of the treaty. The Finnish government has endorsed the goals of the treaty (and contributed to mine action funding, US$5 million in 1999) and has indicated its desire to sign in 2006.[13] However, this appears to be on the basis of alternatives to APLs being developed, a project likely to cost millions of dollars and unlikely to be completed in such a short time frame. Finland claims that it cannot abide by the treaty's commitment to destroy its stockpiles of APLs (the government has not been forthcoming with precise numbers) within a four-year period.

However, the overriding reason for Finnish reluctance about the treaty is based on security concerns and strategic doctrine, stemming from its historically prickly relations with Russia (and before that the USSR). Relations between Russia and its neighbors in the Baltic are the crucial regional issue. Finnish military doctrine calls for the maintenance of a central defensive role for landmines of all kinds, mainly due to the geographical nature of the country. It is argued that without an adequate replacement for APLs, Finland's ability to independently defend itself from attack would be seriously compromised. While it is easy for other European states to deride Finnish intransigence and ascribe it to outmoded Cold War philosophy, Finland can argue it is simply acting according to the geopolitical realities of its situation, away from the relatively cozy surroundings of Brussels and other Western capitals.

Russia has not only failed to sign the Ottawa Treaty but is also both an active producer and user of APLs. However, an export moratorium has been in force since 1994. The conflicts in Dagestan and Chechnya since late 1999 have seen widespread use of APLs by both sides. It is clear that the Russian military still considers them a valuable weapon in its fight against the mobile guerrilla forces of its enemy. In addition, with an estimated stockpile of between 60 and 70 million APLs, signing the treaty and undertaking the destruction of such a huge quantity would place a considerable financial burden on the struggling Russian economy.

Russia has maintained that it favors a more holistic approach to the question of APL controls, through its inclusion in talks on the Convention on Conventional Weapons or the Conference on Disarmament. Moreover, Russia argues that due to its unique geography and the range of threats against which it has to defend itself suggests it cannot afford to forsake any potentially useful weapon in its arsenal. No doubt, the nonsignature of China and the United States is also a prime consideration, and reason enough for some in Moscow to scorn the Ottawa Treaty. But the global strategic balance is less significant for determining the utility than the brute realities of managing a long, frequently contentious border with a neighbor that is both powerful and periodically hostile (China) and of managing counterinsurgency operations against separatist militants within the borders of the Russian Federation.

Russia's continuing nonadherence places the smaller states of the region—Estonia, Latvia, and Lithuania—on the horns of a dilemma. The three Baltic states have a recent shared history of invasion and domination by Russia and a mutual distrust over its future direction. To assuage these fears, they have sought membership of both NATO and the European Union as quickly as possible. This in turn has only served to antagonize Russia and resulted in a form of nascent security dilemma. The Russians fear any attempt by the Baltic states to mitigate the wide disparity in power between them that would involve an alliance with the major Western powers.

Lithuania actually signed the treaty in February 1999, but with little hope of ratification in the near future. Again, the government cites the regional security context and concern over the nonsignatures of its neighbors as the primary reasons for the delay. Lithuania's precise stockpile of APLs is unknown (like the other Baltic states inherited from the Soviet Union) but is presumed small and certainly inadequate to halt any potential invasion in any case. Another concern of Lithuania is the Russian enclave of Kaliningrad, a major port and military center that is only accessible to Russia through Lithuanian territory.

Latvia has not signed the Ottawa Treaty, citing its local security environment, although it has long endorsed its goals rhetorically. In fact, Latvia suggests it already meets the requirements of the treaty. The government claims a stockpile of only 4,500 APLs, and the military maintains its importance in territorial defense. According to the Latvian government, the presence in Latvian territory of unexploded ordnance remaining from World War II as well as the perceived lack of international assistance to rid the country of this problem constitute obstacles to Latvian adherence to the Ottawa Treaty.

Though it has yet to sign the Ottawa Treaty, Estonia probably complies with its provisions as it has strong domestic legislation outlawing the export and transit of APLs, and a stockpile of less than one thousand. The government shares the view of several other nonsignatories (including Russia) that the issue can only be satisfactorily dealt with under the auspices of the Conference on Disarmament.

The three Baltic states are policy followers, not policy leaders, on the issue of the Ottawa Treaty. It appears Finland is the state they look to for guidance, and Russia the state they fear. Whether they become members of the European Union (likely) and NATO (rather less so) within the next decade, the fundamental inequality of military power and the utility of APLs as a cheap defensive military weapon will mean these states will maintain some APLs. The logic of the Baltic situation is shared to some extent with Belarus, a nonsignatory with a vast stockpile, and Ukraine, a signatory and probable ratifier in the medium term. Only a coordinated diplomatic effort will likely be successful in breaking the deadlock on the landmines issue in the Baltics. If it can be disengaged from these wider concerns, then the possibility of a settlement exists. However, no resolution can be made without Russia, and in present circumstances, it would appear unlikely that Moscow's signature will appear on the Ottawa Treaty in the short to medium term. It is important to be cautious, however. Russia's signing of the Ottawa Treaty might simply serve to embarrass its neighbors, but the military logic against general Baltic signature and ratification (absent new technologies) would remain the same.

Conflict and Resistance in Southeastern Europe

The southeastern corner of Europe is another exception to the general rule of compliance with the Ottawa Treaty. Here, two nodes of hostility and suspicion appear to underlie the reluctance of states to sign and ratify the treaty. One of these is the long-standing antagonism between Greece and Turkey. Greece agreed to sign the Ottawa Treaty shortly before the Ottawa conference but at the time indicated that it would ratify it at its own pace, doubtless expecting there to be the delays in ratification that usually occur in such accords.[14] Greece is also constrained by having to adhere to the EU Joint Actions on landmines that have prohibited transfer and production of the weapons. The Greek position is directly related to Cyprus and the wider dispute with Turkey over the Aegean Sea. It is also concerned with the cost and difficulty of removing APLs deployed during its civil war. In EU terms, Greece is certainly the poor relation, contributing a paltry US$80,000 in mine action aid in 1999.[15] In 1997, Greece agreed with Bulgaria to demine their border, although this has yet to be completed on the Greek side.

Turkish nonparticipation has wider implications. It is the largest state applying for EU accession as well as a longtime NATO member, but most of all it is strategically crucial because of its location adjacent to middle and central Asia and its status as a secular state in the Islamic world. These factors alone make any security issues involving the country extremely delicate, and even more so given the dispute with Greece. Turkey's problem with Kurdish insurgency is another problem. In addition, in almost all cases, Turkey borders on states with which it has difficult relations or which itself is a conflict-prone area, namely, Syria, Iraq, Iran, Armenia, and Georgia. Turkey is believed to possess a large stockpile of APLs (although an export moratorium is in place) and cites regional security concerns as the reason for its nonsignature of the Ottawa Treaty, including its ongoing conflict with the Kurdish Workers Party. In reference to APLs, the Turkish government legitimately calls attention to the fact that of the seven countries bordering Turkey only Bulgaria is a party. Turkey has sought to reach agreements with its neighbors on demining its borders, with some success, including a 1999 accord with Bulgaria followed by a similar arrangement with Georgia signed in January 2001.

In addition, a form of détente between Greece and Turkey has developed since 1999 when Greece dropped its opposition to Turkish application for EU membership. Following a general improvement in relations, a breakthrough in the stalemate concerning landmines appears to have been made in April 2001. After negotiations in Ankara, Turkish Foreign Minister Ismail Cem, and his Greek counterpart George Papandreou announced that the two countries had agreed to demine their common border. Furthermore, both agreed to ratify the Ottawa Treaty and submit their documents to the United Nations simultaneously. It remains to be seen when this will happen, but the announcement appears to be a genuine victory for the antipersonnel landmine lobby.

The Balkans: Europe's Mine Victims

The Balkans is the most heavily mine-affected area of Europe. A decade of war has exacted a heavy price from the civilian population. Regular media reports of the civilian mine victims and particularly of peacekeepers injured by APLs contributed much to the growing sense of moral outrage regarding their use in Europe. As such, it is important to look at the area as a test of European will, not only to prevent future problems involving landmines but to solve present ones.

Before the breakup of Yugoslavia, half of the defense production of the country was situated in Bosnia and Herzegovina, giving a ready supply to the ensuing conflict. Bosnia and Herzegovina is party to the Ottawa Treaty. It destroyed its stockpile of APLs in 1999 although this was done largely to comply with the Dayton Agreement. Most of these mines belonged to the Republika Sprska: 370,000 compared to the 90,000 eradicated by the Bosnian Federation. However, with tension still existing in arrangements for the future of Bosnia, it would not be surprising if each side has secretly stored APLs for use in any further potential conflict, despite the efforts of Stabilization Force (SFOR) inspectors. However, the biggest obstacle for Bosnia with regard to landmines is the question of mine clearing. It still needs international assistance to clear the estimated 18,000 mined areas containing 740,000 landmines.[16]

To facilitate this, international aid has flooded into Bosnia, producing a maze of operations from national governments, NGOs, and supranational organizations, differing greatly in funding, scale, and success. The physical demining is also carried out by a variety of agencies: the military of the Bosnian entities after training by foreign SFOR troops, SFOR soldiers themselves, indigenous and international NGOs, and private demining companies. Unfortunately, the sheer complexity of the situation has led to widespread misappropriation of these funds, and also mistakes. In 1998, a British newspaper reported that a 230-strong team of mine clearers sent by the European Union to Bosnia was not used because a bureaucratic error did not budget for the expenses of the operation—after spending US$5 million training and equipping them.[17]

Croatia is also seriously blighted by landmines, although it retained no indigenous APL-producing capabilities upon the breakup of Yugoslavia. It is estimated that almost 8 percent of Croatian territory is mine affected, and possibly up to 1.5 million mines remain to be cleared.[18] Croatia ratified the Ottawa Treaty in May 1998, but has made a slow start in destroying its sizable stockpile. This is the major concern regarding Croatian adherence to the treaty, along with the fact that it intends to retain 17,000 APLs for training purposes. This is a far higher figure than other countries have maintained, typically numbering below 5,000. It remains to be seen if this policy will be reconsidered under international pressure.

Croatia has also been the recipient of international funding in mine action funding, as well as committing domestic expenditure to the problem, US$24.4 million in 1999.[19] Another noteworthy aspect of Croatian landmine policy is its hard line on the joint operations issue, opposing any usage or transit of APLs by forces working with the Croatian military.

The situation in Kosovo has also garnered much international attention. Although the extent of the problem is not on the same scale as in Bosnia and Croatia, an added danger for the civilian population is the presence of thousands of "bomblets" (with an effect similar to an APL) dropped by NATO aircraft during the 1999 conflict with Yugoslavia. Both the Yugoslav army and the Kosovo Liberation Army used APLs during 1998 and 1999. Yugoslavia is not a party to the Ottawa Treaty and maintains a considerable stockpile, and the Kosovo Liberation Army has continued using them to intimidate the Serb population in Kosovo. The present conflict in Macedonia also suggests ethnic Albanian groups are actively deploying APLs.

As with Bosnia, myriad governmental and nongovernmental funding has been poured into Kosovo, with much the same result in terms of corruption. However, specifically on the issue of landmines, the international community seems to have learned a few lessons and the funding in this area appears more streamlined and targeted, much of it through the UN Mine Action Coordination Center based in Pristina. Importantly, the center's activity is incorporated into the wider development strategy for Kosovo, rather than being treated as a separate issue. A UN fund for Kosovo raised US$7.5 million by June 2000, of which around 80 percent came from EU members or the European Union itself.[20]

Loopholes

Although the Ottawa Treaty has been a relative success in Europe, some notable problems have emerged. As is inevitably the case with any legal document, loopholes and different interpretations of both the text and the spirit of the treaty remain. It is crucial to examine these difficulties as they have the potential to seriously undermine its accomplishments. As we investigate this area further, it again becomes clear that the APL issue cleaves many greater security matters.

Blurring Compliance in Joint Military Operations

The use of APLs during joint operations is possibly the most controversial aspect of the Ottawa Treaty. Today, few military actions are wholly unilateral. The experience of the 1990s suggests that in the future the coordination of national militaries will be necessary for the successful undertaking of most military expeditions. From peacekeeping to war fighting, whether under NATO, United Nations, or other auspices, European armies are unlikely to act alone (with the sole exception of Russia or further conflicts among and within the states of southeastern Europe). The crux of the matter results from a context in which a party to the Ottawa Treaty undertakes a joint military operation with another state that is a nonsignatory. In practice, from the European perspective, this dilemma involves the United States—the most high profile of the nonsigners. Furthermore, the joint operations issue touches on the matter of the independence of national armed forces to decide their own strategic deployment of their forces, an important consideration even among closely allied countries. The controversy revolves around the extent to which signatories are permitted to engage in joint operations that may involve another countries' landmines, and the extent to which assistance given to a nonsignatory in such joint operations is a violation of the Ottawa Treaty.

The opinions of European countries on this issue is difficult to ascertain, as it inevitably involves certain operational details of the sort all armed forces are loath to divulge. However, certain government statements provide an insight into the differing attitudes we find across Europe, and are an indication of the challenge this issue presents to the effectiveness of the Ottawa Treaty. On one end of the spectrum stands France. The French government has made clear that it will not take part in any operation using APLs:

> France will prohibit the planned or actual use of antipersonnel mines in any military operation whatsoever by its military personnel. Furthermore, France will refuse to agree to rules of engagement in any military operation calling for the use of antipersonnel mines.[21]

In addition to this strong approach, France has sought to formulate a similar policy to encompass all NATO missions. This has obviously floundered somewhat in the wake of American objections, but the pressure of such a hard-line French attitude exemplifies some of the fault lines within NATO.

The German government also appears to take a strict approach to the question of joint operations with nonparties to the Ottawa Treaty, although with perhaps a little more latitude than in the French case. Domestic legislation prohibits German military personnel from any participation in an operation involving APLs, under any circumstances. However, the German government is not clear on its position in the event of a joint operation with a nonsignatory state using APLs. Although German troops may not physically be involved in minelaying, they could still be indirectly endorsing the action by taking part in a joint operation with a state behaving in such a manner. This could be interpreted as contravening Article 1.1c of the Ottawa Treaty.[22]

The United Kingdom takes a more lenient line on the joint operations issue, and has received criticism for potentially undermining the goals of the treaty. In May 2000, the Ministry of Defense released a statement admitting that the British military had, over the previous three years, been involved in fifteen joint operations in which APLs were used (mostly in the Balkans). However, the government stressed that in no instances were British personnel involved in actually using APLs. In addition, the United Kingdom issued a declaration in 1998 on the subject of joint operations in which nonsignatories may use APLs, in the hope of making British personnel immune from prosecution for the "mere participation in the planning or execution of operations, exercises or other military activity."[23] Again, this would appear to flout both the spirit and the letter of the Ottawa Treaty.

The smaller states have less well-defined positions, although the Netherlands has made statements endorsing the French position, whereas Portugal and the Czech Republic have indicated a laissez-faire attitude toward the use of APLs by nonsignatories in joint operations. This area is still clouded in confusion and while the United States remains outside the Ottawa Treaty, it may prove to be a major stumbling block of the treaty. The range of opinions on the joint operations issue within Europe is damaging to the hopes of developing a coherent and workable level of agreement, and this is only exacerbated by the continued tension with the United States on the entire antipersonnel mines problem.

New Technologies, Old Evasions

While states may have pledged to rid their arsenals of APLs as defined by the Ottawa Treaty, many are seeking to produce new weapons that perform the same function of "area denial" to opposing forces. Such technologies were a subject of debate in the aftermath of the treaty, especially the status of "antihandling" devices fitted to antivehicle mines that are deemed admissible. But the fact that such devices may behave like APLs, and explode due to an unintentional act by a person, has led some in the anti-APL lobby to suggest they should also be banned. Many European countries produce antitank mines, notably the United Kingdom and Germany.

However, a new generation of military hardware as well as strategic concepts threaten to bypass the Ottawa Treaty. These armaments take differing forms: grenade launchers, multiple mortar delivery systems, automated machine guns, and dart guns; all utilizing high-tech combat identification systems, artificial intelligence, and satellite systems.[24] High-tech alternatives to APLs do pose potential problems because these alternatives may behave just like APLs when deployed, and are thus subject to the same moral objection of nondiscrimination. However, because they are high tech and considerably more expensive than APLs, they will be more costly and difficult to produce or acquire. As a result, such alternatives are unlikely to pose the sort of menace to civilians around the world that APLs have.

Conclusion

The general outlook in Europe, then, is one of compliance with some exceptions at the periphery of the continent and some controversies regarding loopholes. Neither the exceptions nor the loopholes can detract from the overall benefits that the Ottawa Process and the treaty have brought. The attitudes and actions of the European states have been transformed. A realist would no doubt observe a recurring theme of states behaving according to their own security concerns. Those states with no need for APLs for various strategic or political reasons, such as the Benelux countries, have accordingly been able to implement the treaty with little dissent and some degree of self-congratulatory fanfare. Those states not so conveniently positioned by geography have been noticeably reluctant to step into line, as is the case in the eastern Baltic and the Balkans and in the Greek–Turkish standoff.

We have noted the role of the European Union. In the European Union, the drive to ban landmines, and the entire process surrounding it was dominated by states.[25] However, the European Union as a group has successfully built a degree of expected behavior among its members, and, perhaps more importantly, among its prospective members for whom the Ottawa Treaty is implicitly another hurdle for them to jump in order to be members of the European Union. The pressure to be a "good citizen" of the international community is felt particularly strongly in the former communist states of eastern and central Europe. In the European Union context, the Ottawa Treaty enjoys the full support of France, Germany, and the United Kingdom, a relatively rare occurrence and a guarantee of its wider success. Furthermore, the European Commission has had a more active role to play in the Ottawa Process since the signing of the treaty, since it can bring to the table resources for humanitarian demining as well as research into new mine detection technologies.

Europeans, with the exception of those living in the territories of the former Yugoslavia, were generally not victims of the proliferation of APLs. As a result, the significance of European adherence or nonadherence to the Ottawa Treaty lies in abiding by the ban and providing support to deal with the devastation of mines in other parts of the world. In this context, the Ottawa Treaty has been a qualified and major moral, financial, and political success.

Notes

1. See David Long and Laird Hindle, "Europe and the Ottawa Process: An Overview," in *To Walk without Fear: The Global Movement to Ban Landmines*, ed. Maxwell A. Cameron, Robert J. Lawson, and Brian W. Tomlin, (Oxford: Oxford University Press, 1998): 248–268.

2. International Campaign to Ban Landmines (ICBL), *Landmine Monitor Report 2000*, Country Report: France, available at http://www.icbl.org/lm/2000/report/LMWeb-22.php3#P14027_1867830.

3. ICBL, *Landmines Monitor 2000*, Country Report: Germany.

4. ICBL, *Landmines Monitor 2000*, Country Report: United Kingdom.

5. For an account of the Italian campaign against landmines, see Cameron, Lawson, and Tomlin, eds., *To Walk without Fear* (see note 1).

6. ICBL, *Landmines Monitor 2000*, Country Report: Italy.

7. ICBL, *Landmines Monitor 2000*, Country Report: Belgium.

8. Eurpoean Communities, *The Response of the European Union to the Anti-Personnel Landmines Challenge* (Arlon, Luxembourg: European Communities, 2000), 5. It should be noted this figure includes the individual member state contributions, not simply EU spending.

9. See David Long, "The European Union and the Ban on Landmines," *Journal of European Public Policy* 9, no. 3 (2002), 426.

10. European Communities, *The Response of the European Union*, 8.

11. European Commission, *European Parliament and Council Regulation against Anti-Personnel Landmines* (Brussels: European Commission, December 20, 2000), article 10, 13.

12. See Long, "The European Union and the Ban on Landmines."

13. ICBL, *Landmines Monitor 2000*, Country Report: Finland.

14. Long and Hindle, "Europe and the Ottawa Process," 261.

15. ICBL, *Landmines Monitor 2000*, Country Report: Greece.

16. ICBL, *Landmines Monitor 2000*, Country Report: Bosnia and Herzegovina.

17. "EU Blunder Leaves Mines in Place," *Observer*, August 16, 1998, available at www.icbl.org/media/1998/.

18. ICBL, *Landmines Monitor 2000*, Country Report: Croatia.

19. Ibid.

20. ICBL, *Landmines Monitor 2000*, Country Report: Kosovo.

21. ICBL, *Landmines Monitor 2000*, Country Report: France. Statement by the minister of defense in June 1998.

22. Article 1.1c of the *Convention on the Prohibition of the Use, Stockpiling, Production, and Transfer of Anti-Personnel Mines and on Their Destruction* (1997) states, "Each State Party undertakes never under any circumstances: c) To assist, encourage or induce, in any way, anyone to engage in any activity prohibited to a State Party under this Convention."

23. Quote from "Declaration on Joint Operations with Non-Signatories of the Mine Ban Treaty," in the ICBL's *Landmine Monitor 2000*, Country Report: United Kingdom, available at http://www.icbl.org/lm/2000/uk.html.

24. Steve Wright, "More Efficient Killing fields," *Guardian*, March 8, 2001. For more on this, see http://www.landmineaction.org/clusterb.htm.

25. See Long, "The European Union and the Ban on Landmines."

7

Perspective from a Mine-Affected Country: Mozambique

CARLOS DOS SANTOS

MOZAMBIQUE'S INVOLVEMENT WITH THE BAN LANDMINE MOVEMENT and the priority it has given to the issue of antipersonnel landmines is closely linked to the country's recent history. Mozambique became independent in 1975 after ten years of liberation struggle against Portuguese colonialism. Subsequently, the country suffered direct invasion from both the apartheid and the minority regimes of Southern Rhodesia (now Zimbabwe). Both regimes supported the rebel movement, which destabilized the country for more than sixteen years. In these wars, different generations of landmines were emplaced throughout the territory of Mozambique. This chapter will begin by looking at the magnitude of the problem in this developing nation. It will then discuss Mozambique's commitment and contribution to the ban landmine movement as well as the interaction with the international community.

The Magnitude of the Problem

It is estimated that Mozambique has between two and three million landmines emplaced in the country.[1] Some of these landmines were planted by the Portuguese colonial army, others by the rebel movement, and still others by the government armed forces to protect socioeconomic infrastructure and other strategic areas. While the number of emplaced landmines is now being questioned following some surveys,[2] the fact is that there is a significantly large number of antipersonnel landmines scattered all over the country, causing serious damage and instilling fear. Most of these landmines have not been accurately mapped and the areas where they were placed were not marked. "From 1997 to 2000 there were hundreds of accidents with landmines and other unexploded ordnance, which resulted in 801 mine victims."[3] These are only the latest cases. Thousands of Mozambicans were mutilated by landmines during the armed conflict in the country and they require assistance to reclaim their livelihoods. The government has drawn up, with the assistance of cooperating partners, a national assistance strategy for victims of landmines. The strategy encompasses areas such as health, job creation, and social reintegration of the victims.

The landmine problem in Mozambique has been compounded by the recent unprecedented floods in large areas of the southern and central regions of the country during the 2000 and 2001 rainy seasons. Landmines were moved by floodwaters from the original emplacement areas, some of which had been demined or demarcated with warning signs. New surveys are being conducted as this book is being written and demining of those areas constitute priority action in the postflood reconstruction program.

At the opening of the First Meeting of States Parties to the Ottawa Convention, the president of the Republic of Mozambique characterized the problem, inter alia:

> In view of the three generations of landmines implanted in our territory . . . my people live in uncertainty and permanent fear, which prevent them from effectively using vast areas of arable land. . . . Demining and destruction currently take place at the pace of only 11 thousand per year, thus requiring approximately 160 years to clear all of them.[4]

There is a serious impact of landmines on development as well as on the resettlement of displaced persons and refugees returning from neighboring countries following the 1992 Peace Agreement between the government and the rebel movement. There was, therefore, not only a sense of duty but also of urgency to deal with the problem of landmines in all its different aspects.

Mozambique's Commitment and Contribution to the Ban Landmine Movement

The predicament in which the country found itself in the aftermath of years of war and a sense of responsibility generated the commitment and determination of Mozambicans to address the landmine issue. While the debate was gaining momentum in the international arena, the government of Mozambique was adopting a landmark decree (18/95 of May 3) establishing the National Demining Commission, with the task of defining policies, strategies, organization, leadership, control, and supervision of all demining activities in the country. This body was later replaced by a more permanent institution, the National Demining Institute, which is to provide leadership, coordination, planning, priority setting, and monitoring.

Demining activities in Mozambique are being carried out by a number of nongovernmental organizations and commercial companies. According to an unpublished report of the National Demining Institute, from 1992 to 2000 the total number of destroyed landmines and other ordnance was 71,476 antipersonnel and antigroup landmines; 538 antitank landmines; 34,386 unexploded ordnance; 495,317 pieces of ammunition of different calibers; and 283,277 metallic fragments. The abovementioned activities have resulted in the clearing of 8,129 kilometers of roads, 1,852 kilometers of power lines, 90 kilometers of railway line, and 61,068,551 square meters of socioeconomic infrastructure areas.[5] This has had a significant impact on development in the country.

Mozambique's early engagement and practical experience in demining activities proved to be a valuable asset to the international process to ban landmines. Mozambique could speak credibly on the different aspects and impact of antipersonnel landmines. The government was prepared and committed to work with all partners and stakeholders at national, regional, and international levels. Mozambique's contributions to the process were aimed at building consensus among governments, intergovernmental organizations, and nongovernmental organizations, and all relevant actors around the vital issues. These include the banning of landmines, providing assistance to the victims of landmines and to the affected countries to undertake demining operations and destruction of stockpiles, and promoting the development and sharing of appropriate technologies for demining. The focus was mainly on what could effectively and urgently be done to alleviate the suffering of the people in the affected countries like Mozambique.

With Africa being one of the most affected continents by the scourge of landmines, it was essential that the whole continent rally around the landmine ban cause. Mozambique, together with some active countries of the region, mobilized the other nations to support the international efforts. Such mobilization and the conferences that were jointly organized with the International Committee of the Red Cross resulted in the overwhelming support from the Organization of African Unity.

At the subregional level, Mozambique has worked with the other members of the Southern Africa Development Community. This organization has established a Committee on Demining, which is chaired by Mozambique. All countries of the subregion are committed to work together toward the full implementation of the provisions of the Ottawa Convention, particularly in improving demining technologies, training demining experts, and providing victim assistance and civic education on the danger posed by landmines. The prevailing conflicts in Angola and the Democratic Republic of the Congo represent serious challenges in this regard. The expressed political will from the governments of the region are reassuring.

The government has also encouraged and supported initiatives from civil society organizations within the country and their interaction with international partners. This has had a positive impact in awareness raising and implementing specific projects. Mozambique was among the first states to sign and ratify the Ottawa Treaty thus contributing to its early entry into force. In compliance with article 7 of the Ottawa Convention, Mozambique has reported the size of its stockpile as 37,818 landmines.

Interaction with the International Community: Cooperation, Advocacy, and Assistance

In times of war and in times of peace, Mozambique has promoted and developed cooperation with partners and relevant actors in the international arena. During the years of war, Mozambique sought cooperation and assistance in searching for peace and in providing much-needed help to displaced people and returning refugees and all those affected by war. As a corollary of those efforts, the 1992 Peace Agreement was signed in Rome, inviting the United Nations to assist and monitor its implementation. Consequently, the UN Security Council decided to dispatch a peacekeeping mission to Mozambique. The mission's mandate included demining operations. The first demining operations undertaken in the country were under the United Nations Operation in Mozambique. UN activities continue to date through the Accelerated Demining Programme under the auspices of the United Nations Development Programme and the Department of Humanitarian Affairs.

Mozambique had the commitment and determination to act. The government took the necessary policy and institutional steps but required assistance in human, material, and financial resources to carry out the task. The generosity of the international community corresponded to the country's commitment and determination. Assistance came from several governments, the United Nations, and other intergovernmental and nongovernmental organizations. Donor partners were willing to put money where they believed it would be of good use. With the expertise that Mozambique has developed thus far, the country is also beginning to give assistance to other countries and regions in need. Mozambicans are proud to be part of the solution and not remain part of the problem.

Mozambique cooperated and continues to cooperate with partners and relevant actors in advocacy for the universalization of the Ottawa Convention, encouraging nations to accede to it expeditiously so that the goal set in it of eradicating the scourge of landmines by 2009 is met. The holding in Maputo, Mozambique, of the First Meeting of States Parties to the Ottawa Convention was yet another testimony of the international community's recognition of the nation's commitment and dedication to the cause. The author of this chapter was privileged to serve as the secretary-general of the conference. Mozambique also cochaired one of the Standing Committees of Experts (Mine Clearance) established by the first meeting, which sustained the momentum during the intersessional period.

The holding of the First Meeting of States Parties to the Ottawa Convention in Mozambique—an affected nation—symbolized the determination of the ban landmine movement to work with and assist affected countries and regions that show their willingness to contribute not only to the solution in their part of the world but also on the entire planet.

The First Meeting of States Parties was essential in the global process, for there were doubts as to the possibility of implementation of the treaty. The Maputo Declaration and the statements made by the high-level delegations reaffirmed the commitment and dedication of those nations and other actors forming part of the global movement. The First Meeting of States Parties was equally a unique experience for Mozambique, a least-developed country facing tremendous socioeconomic difficulties, being able to work with the United Nations Secretariat and cooperating partners to host such a successful event. Delegates were able to experience firsthand the problem of landmines and learn about the efforts to solve it through international cooperation and assistance.

Another factor of significant importance in the demining process in Mozambique is the involvement of the different UN funds, programs, and agencies in tackling the problem. They make contributions in raising awareness of children and communities, psychosocial rehabilitation, reintegration programs, resettlement programs, and capacity building to enable the country to deal with problems in the long run. In addition to the United Nations Development Programme, the United Nations Children's Fund, the Office of the United Nations High Commissioner for Refugees, the World Food Programme, the World Health Organization, the Food and Agriculture Organization, and the United Nations Office for Project and Services, among others, have played a pivotal role in support of the government's efforts. It is thus clear that, the difficulties relating to resources notwithstanding, Mozambique has played a significant role in its interaction in the international arena and is moving in the right direction toward the resolution of the landmine problem and is providing adequate assistance to the victims of this inhuman instrument of war.

The challenge, however, remains great. Mozambique will require continued and adequate assistance, particularly in building capacity to deal with the problem in the short, the medium, and the long term. The government has taken the initiative of establishing a National Fund for Demining with the view to lending greater autonomy and transparency into the management of the financial resources. The National Demining Institute is charged with the task of ensuring performance and quality control of those involved in demining. The demining plans are in keeping with national, provincial, district, and community objectives and priorities. Mozambique's motto is "For a Country Free of Landmines." The substantial contributions Mozambique has lent to the landmine ban movement will certainly help sustain the movement and push the agenda forward toward the total eradication of landmines. The success of the process will be judged by the degree of improvement of the living conditions in the affected communities and countries, preventing new victims, as well as providing concrete assistance to victims.

Notes

1. United Nations Secretary-General, "Report of the Secretary-General on Assitance in Mine Clearance," September 1995, available online at http://www.mineaction.org/un_mine_action/_refdocs.cfm?doc_ID=287.

2. Ilaria Bottigliero, ed., *120 Million Landmines Deployed World Wide: Fact or Fiction?* (Geneva: Fondation Pro Victimis, 2000).

3. Mozambique National Demining Institute, "Report on National Meeting with Demining Operator, Nampula, August 30–31, 2001," available at http://www.ind.gov.mz/en/.

4. *Statement by the President of the Republic at the Opening of the First Meeting of States Parties to the Ottawa Convention*, May 3, 1999, Maputo, Mozambique.

5. Mozambique National Demining Institute, "Report on National Meeting."

8

Victim Assistance: Landmine Survivors' Perspectives

Raquel Willerman

T HERE ARE AN ESTIMATED 300,000 LANDMINE SURVIVORS WORLDWIDE. more than half the people involved in a landmine accident die before reaching medical care. Landmines have killed more people than nuclear, chemical, and biological weapons combined. With over eight thousand new victims reported in 2000 and thousands more whose accidents went unreported, the total number of landmine survivors continues to grow. It is estimated that at least 80 percent of survivors are civilians and 25 percent are children.[1]

Resources in nearly every mine affected country do not come close to meeting the needs of survivors. Less than 10 percent of survivors today receive appropriate medical care and rehabilitation services. The economies of most mine-affected countries rank among the least developed of the world. Available funding from the international community for the care and rehabilitation of survivors is well below even conservative estimates of the amount of money required to cover basic needs. The situation that most landmine victims live in is an affront to basic human rights.

Addressing the harsh reality of survivors on a global scale means providing comprehensive rehabilitation[2] for hundreds of thousands of survivors and creating positive change in laws and policies that protect the rights of survivors and other people with disabilities. Landmine Survivors Network (LSN) believes that survivors are central to both tasks; they should be the primary articulators of their needs and given the tools and opportunities to advocate for their human rights and improving their lives. In practice, however, victim assistance is often implemented without consulting survivors, makes assumptions about survivors' needs, and denies survivors the opportunity to participate actively in their recovery.

This chapter thus presents survivors' perspectives on trauma recovery and chronicles the advocacy efforts of survivors who have provoked positive changes in laws, policies, and social attitudes. It is a guiding principle of LSN to continuously seek the input of survivors in planning, implementing, and evaluating programs as well as creating opportunities for survivors to be effective advocates for their human rights.

Landmine Survivors Network

During negotiations of the Mine Ban Treaty, two American landmine survivors, Jerry White and Ken Rutherford, realized that there were not enough opportunities for landmine survivors to communicate their needs and demand their right to have their needs addressed. At that time, one of the slogans of the International Campaign to Ban Landmines (ICBL) was "To speak for those who cannot speak for themselves." Jerry and Ken decided that the time had come for survivors to speak on their own behalf.[3]

In 1997, White and Rutherford created LSN with a mission of empowering people affected by landmines to recover from trauma, reclaim their lives, and achieve their basic human rights. LSN hires and trains landmine survivors as community-based outreach workers who educate, inspire, and offer support to others who have experienced limb loss, as well as links survivors and amputees to health care, rehabilitation, peer support, and opportunities for social and economic reintegration. LSN's philosophy is that each survivor must make the decisions necessary for his or her own recovery, so the LSN outreach worker and the survivor together devise a plan for healing and recovery.

LSN also helps survivors advocate for their own rights. In many countries, mine victims lose more than a leg or an arm; they often lose their place as valued and respected members of society. LSN works with survivors, organizations, and governments to create opportunities that allow survivors to improve their lives and the lives of others.

Since 1997, LSN has established Amputee Peer Support Networks in seven mine-affected countries: Bosnia and Herzegovina, Jordan, El Salvador, Ethiopia, Eritrea, Mozambique, and Vietnam. Nearly one hundred local people are employed in the networks; the majority of them are landmine survivors or people with disabilities.

Trauma Recovery: Survivors' Voices

To determine survivors' full range of needs and seek their input about how to meet those needs, LSN interviewed survivors all over the world who describe their trauma and key factors in their recovery process. LSN outreach workers conducted in-depth interviews with landmine survivors, family members, and service providers from six mine-affected countries: Bosnia, El Salvador, Eritrea, Ethiopia, Jordan, and Mozambique. Survivors were asked to describe their experiences in their own words. LSN researchers observed that certain factors were repeatedly mentioned in survivors' testimonies as contributing to successful recovery from trauma:

1.   A *resilient attitude* toward the limb loss and the future;
2.   Ongoing access to *medical care and rehabilitation*;
3.   Emotional and material support from *family and community* members;
4.   Relationships with *peers* who serve as amputee/disabled role models and sources of information;
5.   Opportunities for *social participation*, including access to community events such as sports and recreation;
6.   Ability to be *economically productive* and provide for one's own and one's family's basic needs.

Survivors' Attitudes

LSN hears over and over again that after the landmine accident and the resulting disability, the survivor contemplates suicide. A landmine survivor from El Salvador said:

> When the soldiers arrived to take me to the hospital, I took the gun from one of the soldiers and begged the soldier to kill me with it. "Please kill me, please kill me," I said. I was desperate to die.

When a survivor cannot muster a positive attitude toward the future, emotional support from family, community, and other landmine survivors becomes critical. However, when a survivor has a hopeful and forward-thinking outlook, he or she provides an inner road map for his or her recovery. One landmine survivor said:

> I set many goals for myself. I knew that if I did nothing, then I would not recover. I will always be disabled but I can give myself the courage to recover.

Medical Care and Rehabilitation

Good medical care and rehabilitation provide a strong basis for recovery. Regaining physical health and mobility affects psychological, social, and economic well-being as well. One survivor describes regaining his mobility:

> I got a new prosthesis and I am ready to live a new life. I can go to the hospital by myself. I can walk five to seven kilometers. It is an amazing feeling for someone who has lost a leg to get a prosthesis and start thinking about the future.

Family and Community Support

Family support can be a key factor in recovery from trauma. Plamenko Priganica, a landmine survivor and director of LSN Bosnia, credits his family for his recovery:

> I have a wife and three beautiful kids. They have given me my most important support in my life after my accident.

A survivor from El Salvador said:

> My family took care of me, they stood by me, gave me advice, and counseled me not to feel bad. They told me they were going to help me no matter what happened.

Hamat Bourdjo is a landmine survivor from Chad. As a deminer, he had lifted thousands of mines and unexploded ordnance from the ground before stepping on a mine and losing both legs. The people living in the community where Hamat had been demining took up a collection of money for him. They knew his military pension would not cover his basic needs.

> Everyone in the community knew I had been risking my life for them. So they took up a collection and presented me with the money. At the time, I didn't know how I would feed my family. But that money helped me get a garden going and now I work in the garden. I don't know what would have happened to me if my community hadn't been there for me.

However, not all landmine survivors are lucky enough to have the support of their family and community. Children who have suffered a landmine accident are sometimes abandoned to orphanages because their

parents feel the children will not be productive or are no longer mar-
riageable. It has been estimated that nearly half of all landmine survivors
are abandoned by their spouses. When survivors feel valued by their family and community, they are more likely to recover from their injuries and
lead "normal and healthy" lives. Survivors' experiences within their immediate families often mediate or affect experiences within wider circles
of the community or the society at large.[4]

Peer Support

A person who suddenly loses a limb in a traumatic event, such as a landmine explosion, is usually burdened with the same misconceptions about
amputees that most able-bodied people carry. That is, the new amputee
may believe he or she will never walk, play sports, work, marry, or leave
the house ever again. Therefore, it is crucial that the new amputee meet
with another person who has also lost a limb and who has already made
significant progress toward recovery and reintegration back into the community. Adnan Al Aboudy, director of LSN Jordan, said:

> I was lying in the hospital bed with both my legs cut off. I said to
> myself, "OK, I will never walk again." And I tried to start accepting
> that. Then I received a visit from someone who also was missing
> both legs. And he was walking on these prosthetic legs. That was
> the first time I thought, "OK, maybe I will walk again."

Margaret Arach went to visit a young boy about ten years of age in the
hospital. The boy's father sat gloomily at the edge of the bed:

> "Hello, I hear you have just lost your leg to a landmine. Is that true?"
> Margaret asks.
>
> "Go away" says the father grimly.
>
> "Oh, but I would like to talk to you. I think we could have a good
> talk."
>
> The boy shouts, "Go away! What do you know about losing your
> leg? My life is over!"
>
> "Yes, his life is ruined," confirms the father.
>
> "Ah, well I know a little bit." And Margaret shyly lifts up her skirt
> enough to reveal her artificial leg.
>
> The boy's face lights up and he says, "You are walking! How can you
> walk like that? Show me that leg again. I can't believe it is fake."

Margaret Arach finds that doing peer visits energizes her and gives her, as well as the new amputee, renewed hope for life.

> The way I have accepted my disability and carry on with my life has touched many amputees, and it gives me zeal to reach as many as I can.

Research indicates that social support can reduce symptoms of stress after trauma and is most useful if it happens among peers who have experienced the same trauma.[5] Studies show that talking about the traumatic event has significant health benefits including a boosted immune response and fewer visits to doctors.[6] The peer visitation system is predicated on the fact that the "helper" and the "beneficiary" are inherently equal, although one has had more time to recover and has received training in peer visitation. The friendship, exchange of information, and prospect of finding a community of survivors to belong to are simple yet crucial resources for landmine survivors and other people with disabilities. Peer support can also be one of the most cost-effective forms of victim assistance.

Social Integration

Adnan Al Aboudy, the man who thought he would never walk again, is a sports enthusiast. He skis and swims and is a champion Ping-Pong player, and, in 1998, he competed in the Paralympic Games for weight lifting. Adnan's love of sports has inspired the creation of Jordan's first amputee swim team. Adnan believes that participating in sports is one of the best ways to reclaim your life, both physically and psychologically, because sports focus on abilities, not disabilities.

LSN, in partnership with the Jordan Sports Federation for the Disabled, held a regional tournament with amputee swimmers from Lebanon, Iraq, and Palestine, as well as the top nine swimmers from Jordan. Adnan tells how the tournament brought about a change in the amputees:

> The first time the survivors appeared in front of a crowd not wearing their prostheses was a great challenge to them. As they competed, the feeling of pride overcame the feeling of shame.

Messages or attitudes that people with disabilities cannot be physically active or strong are often internalized by survivors. However, when testing his or her strength, endurance, and skill through sports, the survivor is better able to see the error in such messages. A review of the literature on sports for disabled people revealed that peo-

ple who were active in sports perceived fewer psychological limitations.[7] In addition, sports can alleviate the isolation that many people
with disabilities experience. In fact, Seppo Iso-Ahola and Chun Park
suggest that it is the social support and activity generated through
sports that alleviate mental and physical stress, as opposed to the sport
itself.[8] Adnan agrees:

> The importance of the tournaments were that these were the first
> times that amputees from the different regions of Jordan, and then
> from different countries in the Middle East, could meet. This gave
> them a tremendous feeling of belonging and support.

For many landmine survivors and other persons with limb loss,
sports improve their physical and psychological well-being.

Economic Productivity

Without the ability to meet basic needs, survivors describe feeling de-
pressed, angry, and hurt. Unemployed survivors may not have the resources to obtain adequate health or prosthetic care. A family that
struggles to provide food and shelter may view a prosthesis as an unaf-
fordable extra. In addition to earning an income and providing material
necessities, survivors have a psychological need to regain the breadwinner
role or have productive status within the family and community.[9]

The opportunity to be productive can positively affect physical, psychological, and social aspects of recovery. An American survivor describes his experience after being injured in a war. Still on crutches and
unable to walk, a general told him, "Let me know when you're ready,
there's still a lot to do. I've got a big job for you." This made a big difference for the survivor who described the general's attitude and offer of
employment as "instant rehabilitation."

Many survivors languish for years before finding employment. Naj-
muddin is a landmine survivor from Afghanistan who did not receive
prosthetic legs until six years after his accident. He describes the most
painful part of having to remain at home:

> Of course to be five years at home without legs was extremely de-
> pressing. It is not easy to accept losing part of your body. But to be
> at home without a job is really, really difficult.

Many survivors say that work is their primary concern for getting
on with their lives and recovering fully from trauma. A survivor from El
Salvador said:

I don't need anything else except to work in a regular job, to work like a normal person! With my diploma for repairing bicycles, I am capable and ready to work like any other person.

Trauma recovery depends on a dynamic relationship among many factors. Although every survivor's path to recovery will be unique, LSN's trauma research indicates that victim assistance programming and humanitarian interventions for landmine survivors should promote access to a wide range of services that include psychological and emotional support, social and economic reintegration, family and community education, and access to positive amputee role models.

Survivor Advocacy

Survivor testimonies have had a significant impact on the landmine ban movement since the early days of the campaign. The voices of survivors were first heard at the international level at the Conference on Conventional Weapons in Vienna in September 1995. The testimonies of survivors from Afghanistan, Cambodia, and the United States gave powerful arguments for banning landmines. It was the call to action from survivors at the June 1997 landmine conference in Brussels that focused treaty drafters on the need to include humanitarian provisions to address the needs of mine victims. The twelve survivors present at the Brussels conference were appalled that the first draft of the treaty did not mention victim assistance. An excerpt from the statement they issued reads as follows:

> We ask you to re-read the current draft of the Treaty and consider how it appears to us landmine survivors. There is virtually nothing in it to urge governments to take responsibility for the victims. . . . To this day, the real needs of mine-affected communities are not being addressed.

The persistence of the survivors and the moral rectitude of their demand led to article 6.3 being added to the final draft of the Mine Ban Treaty, which obliges signatories to "provide assistance for the care and rehabilitation, and social and economic reintegration of mine victims." The Mine Ban Treaty is the first arms control treaty in history to include a provision for humanitarian assistance to the victims of the weapon banned by the treaty.

Landmine survivors won a great battle through article 6.3, but there are many more battles survivors and their allies will have to fight. The reality is that survivors and other people with disabilities face daunting obstacles in reintegrating into their communities on an equal basis with others because of disability-based discrimination. Negative attitudes toward people with disabilities can be more disabling for the survivor than the landmine injury. Examples of false yet pervasive messages and attitudes that undermine the value of disabled people as human beings are disabled people are inactive, disabled people cannot be productive, disabled people are a burden to their families and communities, no one would love a disabled person, it is better to be dead than disabled. These messages are based in fear and ignorance, not in reality.

To help combat negative attitudes toward disability and to fulfill the promise of the Universal Declaration of Human Rights that all people are "born free and equal in dignity and rights," LSN is building an international network of landmine survivors and other people with disabilities who actively promote their own rights and the human rights of their peers, and who serve as advocates for local, national, and international laws and policies that affect their lives.

In 2001, LSN launched Raising the Voices, a human rights advocacy and leadership training program for landmine survivors and other people with disabilities from mine-affected countries. The training takes place in the context of the monitoring and implementation processes of the Mine Ban Treaty and is coordinated by LSN on behalf of the ICBL. Raising the Voices builds skills, knowledge, and capacity in human rights, social justice advocacy, the history of the Ottawa Process, the Mine Ban Treaty, and public speaking. Participants are encouraged to build relationships with key allies who are essential to their advocacy efforts in their home countries, including government representatives, ICBL campaigners, and Landmine Monitor researchers.

In 2001, Raising the Voices trained eight landmine survivors from Nicaragua, El Salvador, Colombia, Ecuador, and Chile. In 2002, the program trained fifteen landmine survivors from Chad, Rwanda, Senegal, Eritrea, Uganda, Angola, Mozambique, Ethiopia, Sudan, and South Africa. Landmine survivors from Asia are being trained in 2003.

Raising the Voices graduates continue their advocacy work beyond the meetings of the Mine Ban Treaty. Nelson Castillo, an Ecuadorian graduate of the program, was instrumental in enacting a new law that allows disabled military personnel to continue serving their country rather than be discharged without a pension or retraining. Nelson accomplished this through human rights education and raising awareness within the military system.

Another Raising the Voices graduate, Jean-Claude Bassene from Senegal, helps disabled children in his province go to school. In Senegal, many parents keep children with disabilities out of schools and out of sight. The local superstition in small villages is that a disabled child brings shame and bad luck to the family. Jean-Claude speaks to the parents of disabled children to convince them that education is the key to their child becoming a productive member of the family. Working in close coordination with the schools and a scholarship program for children with disabilities, Jean-Claude has successfully enrolled several disabled children in school.

Some interventions that promote trauma recovery for survivors can also have the effect of helping change attitudes toward people with disabilities. Adnan Al Aboudy comments on the effect that watching disability sports had on able-bodied people:

> Spectators were amazed seeing single and double amputees swim. The tournaments shed light on the capabilities of amputees in general and focused attention on their needs.

Peer visits are also a good way to combat negative attitudes that the survivor may have internalized about disabled people. Margaret Arach knew that part of her recovery was tackling the negative attitudes she had learned when she was an able-bodied person. She tries to help new landmine survivors understand how damaging and how false these attitudes really are.

> Being disabled has opened my eyes to the plight of disabled people. I now identify with disabled persons. I know that with disability comes low self-esteem. This comes from negative attitudes some of our community have towards people with disability. I want to tell them that it doesn't have to be this way. But I can see in their eyes that they believe it does.

Practicing Inclusion: Implications

Initial thrusts of the campaign to ban landmines focused on a universal and total ban of the weapon and did not include a provision for victim assistance. In fact, early attempts of survivors and others to address victims' needs in the treaty were met with skepticism by some campaigners and government representatives who felt that the issue of humanitarian assistance detracted from the main goal of a total ban. The survivors who advocated for the victim assistance provision were persistent and organized, gained access to the relevant negotiations, knew about international humanitarian law and human rights, and relied on available resources and sympathetic allies.

The Ottawa Process holds several lessons for future humanitarian treaties. From the point of view of survivors, the lesson of inclusion is most important. Inclusion means the proactive efforts that provide survivors a seat at the negotiating table and a voice in the process. We must remember that few survivors enjoy comprehensive medical and rehabilitative care or have access to educational and economic opportunities. Inclusion means creating opportunities for survivors to build the skills and knowledge that will allow them to substantively participate in international conferences, developing materials directed at strengthening survivors' capacity to advocate for themselves, making sure buildings are physically accessible, and devoting the resources to accommodate needs.

Survivors and other victim assistance players still have much work to do to make sure that governments comply with their victim assistance obligations and that landmine survivors around the world have the opportunity to improve their lives. LSN believes that the next important challenge for survivors and other people with disabilities will be to help bring about an international convention on the rights of people with disabilities. While conventions exist protecting the human rights of marginalized groups such as women, children, and indigenous peoples, there is no convention that specifically targets the human rights of people with disabilities.

An international coalition of landmine, disability, and human rights groups, as well as other key organizations, is emerging to campaign for a UN convention on the rights of people with disabilities. The governments of Mexico, Ireland, South Africa, Jordan, and Ecuador are currently among the key promoters of the convention and the United Nations is also showing leadership on this issue.

The campaign for the convention is, in several important ways, modeled on the International Campaign to Ban Landmines and the Ottawa Process. First, the campaign for a UN convention is working to secure broad participation of civil society in the convention process, following the example of the historic collaboration of civil society and governments during the Ottawa Process. Second, the coalition is working to ensure full participation of people with disabilities in the development of the convention. The coalition is looking to landmine survivors who participated in the Ottawa Process and the subsequent monitoring and implementation of the Mine Ban Treaty as leaders in the movement to bring about a convention.

Victim assistance actors need to listen to landmine survivors and create opportunities for their voices to be heard. The Ottawa Process has taught us that survivors' voices can change the world.

Notes

1. Main sources for statistics on casualty rates are Landmine Monitor, non-government organization and international organizations such as the International Committee of the Red Cross, the World Health Organization, Handicap International, and the U.S. government. The International Campaign to Ban Landmines' Working Group on Victim Assistance, chaired by Landmine Survivors Network, produces *Portfolio of Victim Assistance* that gives a snapshot of victim assistance programs and services worldwide.

2. According to the *International Campaign to Ban Landmines (ICBL) Guidelines for the Care and Rehabilitation of Survivors,* comprehensive rehabilitation includes medical care, physical rehabilitation, psychological and social support, employment and economic integration, capacity building and sustainability, legislation and public awareness, access, and data collection.

3. Jerry White and Ken Rutherford, "The Role of the Landmine Survivors Network," in *To Walk without Fear: The Global Movement to Ban Landmines,* ed. Maxwell A. Cameron, Robert J. Lawson, and Brian W. Tomlin, 99–117 (Oxford: Oxford University Press, 1998).

4. B. S. Richie, *Peer Visitation Programs and Trauma Survival* (Washington, DC: Landmine Survivors Network, 1998).

5. Ibid.

6. R. J. Booth, K. J. Petrie, and J. W. Pennebaker, "Changes in Circulating Lymphocyte Numbers following Emotional Disclosure Evidence of Buffering," *Stress Medicine* 13, no. 1 (1997): 23–29.

7. G. W. Van Der Gugten, "Sport as a Tool in Rehabilitating Persons with Physical Disabilities," *ICHPER-SD Journal: The Official Magazine of the International Council for Health, Physical Education, Recreation, Sport, and Dance* (Summer 1997): 50–55.

8. S. E. Iso-Ahola and C. J. Park, "Leisure-Related Social Support and Self-Determination as Buffers of Stress-Illness Relationship," *Journal of Leisure Research* 28, no. 3 (1996): 169–187.

9. B. S. Richie, A. Ferguson, Z. Adamaly, D. El-Khoury, and M. J. Gomez, "Paths to Recovery: Coordinated and Comprehensive Care for Landmine Survivors," *Journal of Mine Action* 6, no. 3 (2002): 66–69.

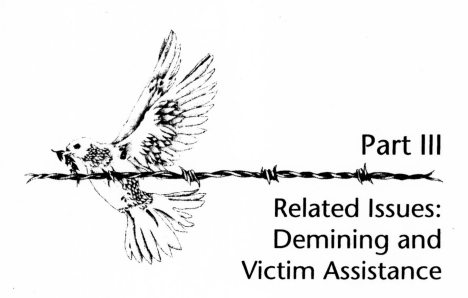

Part III

Related Issues: Demining and Victim Assistance

9

Political Minefield

Michael J. Flynn

IN THE EARLY 1990S, BRIGADIER GENERAL PATRICK BLAGDEN, THEN MINE clearance chief for the United Nations, was under pressure to come up with estimates of the number of antipersonnel mines that had been laid in various countries. The United Nations and its advisers used a simple rule of thumb to estimate that there were 100 million landmines worldwide. Afghanistan, for instance, was thought to have, 10 million.

Such a number, Blagden told me in a 1999 interview, was patently false. As Mike Croll, a British Army engineer and former deminer, explains in his 1998 book *The History of Landmines*, had there actually been 10 million mines in Afghanistan, it would have meant that the Soviets had laid three thousand mines per day, every day for nine years.[1] Nonetheless, the numbers were enormously influential. They not only spurred the United Nations to commit resources to landmine clearance, they also attracted the many nongovernmental organizations who in the 1990s turned their considerable attention to persuading most of the world's governments to sign a treaty banning antipersonnel mines. On March 1, 1999, the Convention on the Prohibition of the Use, Stockpiling, Production and Transfer of Anti-Personnel Mines, and on Their Destruction entered into force. The treaty, signed by 150 countries, has so far been ratified by 141.

A version of this chapter first appeared as an editoral in the *Bulletin of the Atomic Scientists*, March/April 1999.

The successful completion of a treaty outlawing landmines would seem like a happy ending to a tragic story-with the moral that through grit and determination ordinary people could end a scourge that kills innocent civilians long after conflicts have ended.But in the years immediately following the treaty's signing, a rift developed between the "banners" and the deminers—between those who lobby governments and go to meetings, and those who work in the field. Deminers claimed the landmine campaign absorbed funds that would have been better spent actually clearing mines— that the banners' efforts and financial resources were spent on holding international conferences and conducting "public education" campaigns. Meanwhile, many organizations, flush with success, began turning their attention elsewhere, to a new campaign to end the international trade in small arms.

A Matter of Priorities

Although none of the world's chief mine-producing nations—Russia, China, the United States, and North Korea—signed the ban on antipersonnel mines, the treaty has been hailed as a remarkable achievement for the International Campaign to Ban Landmines (ICBL), a coalition of more than one thousand nongovernmental organizations, charities, and likeminded governments. The campaign's coordinator, Jody Williams, was awarded the Nobel Peace Prize in 1997, soon after the treaty was signed. As a result of the campaign, the use of mines is now regarded with widespread antipathy.

On the other hand, both the campaign and the treaty have had their critics. A key point of contention concerns the use of inflated numbers of landmines, which the campaign and organizations like the International Committee of the Red Cross and the United Nations frequently cited. Many deminers charge that using such misleading figures—saying that there are 110 million antipersonnel mines in the world, that it will take one thousand years to get rid of them, and that millions more are going in the ground than are being taken out—actually undermined mine clearance efforts.

Mine clearance, say the deminers, is the one activity that prevents more people from being killed or injured and the one effort that enables once-strife-torn localities to resume farming. The numbers used by the campaign, they add, make demining look like Mission Impossible.

Paul Jefferson, a British mine clearer who was injured in a mine accident, told me that "by inflating figures, the campaign makes the issue look as if it doesn't have a practical solution."

In a *Wall Street Journal* article, Jefferson wrote, "Government ministers, donor institutes, and the public accept [these figures] unquestioningly. The clearance problem is thus seen as intractable . . . something beyond our capabilities to address. Instead, people support a landmine ban, feeling that at least they are doing something."[2]

Croll wrote in *The History of Landmines* that signing the treaty may turn out to be an empty gesture. Countries may sign the treaty, but in extremis they may look after their national security interests before honoring a voluntary treaty. Countries that use antipersonnel mines may be stigmatized in popular opinion, but in war the opinion of outsiders counts for little.[3] (The treaty, like most treaties, has an escape clause. Each party has the right to withdraw as long as it includes "a full explanation" of its reasons for withdrawing and it is not currently engaged in armed conflict.)

Tim Lardner, a deminer who worked for several years in Cambodia, told me that he agrees with Croll: "Most deminers accept the ban as an ideal, but if you look at . . . where most of us are working, you will find that [they] are places where a piece of paper stating that it is naughty to use mines is really not of too much interest." As an example he cites the Cambodian government, which continued laying mines after it had signed the treaty.

Such comments lead to a central question: If a political ban against landmines cannot prevent some countries from using the devices, then shouldn't attention have been refocused on mine clearance? And another question: Did it make sense to continue pouring money into the campaign as opposed to on-the-ground demining?

Croll writes: "Many individuals working in mine clearance felt that the ICBL represented something of a double-edged sword. Certainly the campaign brought a great deal of publicity to the issue, but it . . . distorted the size and the shape of the problem and distracted attention from the crux of the issue."[4]

Troublesome Numbers

How many mines are actually still in the ground? Nearly everyone agrees on the actual answer to that question: No one really knows.

"The very nature of mine warfare in the late twentieth century," says Laurie Boulden, an arms analyst who studied demining in southern Africa, "has made it difficult to take an accurate census of deployed landmines." In "so-called conventional wars," she explained to me, "traditional military procedures and international treaties set out rules for landmine marking and removal. Those conventions . . . have little bearing on the civil and guerrilla wars of this generation."[5]

Croll agrees. With very few records to go by and no distinguishable front lines to use as guides for locating minefields, "mine clearance [in the 1990s] has frequently been likened to finding a needle in a haystack. But in Cambodia, for example, finding the haystack was a problem in itself."[6]

Despite the impossibility of accurately quantifying the landmine problem, coming up with an assessment was critical to getting demining programs under way. Blagden, the UN's clearance officer in the early 1990s, told me that the reason why his figures "were calculated by rule of thumb at short notice [was] mostly because we had to prepare programs and make budgets—without having proper access to the countries concerned. Today's wisdom," Blagden added, would call for a "level one [minefield] survey." But "the 1993 real-life situation was that we had no money for a survey until the plan had been approved—a perfect Catch-22 situation."

Blagden says that the first global estimate to be announced publicly was "probably" the one the UN demining office produced in 1992. Its estimate of up to 100 million mines deployed worldwide was based on assumptions about the numbers in Cambodia, Afghanistan, Mozambique, and Kuwait. Using a guesswork benchmark of 10 million mines in Afghanistan, mine clearance officials began making estimates for other countries. Croll says: "It was felt that Cambodia was not as heavily mined as Afghanistan, and a figure of seven million was produced. Similarly, Mozambique was considered to be not nearly as heavily mined as Cambodia and a figure of two million was adopted."[7] Mine clearance officials soon realized they were wrong. Mozambique, for instance, probably "had fewer than 300,000 mines," says Croll. But, he explains, "the United Nations continued to state the figure of two million officially in order to mobilize donor funding for the clearance program."[8]

Blagden, who admits that he was principally responsible for many of the initial UN estimates, says he "knew all along that they were flagrant estimates, but such estimates were needed at the time to get the whole mine clearance process started. If I went in high, it was because in the UN system it is easier to hand money back if you overestimate than to get more if you underestimate." Besides, he says, "those who remember my briefings at the time will recall that I always began by saying 'all the figures I give are wrong. They are worst-case estimates for planning purposes. I can only say that there may be as many as n mines in Angola, Mozambique, or wherever.' The fact that the caveats seemed to disappear, and such figures became de facto totals is unfortunate, but beyond the control of the United Nations."

Once the inflated figures had been repeated often enough, says Jefferson, the former deminer, "[i]t was in nobody's interest to be truly objective. The incentive will always be to exaggerate figures. Why make the issue less dramatic?" There is also, he says, "a complicity to allow figures to escalate."[9] Aid agencies wanted to keep the funds flowing, the ICBL wanted to mobilize public outrage for its political agenda, and journalists wanted a dramatic story.

In recent years, the trend has been toward lower estimates. For example, the U.S. State Department, in a revised 1998 edition of its report, *Hidden Killers: The Global Landmine Crisis*, estimated that the global number of mines might be closer to 60 million rather than 100 million. According to estimates released in January 1999 by HALO Trust, a British mine clearance charity that heavily criticized the inflated figures, the combined total for Afghanistan, Angola, Cambodia, Mozambique, Croatia, and Bosnia (countries in which HALO has been demining for several years) was between 1.6 million and 2.5 million mines. But the UN landmine database continued to estimate that 40 million mines were still in the ground in those same six countries.

Do the Numbers Matter?

Most deminers say the numbers, by themselves, don't matter—the important thing is to get mines out of the ground quickly and efficiently. Progress should be measured by how much land is cleared, not by how many mines are removed.

"Realistically," Tim Lardner, the deminer who worked in Cambodia, told me, "it doesn't matter to my deminers on the ground whether there are no mines or whether there are one thousand mines in the five hectares of land they are told to clear." Experts say it takes the same amount of time to clear a square kilometer of land with one hundred mines as it does to clear one with one thousand mines. Disposing of mines once they are found is relatively easy; combing every square inch of a suspected minefield is tremendously time-consuming.

So why all the fuss about numbers? The answer is money. Money that could be used for mine clearance, the deminers say, was "hijacked." The ICBL's media campaign, they argue, diverted funds from mine clearance by persuading potential donors that clearance is an open-ended, intractable problem.

"It is becoming more difficult to convince donors to fund [demining] because the problem is perceived as insurmountable," Lardner told me in a 1999 interview. Deminers cite a decision by billionaire financier George Soros as an example. In 1996, he announced that he would not fund mine clearance until it became more cost-effective. His foundation, the Open Society Institute, donated $3 million to the ICBL instead.

Another example is The Diana, Princess of Wales Memorial Fund, which was established immediately after Princess Diana's death to support her favored causes, including demining. As of 1999, the fund had given away $20 million, including $1.6 million to the landmine campaign. Not a penny had gone to actual mine clearance, according to Tim Carstairs of the British-based Mines Advisory Group. After the princess's death, the intense media focus on landmines generated millions of dollars for the fund, he told me. But the fund chose "to focus only on victim assistance." In the meantime, the public thought "we [were] receiving money." Carstairs said that "the ICBL brought a lot of attention to the mines issue and we thought that our resources would increase as a result. But that just [wasn't] the case."

Private foundations may not be the only entities influenced by misleading statements that it will take one thousand years to clear all the mines or that it costs $1,000 to clear each mine. Many demining agencies say these estimates have also had an impact on how donor governments—the source of most antilandmine funds—choose to spend their demining dollars. In particular, the mine clearance charities are concerned that governments spend too much money in the search for new demining technologies.

The agencies say it is unlikely that any "silver bullets" will make demining much easier. In a joint statement on funding released in November 1998, three agencies—the Mines Advisory Group, the Norwegian Peoples Aid, and Handicap International, which together claim to represent one-third of the world's demining capacity—predicted that despite the need for new technologies to improve the speed, safety, and cost-effectiveness of demining, we are convinced that existing methods will remain dominant for years to come and should be supported accordingly.

A Matter of Opinion

"The ICBL's publicity machine hijacked the issue of demining, turning a practical problem into a bureaucratic, legalistic, and media gravy train," said former deminer Jefferson soon after the ICBL won the Nobel Prize in 1997. "It provides employment and kudos for bureaucrats, aid workers, lobbyists, lawyers, and administrators, which would not matter were it not for the counter-productive aspect. It diverts resources and attention from the real problem."[10]

This sort of criticism angers ban supporters, who prefer to view the campaign and mine clearance, in Jody Williams's words, as "mutually reinforcing goals." Yet, says Croll, critics characterize the campaign's grand achievement—the treaty—as "parchment pacification, encouraging a false sense of security, and not reducing the casualties caused by mines by a single leg."[11]

Nevertheless, not all deminers believe the ICBL has had a negative impact on demining. Dave McCracken, a deminer who heads the Vietnam Veterans of America Foundation's (VVAF's) landmine survey team, thinks the campaign brought more money to demining than ever. And he told me that many deminers fail to realize that mine clearance is just one part— albeit a crucial one—of what he calls "mine action," which includes demining, advocacy, mine marking, mine awareness, victim assistance, and training. Funds are needed for each of these initiatives. Deminers, he says, should not assume that their work is the only objective. As for criticism of the treaty, McCracken argues that "if the only thing it achieves is destruction of the 120 million mines stockpiled around the world, then it will have been a worthy cause and will have saved lives."

Meanwhile, the VVAF—which cofounded the campaign—announced in 1998 that it was shifting its focus: "The VVAF's Campaign for a Landmine Free World now moves beyond calling for a ban" and is focusing on minefield surveys and victim assistance.

Blagden also doubts that the ICBL's use of high-end estimates is the cause of donor reticence. He told me that "mine clearance is dirty and dangerous, and people die and are mutilated. Few organizations care to be associated with that. Much better to fund training, awareness, surveys, setting up of management headquarters—anything except the dirty bit."

Further, at least one demining organization, HALO Trust, said it had very little trouble raising funds. In a 1999 interview, HALO's Guy Willoughby, an outspoken critic of exaggerated numbers, said his organization was doing just fine. Why, then, has he spoken out so often about inflated estimates? "You work for a scientific journal," he told me. "You can appreciate the need for accuracy."

Irreconcilable Differences?

Tim Lardner thinks that—funding aside—the rift dividing deminers and banners is caused by a fundamental difference in the two groups' approach to the landmine problem: "Most banners are idealistic thinkers and probably have a longer-term perspective of things." Deminers "tend to be more pragmatic and, unfortunately, often short-term thinkers. The fact is, most deminers are ex-military and are trained in a specific way— here's the problem, solve it, deal with the consequences later."

If there is no love lost between the two camps, says Blagden, that is only natural. "The mine clearers see themselves doing dangerous work in horrible countries with little recognition. . . . They believe that the honors and plaudits are going to a few outspoken self-promoters eating huge lunches in classy hotels in safe capitals. An exaggeration, but [one] with a grain of truth."

While many deminers regard the campaign as time and money poorly spent, others are willing to give it credit. "The future effects of the ICBL in practical terms will be extremely limited," writes Croll. But, he continues, "the campaign is ultimately heartening. Armies will be more prudent when employing mines and the well-publicized difficulties of clearance may result in improvements in the marking and the recording of minefields. The most important effect of the ICBL is that it mobilized public opinion and brought the horrors of war to the public."[12]

Notes

1. Mike Croll, *The History of Landmines* (Barnsley, UK: Pen and Sword Books, 1998).

2. Paul Jefferson, "A Political Minefield," *Wall Street Journal*, October 15, 1997. Available at www.centerforsecuritypolicy.org/index.jsp?section=papers &code=97-P_lstat1.

3. Croll, *The History of Landmines*.

4. Ibid., 136.

5. See also Laurie Boulden, "Harvest Season," *Bulletin of Atomic Scientists 53*, no. 5 (September/October 1997), available at http://www.thebulletin. org/issues/1997/so97/so07boulden.html.

6. Croll, *The History of Landmines*, 136.

7. Ibid., 131.

8. Ibid.

9. Jefferson, "A Political Minefield."

10. Ibid.

11. Croll, *The History of Landmines*, 136.

12. Ibid., 152.

10

Tackling the Global Landmine Problem: The United States Perspective

Stacy Bernard Davis and Donald F. "Pat" Patierno

THE UNITED STATES HAS A STRONG TRADITION OF LEADERSHIP IN GENERAL humanitarian issues and specific emergencies. Americans have long been committed to extending a helping hand to those struggling to make life better for themselves and their families, because a safe and secure world benefits all people. Achieving regional and global stability is an important goal as we help others recover from disaster. It is important to help the growth of democratic values and support equal opportunity for all peoples. In the humanitarian area, the United States is committed to helping stem the spread of HIV/AIDS, empowering women in developing nations, helping prevent childhood diseases and malnutrition, and removing landmines and other remnants of war.

With the growing frequency of conflict in the past half century, the U.S. government is acutely aware that the postconflict landscape must be cleared not only of landmines, but also of other destabilizing hazards and excess weapons of war, such as unexploded ordnance (UXO) and small arms and light weapons. The U.S. government is dedicated to meeting the challenge of removing the millions of landmines and explosive remnants of war that pose an immediate threat in approximately one-third of the world's nations and caring for the survivors of landmine accidents and their families. Since 1989, with the inception of U.S. mine

125

action assistance in Afghanistan, the United States has financed training, equipping and operating costs for mine-clearance teams, mine risk education, landmine surveys, and assistance to landmine survivors in close to forty countries around the world, investing more than $600 million in the past fifteen years.

Why the United States Engages in Humanitarian Mine Action

We should begin by asking a fundamental question: Why has the United States been so engaged in humanitarian mine action? The answer, simply put, is that such engagement is in the best interest of the United States in achieving its foreign policy goals. For several years, humanitarian engagement has been a core precept of the U.S. National Security Strategy.[1] Among its other fundamentals, the most recent (September 2002) National Security Strategy champions aspirations for human dignity and highlights the need to work with others to defuse regional conflicts. These two fundamental components compel us, as citizens, and as a government, to seek to restore stability by:

- alleviating human suffering;
- remedying the economic and social root causes of conflict that force people to become internally displaced or flee to other countries.

Foreign and domestic policy considerations are enormously intertwined in today's world, and that integration is particularly true of our humanitarian engagements. While we categorize most of the assistance we provide to other nations as foreign aid, we should recognize that in providing such assistance we are aiding the United States as well.

The removal of landmines and UXO, the education of at-risk populations, and rehabilitation and reintegration of survivors provide a case in point. As Secretary of State Colin L. Powell stated, landmines

> pose a constant threat to the safety of local populations long after the guns of war have been silenced. In addition, they hinder post-conflict reconstruction and recovery by preventing refugees and displaced persons from returning to their homes, taking valuable land out of production, depriving societies of valuable infrastructure, disrupting the free circulation of people and goods, and preventing deployment of peacekeeping forces.[2]

When the United States assists other countries in clearing landmines and caring for refugees, we serve America's long-term interests and remain true to the values upon which our country was founded, and which are espoused in our National Security Strategy. U.S. support for humanitarian mine action around the world enhances our reputation as a nation committed to the free movement of people as well as goods and services and the freedom to cultivate land and to produce, sell, and consume its bounty. Over time, humanitarian engagement contributes to internal and regional stability, instilling confidence in governments to reach out and interact rationally with others and to avoid potentially explosive escalation of regional disputes.

Landmines and Unexploded Ordnance: The Problem

Our understanding of the landmine problem and the closely related problems caused by unexploded ordnance is much greater today than in 1989, when the United States initiated humanitarian mine action assistance. The landmine problem is no longer defined by the sheer number of landmines, but rather by their impact, that is, number of casualties inflicted, the amount of land rendered unusable, and the degree of economic infrastructure made inaccessible. In its most recent attempt to catalog the problem, the U.S. Department of State collected data from its embassies around the world, the United Nations, the International Committee of the Red Cross, and other reputable sources. The results of this effort were published in a State Department report, *Hidden Killers 2001*, which detailed how landmines still kill or maim thousands annually and how an estimated 50 million landmines remain in nearly sixty countries around the world, affecting domestic and regional stability, as well as families and individuals and their livelihoods. Millions more remain in stockpiles, presenting a potential threat.[3] While this data reflects a downward trend in the reported numbers of casualties and land affected, continued effort is necessary to overcome the challenge presented by the vast remaining number of hidden killers.

U.S. Humanitarian Mine Action Program

With that as background, we will outline the U.S. Humanitarian Demining Program, which has been one of our government's success stories over the past decade.

Modern warfare no longer targets only military forces. With increasing frequency, noncombatant civilians are the victims. At the start of the twentieth century, almost all wartime casualties were soldiers. Most wars fought were between countries, such as World War I and World War II. Now, in the twenty-first century, the overwhelming preponderance of the casualties of war and other forms of conflict are civilians, whose injuries are not necessarily sustained during the period of conflict. As the twentieth century passed its midpoint, many conflicts erupted that were no longer government against government, but were internal or guerilla wars. Rules and laws codified in international agreements were ignored, and civilians increasingly bore the brunt of the fighting. Vietnam, Cambodia, Angola, Nicaragua, and Mozambique are just some examples of countries where civilians suffered disproportionately to armed forces in conflict. Furthermore, the increasing use of landmines in these newer types of conflicts, aggravated by their indiscriminate deployment, has resulted in civilian casualties occurring long after the fighting ceased.

The United States has responded to the humanitarian challenge posed by the presence of landmines and unexploded ordnance with an ambitious program that has very clear goals and objectives. The United States seeks to relieve human suffering and promote U.S. foreign policy interests by:

- reducing casualties among the civilian population of mine-affected nations;
- creating conditions for the safe return of refugees and internally displaced persons to their homes;
- restoring infrastructure that is critical to a nation's capacity for economic recovery and political stability;
- extending U.S. bilateral, regional, and international influence.

No government, international agency, or private group on its own has the capacity to completely eradicate the indiscriminately placed landmines that threaten innocent civilians. Governments must work together and with international, local, and national groups that share the goal of eliminating this threat, and, of course, with citizens of mine-affected countries. Only then can the goal of removing the threat of landmines to civilians be accomplished in a reasonable time frame.

The United States, like other donors, focuses its humanitarian mine action assistance on one or more of the following:

- Mine Risk Education—educating the people, especially children, of mine-affected nations on the dangers of landmines and unexploded ordnance and what to do (or not do) should they encounter such devices;
- Mine Surveys—supporting broad and technical surveys conducted to assess not only the location of landmines and unexploded ordnance, but their likely social and economic impact on communities and regions;

- Mine Clearance—training and equipping indigenous personnel to build a capacity to detect, remove, and/or destroy mines and unexploded ordnance;
- Assistance to Survivors—providing long-term care, including prosthetic support, rehabilitative services, and social reintegration, to survivors of landmine accidents and their families.

The U.S. government coordinates its bilateral mine action assistance activities through close consultation between various agencies. These activities take place under the auspices of the International Operations Policy Coordination Committee's Sub-Group on Humanitarian Mine Action, which is cochaired by the Department of State and the Department of Defense. Other members of the sub-group include the Central Intelligence Agency, the United States Agency for International Development, the Joint Staff, and the Centers for Disease Control and Prevention. The U.S. Humanitarian Demining Program relies on the knowledge and expertise of the mine-affected country itself to help shape the overall U.S. program of assistance, which is provided via a variety of mechanisms.

The Department of State's Office of Humanitarian Demining Programs, which currently oversees programs in over three dozen countries, relies on a system of commercial contracts and grants to nongovernmental agencies to provide training, equipment (including mine detection dogs), and technical advice. The office also directly funds and monitors mine clearance operations in some countries. In addition, the office funds some operational costs of governmental mine action centers, although, to conform to general long-standing U.S. policy, this category of assistance generally does include paying salaries of other government employees. Special Operations Forces (SOF) of the Department of Defense provide training to military personnel in mine-affected countries. The focus of the SOF effort is a train-the-trainer program in mine detection and clearance, which helps build an indigenous capacity to address the landmine and UXO problem over the long term. SOF also provides training on the management of mine action (civil affairs) and on various aspects of medical support to deminers injured in the process of landmine detection and clearance.

Since 1993, the United States has provided assistance to the following countries: Afghanistan, Albania, Angola, Armenia, Argentina, Azerbaijan, Bosnia and Herzegovina, Cambodia, Chad, Colombia, Costa Rica, Croatia, Djibouti, Ecuador, Egypt, Eritrea, Estonia, Ethiopia, Georgia, Guatemala, Guinea-Bissau, Honduras, Iraq, Jordan, Laos, Lebanon, Liberia, Macedonia, Mauritania, Moldova, Mozambique, Namibia, Nicaragua, Oman, Peru, Rwanda, Senegal, Serbia and Montenegro, Somalia, Sri Lanka, Swaziland, Thailand, Vietnam, Yemen, Zambia, and Zimbabwe.

Included in the overall U.S. mine action program is assistance for survivors of landmine and UXO accidents. For over a decade, the Patrick J. Leahy War Victims Fund, administered by the U.S. Agency for International Development, has provided a dedicated source of financial and technical assistance for people living with disabilities, primarily those who suffer from mobility-related injuries, including antipersonnel landmines and UXO. Since 1989, it has provided more than $92 million to twenty-six countries. Aimed at improving the mobility, health, and social integration of civilians who have sustained injury and disability as a direct or indirect result of war and civil strife, the fund's primary objective is expanding access to affordable and appropriate prosthetic and orthotic services. The fund has provided technical assistance grants to the International Committee of the Red Cross, the International Society for Prosthetics and Orthotics, the Pan American Health Organization, and the World Heath Organization, among others. Depending on the needs of the situation, the Leahy War Victims Fund has adapted its response to provide support for a wider variety of interventions. These include support for improving medical and surgical services, developing and enforcing laws and policies regarding people with disabilities, promoting partnerships between nongovernmental organizations and the government, and expanding barrier-free accessible employment and other economic opportunities. At the field level, this has led to a number of exciting developments:

- In Laos, an innovative approach to training service providers has reduced hospitalization and secondary infections of victims of traumatic injuries, many of which previously led to death or amputation.
- In Vietnam, seed money for an initially small program of assistance, focused on barrier-free accessibility, resulted in the passage of a comprehensive national disabilities law, utilizing assistance of many Americans who had been closely affiliated with the Americans with Disabilities Act.
- In South Lebanon, the fund supports an agro-industrial cooperative based on marketing surveys that will benefit many war victims and their families.
- In Angola, a program is helping amputees secure housing and land, allowing them and their families to become self-sufficient.

The programs of the Leahy War Victims Fund consistently exemplify the generous character and tradition of U.S. leadership on humanitarian issues. In carrying out the mission of the United States Agency for International Development, they help people overseas recover from conflict and rebuild their lives.

Mine Action Initiatives:
Partnerships and International Coordination

To reinforce the importance of mine action to the United States, in late 1997, President Bill Clinton launched a global humanitarian demining initiative by creating a Special Representative of the President and Secretary of State for Mine Action.[4] President George W. Bush reaffirmed this commitment. The Office of Mine Action Initiatives and Partnerships in the Department of State's Bureau of Political-Military Affairs supports efforts in the United States and abroad to increase international coordination among donor governments, the United Nations, international and regional organizations, and nongovernmental organizations. The Office also encourages the development of public–private partnerships to increase the participation of civil society and the level of resources devoted to this global challenge.

The challenge is enormous. Even if no new landmines were planted from today forward, the world would still have to remove the threat of the millions of landmines and care for the survivors of landmine accidents and their families for years to come. This poses a serious question for the future: How can the United States sustain donor interest and involvement in mine action over the long term? One answer is to engage everyone, not just governments, in this effort.

In the United States, a number of groups have come together with community-led initiatives to address this global tragedy. The U.S. Department of State has pioneered the humanitarian mine action public–private partnership approach over the past several years, starting with a handful of partners in 1998. Now, more than thirty-five partners workd with the State Department on a variety of mine action initiatives. The Department of State works with individuals, organizations, and foundations to develop imaginative approaches and new resources for mine action. In June 2001, Secretary Powell said, "The engagement of private citizens, civic groups, corporations, foundations, educational institutions and other organizations in partnership with the U.S. government has been one of the most exciting recent developments in mine action."[5] Following are a few examples:

- *Adopt-A-Minefield Program.* The United Nations Association of the USA sponsors the Adopt-A-Minefield program, which works with the United Nations in Afghanistan, Bosnia and Herzegovina, Cambodia, Croatia, Mozambique, and Vietnam.
- *K9 Demining Corps.* The Marshall Legacy Institute's canine corps campaign is a nationwide effort to purchase, train, and deploy mine-detecting dogs around the world for humanitarian demining

purposes. Mine-detecting dog teams have been fielded in Lebanon, Armenia, and Thailand.

- *Warner Bros.* has committed the use of its "Looney Tunes" characters Bugs Bunny and Daffy Duck and created a new character, Rith, a young Cambodian landmine survivor, to produce two animated public service announcements for broadcast in Cambodia to help raise mine awareness education and acceptance of people with disabilities.
- *Roots of Peace*, through its association with California vintners, apparel manufacturers, high-tech firms, and the U.S. Department of State, is raising funds for mine action and public awareness of the global landmine problem in Croatia and Afghanistan.
- The *Polus Center for Social and Economic Development* is Massachusetts'-based, nonprofit human services organization that has supported a number of community-based rehabilitative initiatives in Central America since 1979.
- *People to People International* was founded in 1956 by President Dwight D. Eisenhower to enhance international understanding and friendship through educational, cultural, and humanitarian activities involving the exchange of ideas and experiences directly among people of different countries and diverse cultures. Sri Lanka is the focus of this organization's mine action efforts.

In addition to engaging civil society in mine action through public–private partnerships, the Office of Mine Action Initiatives and Partnerships works to raise public awareness of the landmine issue in the United States and overseas. Education outreach has been a particularly useful means of conveying the importance of mine action to students and teachers. An early partnership, supported by the Office of Humanitarian Demining Programs, resulted in the University of Denver's Center for the Teaching of International Relations preparing three landmines curricula for the upper elementary grades through high school. Fortunately, landmines are far removed from the everyday lives of most Americans, but focusing on this issue can draw students and their parents and teachers into a deeper understanding of the world around them. These curricula introduce schoolchildren to the impact of landmines through social studies, geography, language arts, and other subject areas, including service learning. These curricula are available, for free, on the center's Web site.

The Office of Mine Action Initiatives and Partnerships also works directly with interested schools and universities. More than a dozen educational institutions, from middle schools through the college and university level, have had Department of State speakers make appearances to discuss the global landmine problem. In many cases, the students and their teachers have followed up by developing service learning projects to raise community awareness and funds for mine action. Some examples include:

- *Global Care Unlimited*, a nonprofit charity formed by a motivated teacher and his students at Tenafly Middle School in Tenafly, New Jersey. By heightening local awareness of the global landmine threat, Global Care Unlimited has succeeded in funding the clearance of a minefield near the Ale Husidic school in Tenafly's sister village of Podzvizd in Bosnia and Herzegovina.
- *Maret School* (Washington, DC) teacher Linda Cole began a landmine awareness campaign in 2000 and formed connections with the Croatian Embassy and others in Croatia. During the past three years, her seventh graders have raised money to support one mine-detecting dog and are well on their way to funding a second dog for deployment in Croatia.
- *International Baccalaureate* high school students in the Beaverton, Oregon, School District and their teacher, Doug Kavanaugh, began a landmine effort in 2000 and raised enough funds to clear a minefield in Cambodia.
- *The Landmine Studies Program*, launched in 2000 by Dr. Ken Rutherford in the Department of Political Science at Southwest Missouri State University in Springfield, Missouri, provides comprehensive hands-on, practical, and academic training for students interested in mine action and policy.

Part of the special representative's mission is to increase international coordination and cooperation. In addition to multilateral coordination with the United Nations and other donor governments through the Mine Action Support Group, based in New York, the special representative is pursuing initiatives to increase the attention and resources devoted to mine action, and, in particular, technical solutions to mine detection and clearance. In 2000, the United States, Belgium, Canada, Sweden, the Netherlands, the United Kingdom, and the European Commission established the International Test and Evaluation Program (ITEP) for Humanitarian Demining, an initiative to help institutionalize technology cooperation for humanitarian demining. The ITEP provides a formal, multinational approach for cooperating on the test and evaluation of humanitarian demining equipment and systems. In 2002, a work plan of thirty-seven projects (with three or more countries participating in a majority of the tests) was approved, concentrating on survey, detection, and mechanical equipment. Germany, France, South Africa, and Croatia have since joined the ITEP. The ITEP countries examine currently available technology, such as handheld metal detectors, and determine which are most effective in various kinds of terrain, and delve into higher-tech solutions like ground-penetrating radar. The strengths of different countries working together toward a common goal should help speed the way to improved technological support for mine action.

U.S. Policy on Antipersonnel Landmines

U.S. antipersonnel landmine (APL) policy is currently under review by the Bush administration. However, the United States has been stalwart in its support of restrictions on the use of all categories of landmines. Inspired in part by the U.S. call to action at the United Nations in 1994, the international community has recognized the problems caused by landmines. The international movement to eliminate APLs has brought the landmine issue to a number of fora, such as the Convention on Prohibitions or Restrictions on the Use of Certain Conventional Weapons Which May Be Deemed to Be Excessively Injurious or to Have Indiscriminate Effects (known as the CCW), which the United States signed in 1980. In 1999, the United States ratified the CCW Amended Mines Protocol (which was adopted in 1996). The United States welcomes international efforts to eliminate the humanitarian crisis caused by the indiscriminate use of APLs espoused in the Prohibition of the Use, Stockpiling, Production and Transfer of Anti-Personnel Mines and on Their Destruction, commonly known as the Ottawa Convention. Although criticized for not acceding to the Ottawa Convention, the United States has taken on a leadership role in the CCW, having presented numerous proposals to strengthen the Amended Mines Protocol and to address humanitarian concerns associated with other remnants of war.

The United States is committed to increasing the number of adherents to the CCW and the Amended Mines protocol. The protocol significantly strengthens restrictions against landmine use, including restrictions on landmine transfer. In May 2000, at an informal meeting of experts of parties to the CCW, the United States called for improvements to the protocol, including requiring detectability for all landmines and requiring self-destruction and self-deactivation for all remotely delivered landmines as well as increasing the reliability standards for these mechanisms, and providing a verification and compliance process in cases of alleged violations.

The Amended Mines Protocol to the Convention on Conventional Weapons, with these key restrictions on landmine use, productively engages a number of important APL-producing and exporting countries that have not signed the Ottawa Convention, such as Russia, China, Pakistan, and India (of these, only Russia is not yet a party, though it is in the process of ratifying).

While some would have the U.S. government take a different course on the Ottawa Convention, this disagreement must not deter us from our common goal. The U.S. government is committed to eliminating the threat of the indiscriminate use of APLs to civilians worldwide and caring for the survivors of landmine accidents, as evidenced by its decade-long involvement in mine action, through programs at the State Department, the Defense Department, and the Agency for International Development (as well as other agencies such as the Department of Education and the Centers for Disease Control) and by generously supporting the programs of international as well as nongovernmental organizations.

The United States has joined with the international community to help achieve the objective of eliminating the threat of landmines of all types and has pledged to continue such support via international and private partnerships. As U.S. Secretary of State Powell has stated: "Working together, we can help the next generation of world citizens to walk the earth in safety."[6]

Resources

For more information on the Office of Humanitarian Demining Programs and the Office of Mine Action Initiatives and Partnerships, please see the following Web sites: http://state.gov/t/pm/maip/ and http://state.gov/t/pm/hdp/. The following are links to the U.S. Agency for International Development Leahy War Victims Fund publications: http://www.usaid.gov/pop_health/dcofwvf/reports/index.html (see also the Leahy War Victims Fund 2002 synopsis) and www.dec.org.

For additional information and details about U.S. State Department public–private partnerships, please see some of our partners' Web sites:

- United Nations Association of the USA: www.landmines.org
- People to People International: www.ptpi.org
- Warner Bros: http://looneytunes.warnerbros.com/web/home.jsp
- Vietnam Veterans of America Foundation: www.vvaf.org
- United Nations Foundation: www.unfoundation.org
- James Madison University's Mine Action Information Center: http://maic.jmu.edu
- Landmine Survivors Network: www.landminesurvivors.org
- Humpty Dumpty Institute: www.humptydumpty.net
- Roots of Peace: www.rootsofpeace.org

- Marshall Legacy Institute: www.marshall-legacy.org
- Center for Teaching International Relations: www.du.edu/gsis/outreach
- Landmine Studies, Department of Political Science, Southwest Missouri State University, Springfield, Missouri: http://www.smsu.edu/polsci/landmines/
- HALO Trust: www.halousa.org
- National Committee on American Foreign Policy and Huntington Associates: http://www.ncafp.org
- Clear Path: www.clearpathinternational.org
- Save the Children: www.savethechildren.org/landmines
- Center for International Rehabilitation: www.cirnetwork.org
- Polus Center for Social and Economic Development: www.poluscenter.org
- Grapes for Humanity: www.grapesforhumanity.com
- Global Care Unlimited: info@globalcareunlimited.org
- PeaceTrees Vietnam: www.peacetreesvietnam.org
- CZBioMed: http://www.czbiomed.md
- Health Volunteers Overseas: http://www.hvousa.org
- Wheelchair Foundation: www.wheelchairfoundation.org
- Organization of American States: www.upd.oas.org
- South Florida Landmine Action Group: www.sflag.org
- Julia Burke Foundation: www.juliaburkefoundation.com

Notes

1. The White House, "National Security Strategy of the United States of America," September 2002.

2. Statement by Secretary of State Colin L. Powell in the Office of the Special Representative for Global Humanitarian Demining's Public–Private Partnership brochure.

3. United States Department of State, Bureau of Political-Military Affairs, "Hidden Killers 2001: The World's Landmine Problem," in *To Walk the Earth in Safety: The United States Commitment to Humanitarian Demining*, 3rd ed. (Washington, DC: U.S. Department of State, 2001).

4. In October 1997, Secretary of State Madeleine Albright and Secretary of Defense William Cohen launched President Clinton's Demining 2010 Initiative, naming a Special Representative of the President and Secretary of State for Global Humanitarian Demining and creating an Office of Global Humanitarian Demining at the Department of State, staffed by members of both the State and the Defense Departments. The special representative and the office

were renamed Office of Weapons Removal and Abatement (WRA) in 2001 when President Bush came into office.

5. Statement by Secretary of State Colin L. Powell.

6. United States Secretary of State Colin Powell, November 2001. Quoted in United States Department of State, Bureau of Political-Military Affairs, *Humanitarian Demining Programs Policy and Procedures Manual*, January 2002 edition.

11

Demining: Enhancing the Process

COLIN KING

IN RECENT YEARS, PUBLICITY SURROUNDING THE GLOBAL LANDMINE CRISIS HAS given the issue the high profile it rightly deserves; however, this is not always as helpful as it may seem. The human tragedy inflicted by landmines needs little explanation, and it is relatively easy to convey the urgency of demining for regional development or reconstruction; however, in addition to gaining public attention, publicity often focuses on the enormity of the problem.

In their enthusiasm for the story, journalists have often sought out the most sensational statistics and, when these no longer have the desired effect, have sometimes invented their own. The first guesstimate for the number of mines threatening communities began at 110 million and rose steadily with successive press articles. Multiplied by equally ill-founded estimates of the cost and time required to clear each mine, this yielded spectacular numbers for public consumption; apparently, thousands of years and billions of dollars would be needed.

While the impressive statistics certainly grabbed headlines, the prospect of such an expensive and protracted campaign led many to conclude that global demining was totally unachievable. Further reports stating that more mines were being laid than cleared just added to the sense of hopelessness. Plenty of people cared about the situation, but what difference could they make when faced with such overwhelming odds?

Ironically, the situation was effectively reversed by the success of the Ottawa Process and the resultant Mine Ban Treaty. Media coverage now gave the impression that as a result of international rejection of antipersonnel landmines, the crisis was now solved. This upbeat but equally unrealistic message has been supported by coverage of various technical innovations that supposedly solve the practical problems associated with mine clearance.

Unfortunately, the actual situation does not have the appeal to make headlines or capture the public imagination. Enactment of the Mine Ban Treaty has not removed the mines that threaten communities throughout the world, although it has significantly lessened the continued use of antipersonnel mines. The human tragedy continues, and mines continue to interfere with postconflict reconstruction, but effective mine action programs now exist in virtually every mine-affected region. The fact is that far more mines are being removed than are being laid; the process is indeed slow and costly, but an order of magnitude faster and cheaper than previously believed.

The reality is that the campaign to remove the mines that threaten communities *is* being won and that many nations can look forward to an "acceptable" level of risk within the next ten years. That is not to say that the task is straightforward or without danger; success will come at a cost, including the lives and limbs of deminers. The challenge now facing the operational demining community is to minimize that cost by enhancing the demining process in every way possible.

A good deal of frustration surrounds the subject of demining, much stemming from the sneaking suspicion that technology to improve the process already exists. Almost everybody recognizes that humanitarian demining is slow and dangerous, and most see a need to enhance it. But despite years of research, little has changed in the field. What's going wrong?

Optimizing the process of demining requires much more than the development and incorporation of high technology; it involves a logical and coherent approach to well-defined aims. It also requires the many practical problems that plague field operations to be identified and overcome. The objectives cannot be achieved in isolation; they involve understanding and building on a process that has evolved as a result of hard-learned lessons over many years. Without a detailed understanding of those lessons, the process of refinement will, at best, be inefficient and, at worst, totally misdirected.

Until recently, the operational and scientific communities have been poles apart, with hopelessly inadequate communication between them. Both are partially to blame: demining management for being so engrossed in the minutiae of field operations that they failed to articulate their problems to the developers, and some researchers for having the arrogance to believe that they could contribute to a process of which they had minimal knowledge.

A further obstacle, rarely mentioned, is that some individuals and organizations do not want to collaborate. For example, some of the high-tech research has no immediate prospect of benefiting mine clearance, but attracts consistent, substantial funding and offers potentially lucrative "spin-off." In such cases, there is little incentive to bring a program to completion. Equally, some of the demining agencies, having been disillusioned by a stream of ill-conceived ideas, will now hardly consider the possibility that new technologies could help them.

Focusing on the Aim: What Are We Trying to Achieve?

Throughout the constant struggle for achievement, in both development and clearance operations, it is important to maintain a clear focus on the aims. Perhaps the two foremost issues are the reduction of casualties among the local population—the most direct form of human tragedy—and the reclamation of safe land for the use of that population. For all its good intentions, these are things that a landmine ban, in isolation, can never achieve. Banning landmines today makes it no safer to walk across a field in Cambodia tomorrow, neither is more of that ground usable than it was before. Despite the important role that the ban has in limiting proliferation, practical mine clearance is therefore a fundamental component of the solution to the global problem.

It is also important to consider what "enhancing" the process actually means. Unless new techniques are faster, safer, and cheaper, or fill a "capability gap," they are not truly enhancing the process. Even if they can fulfill one or more of these criteria, they must be readily available (which often means affordable) where and when needed.

Primary Factors

Clearly, equipment and procedures have to be suited to the operational environment, yet all too often this is neither recognized nor assessed during development. All too often, new equipment for detection or clearance is designed without reference to the realities of live minefields, and demonstrated in flat, open environments against unrepresentative targets.

To develop realistic techniques and procedures that will truly enhance the process of mine clearance, two primary factors must be considered:

1. *Mines*—the threat presented by the extensive variety of mines themselves, and the ways in which they are used;

2. *Environment*—the limitations imposed by the real minefield environment, where the conditions often rule out whole categories of techniques and equipment.

Mines

The Overpublicized Blast Mine

Even within the mine action community there is a stereotype landmine image of the small "nonmetallic" antipersonnel blast mine. Many pressure-operated blast mines are plastic cased and have a minimal metal content that does, indeed, make them difficult to detect. However, very few are truly nonmetallic or "undetectable" and the most universal clearance method (using metal detectors and probes) although slow and dangerous, is at least effective.

The antipersonnel blast mine even has a couple of points in its favor. First, the fuse requires direct and often fairly substantial pressure (normally several kilograms). Second, the plastic casing creates a very limited fragmentation hazard and is rarely lethal; there are numerous examples of deminers escaping accidental detonations with minor injuries. Of course, there are exceptions; mines like the Russian PMN, whose large explosive charge and Bakelite casing does create significant fragmentation. To the well-protected operator adhering strictly to standard operating procedures, antipersonnel blast mines are not the greatest threat. If the reliable detection of minimum-metal blast mines were the only major problem faced by deminers, clearance rates would be several orders of magnitude greater than they are.

The Lesser-Understood Fragmentation Mine

To the uninitiated, the high metallic content of the fragmentation mine makes it sound almost deminer friendly: if it's easy to detect, what's the problem? There are several problems. To begin with, stake mines, bounding mines, and Claymore-type directional mines are often initiated by tripwires. Unlike the blast mine, direct contact is not required; this is an area weapon with an area fusing system. While most blast mines require several kilograms of direct pressure, trip wire actuation may take as little as one kilogram. Gone too is the comforting notion of adequate protection. Not only will a mistake with a fragmentation mine invariably result in serious injury or death, but somebody else's mistake may get you killed as well. The detection of trip wires is every bit as important as the detection of minimum-metal mines, yet attracts a tiny fraction of the research effort.

Such is the strength of the blast mine stereotype, that people often overlook the fact that fragmentation mines are normally aboveground to maximize their effect. Being visible, once again, ought to make them safer. Yet in many situations, the reality is that the lethal range of these mines far exceeds the distance at which they can be seen: in other words, they can "see" you before you see them. Mines and trip wires placed well above the ground create a three-dimensional threat, complicating both location and demolition. To the vast majority of the scientific community, minefields are seen as strictly two-dimensional, meaning that an intrinsic element of the problem is (literally) being overlooked.

The "effective range" of fragmentation mines is also debatable: a Claymore, lethal at 50 meters is clearly not safe at 51 meters. The presence of fragmentation mines demands that deminers remain well spread out and are well protected on all sides. But large safety distances make command and control considerably more difficult, while wearing full protection decreases awareness and peripheral vision, increases fatigue, and can make the operator dangerously clumsy. Much of the protective equipment worn by deminers was not designed for that purpose. Most military issue helmets and body armor are too hot and restrictive for prolonged wear in warm climates, and often provide no protection to areas such as the groin and the neck.

Rules of Minelaying

It is the indiscriminate use of mines that is most devastating to communities, and among the "irresponsible" users, there are no rules. Improvisation makes every aspect of the mine threat unpredictable. The use of wooden stakes to initiate deep-buried mines to avoid detection; the linking of claymores to create killing zones; the use of antipersonnel mines to initiate large artillery shells or bombs are all examples of improvisation that a deminer could face in addition to routine clearance.

To further complicate the picture, virtually any mine can be booby-trapped in a variety of different ways. In the former Yugoslavia, World War II British and American mechanical booby trap switches are still in use, complemented by a range of ingenious, well-designed modern devices. The presence of booby traps further limits the number of techniques available to the deminer. Wherever their presence is suspected, buried mines must be uncovered with extreme care and always be pulled out of the ground remotely, or destroyed in place.

Electronic booby traps, which are also used in the former Yugoslavia, can operate on principles such as light, thermal, or acoustic sensitivity; vibration; tilt; inertial; time delay; or break wire. In Bosnia, booby traps like these have been found hidden inside antitank mines, melted into the explosive. In Cambodia, the Chinese Type 72B contains an electronic tilt fuse, but is externally identical to the conventional pressure-fused Type 72. With such a formidable array of potential traps, it is almost impossible to devise universal manual mine clearance drills.

The Environment: Killing Fields, Not Playing Fields

The stereotype image of a flat, grassy minefield is just as misleading and harmful as that of the nonmetallic blast mine. Yet the "football pitch" image is constantly reinforced by the trials, demonstrations, and publicity shots that invariably take place in near-perfect conditions. Even ignoring the special circumstances of Kuwait's oil lakes, the Middle East's drifting sand dunes, Afghanistan's mountains, or the Falklands peat bogs, minefields are rarely simple.

To begin with, there is vegetation. Minefields are not harvested or grazed, and many lie in the sort of hot, wet environment that promotes the rapid growth of foliage. Most of the world's minefields have been in place for years and many have become totally overgrown. Not only does this create a physical access problem, but the inability to spot fragmentation mines and trip wires makes overgrown minefields particularly dangerous. In some areas of Cambodia, more than 80 percent of operational time is spent on the clearance of undergrowth—at the expense of mine clearance. One of the few areas of real progress is the introduction of mechanized vegetation cutters.

The minefields of the real world are often uneven on both a macroscale and a microscale. Rocks of all sizes create problems for the deminer, and even small stones can make probing almost impossible. On the beaches in Kuwait—where it actually was reasonably flat—wet stony sand caused major problems for manual clearance teams. Terrain with steep slopes and large outcrops of rock, common in Afghanistan and the Falklands, simply makes the use of most vehicle-borne systems impractical. Meanwhile, the forces of nature will invariably ensure that mines migrate to the lowest area, given time. That may be a rut or pothole just beyond the reach of a flail hammer or roller, or the bottom of a hill—perhaps outside the known minefield boundary.

Water is normally the most significant of the natural influences, with the capability to carry mines well away from their intended locations. Erosion can undercut mines in one area and bury them deep under silt deposits in another. It can also create obstacles impassable to any mechanical clearance equipment. In the Jordan Valley, the river has cut three-meter gullies through mixed (antipersonnel and antitank) minefields; some mines are left dangling over the cliff edge while others are buried under the collapsed ground. Several miles downstream, the Sea of Galilee must be patrolled daily to check for mines washed up on the beaches. Elsewhere, mine clearance is made almost impossible by tidal action on the beaches of the Falklands, by standing water in the rice fields of Cambodia, and by snow in the minefields of Bosnia. Once again, water does not feature prominently in most equipment test sites and display areas.

Battle Areas

Not surprisingly, mines are often found in and around battlefields, where the ground has been contaminated with the scrap of war. At best, there will be large quantities of metal present: one shell can produce thousands of steel fragments, and each splinter will be large enough to dwarf the signature from a minimum-metal mine. At worst, the area may be cratered, strewn with wire (barbed wire, communication cables, and the guidance wires from missiles), and littered with unexploded ordnance (UXO). Using metal detection, false alarm rates are typically greater than 100 to 1, and can exceed 1,000 to 1; the result is a considerable amount of wasted time and effort.

The failure rate among conventional munitions is generally around 10 percent, and can be far higher. This means that the quantity of UXO often exceeds the number of mines, as was the case among the submunition strikes in the Persian Gulf, where huge numbers failed to function. Most types of UXO are less hazardous than mines, but this is not always so—particularly with submunitions. Once armed, unexploded dual-purpose bomblets such as the American M46 or the Yugoslav KB-1 are far more pressure sensitive than any antipersonnel mine.

Urban Areas

The word *minefield* strongly conveys a rural setting, yet some of the most awkward and dangerous minefields are in urban areas. In most cases the presence of buildings, walls, fences, overhead and underground services, and paths and roads makes the use of mechanical equipment impossible. These obstacles, with their high metallic content, voids, and electric and magnetic fields also rule out the use of most automated detection techniques. Inside buildings, where virtually any type of booby trap may have been used, the clearance procedures are often similar to those needed in a counterterrorist environment. In Afghanistan, the collapse of mud walls and subsequent remining have created layers of mines—sometimes to a depth of several feet.

Another important consideration is infrastructure—or rather the lack of it. Communications and repair facilities are strictly limited in most heavily mined developing countries. There is also an assumption that road and rail networks are universally available for the movement of heavy equipment but, in some areas, routes have become virtually impassable. Even where suitable tracks still exist, few of the bridges can cope with anything more than a light truck. Mobility, survivability, and "sustainability" are therefore key considerations for new demining equipment.

Summary

Most of the factors highlighted in this chapter would create significant problems if they were encountered in isolation but, unfortunately, they are usually superimposed onto one another. The result is a complex, unpredictable tangle of mines, UXO, and trip wires among man-made and natural obstacles. In the Falklands, for instance, there are steep, rocky slopes with soft grassy patches, crossed by streams and littered with wire, shrapnel, and UXO.

At this point, perhaps it is appropriate to return to the principles outlined at the outset of this chapter, remembering that the primary aims are to reduce casualties and to return land to the population. To enable these objectives, the mine clearance component of mine action must be enhanced. Enhancement means safer, faster, cheaper, or a new capability—in other words, finding innovative solutions to overcome existing problems.

On close examination of the real issues, it emerges that much of the technology under development will have, at best, limited application. Sadly, some research has been so misguided that the effort has been totally wasted. The detection of minimum-metal mines, seen by so many as the holy grail of demining, is merely one of many problems faced by the deminer. Gradually, it is dawning on both the scientific and the operational communities that a selection of equipment and techniques are required (the "toolbox" approach), closely tailored to the specific threat in each minefield. Both communities are, at last, beginning to understand the need for communication—even if they still do not fully understand each other's perspective.

There are major practical problems to be overcome in order to enhance the process of demining. The number of permutations arising from the array of mines and variety of environments guarantee that there will be no universal solution. Those who say the process has remained unchanged since World War II are wrong. It has been continually modified through the revision of procedures and the incorporation of new technology; but the overall capability has not been greatly improved. The key to significant enhancement is to ensure that new techniques are well conceived, steered through development with operational input, and applied appropriately.

12

Public–Private Demining Partnerships: A Case Study of Afghanistan

OREN J. SCHLEIN

O NE OF THE UNIQUE FEATURES OF THE LANDMINE BAN MOVEMENT OF THE 1990s was the precedent-setting partnership between civil society and governments to achieve a common goal—the establishment of an international treaty to ban landmines and to protect the rights of all individuals and communities affected by mines. The International Campaign to Ban Landmines spearheaded a unique grassroots coalition of several hundred civic organizations from dozens of countries that, together with the support of governments worldwide, concluded the 1997 Convention on the Prohibition of the Use, Stockpiling, Production and Transfer of Anti-Personnel Mines and on Their Destruction (Mine Ban Treaty) faster than any international treaty in history. The current challenge facing the international community is to continue expanding the public–private partnership paradigm beyond the landmine ban movement to all aspects of the global mine action agenda, including support for the five pillars of mine action: mine clearance, survivor assistance, mine risk education, stockpile destruction, and advocacy for a landmine ban.

The majority of financing for mine action projects to date has come from governments, either funded through the United Nations, bilaterally to mine-affected countries, or directly to mine action operators. Through the 1990s, governments provided unprecedented amounts of money—hundreds of millions of dollars—to support efforts at addressing the landmine problem. Although funding levels remained relatively stable through this period, more recently financial support of mine action programs has been decreasing. The reasons are threefold. First, public perception of the landmine problem has diminished since the signing of the Mine Ban Treaty and the involvement of Princess Diana in the cause. Second, many governments have shifted their funding priorities away from landmines to other humanitarian and development concerns. Finally, an increasing number of mine-affected countries are requesting financial and technical assistance to address their respective landmine problems, reducing the available share of funds to new and existing mine action programs, especially those in the most needy countries.

With the international community now focusing its attention on a field-oriented solution to the landmine problem—particularly now that a majority of states have ratified or acceded to the Mine Ban Treaty[1]—it is critical that adequate funding is secured to support all aspects of mine action. Public–private partnerships are intended to help address this need. Public–private partnerships describes the general affiliation of a broad spectrum of institutional bodies, organizations, and individuals working together to advance a common goal. The landmine community comprises a collection of partners from donor countries and mine-affected countries. They include the United Nations, other multilateral organizations, governments, nongovernmental organizations, and corporations, as well as a large and varied number of civic, religious, and community-based groups. The public–private partnerships that are today supporting mine action have mobilized millions of individuals around the world intent on eradicating landmines and their impact on affected communities. This effort is the embodiment of the relationship between civil society and governments that first emerged during the early growth of the landmine ban movement in the 1990s.

Public–private partnerships add value to aid-related enterprises. In addition to encouraging key stakeholders and other interested parties to work together, they offer unique fund-raising opportunities. Increasingly, major donors, including governments, foundations, and wealthy individuals, will match funds raised through other sources. Another significant strength of public–private partnerships is the opportunity to bring together a diversity of opinions to help formulate programmatic, funding, and communications strategies. For instance, civil society, corporations, and governments may have different perspectives on how to approach aid-related issues. Bringing together these distinctive experiences and points of view can be a complementary exercise that strengthens the overall message and purpose of an aid project.

In spite of these benefits, under certain circumstances competing interests among stakeholders may disturb attempts to forge effective public–private partnerships. Differing organizational histories and approaches to programming and preexisting tensions among such groups may be too difficult to overcome. Although public–private partnerships seek to bridge such differences through collaboration and partnership, emotional and institutional biases may be a significant impediment to cooperation among advocates of humanitarian and development causes. The trend in the aid community in recent years toward public–private partnerships, however, confirms the accepted view that in most cases the strengths of these partnerships outweigh any real or perceived weaknesses.

Adopt-A-Minefield: A Case Study

In 1999, the United Nations Association of the USA (UNA-USA), a New York-based nongovernmental organization, established a new broad-based funding model, after years of near-exclusive government financial support of the landmine issue. What emerged was Adopt-A-Minefield, a global campaign that engages individuals, businesses, and community groups in raising funds for mine clearance operations and survivor assistance initiatives and in raising awareness of the landmine problem. The intent of the campaign is to bring the landmine issue to the public and to create fund-raising and public awareness partnerships across all levels of society. Adopt-A-Minefield was established as a unique experiment to mobilize concerned individuals to donate funds toward a practical solution of the landmine problem in mine-affected countries—the campaign's slogan is "Clear a path to a safer world."

The success of Adopt-A-Minefield has depended on its ability to personalize the landmine issue. It has been able to capture the essence of the tragedy of landmines and to convey this reality to potential donors. The campaign emphasizes the importance of creating links between donor communities and the mine-affected communities that benefit directly from their efforts.

The public side of public–private partnerships is the government, whose reasons for funding landmine projects are typically based on public policy decisions and a desire to support humanitarian and development initiatives. The private sector's commitment to the landmine issue is much more personal and emotive. To respond to the dual needs of the public and the private sectors, Adopt-A-Minefield developed a unique reporting network, which addresses the respective needs and desires of both groups of supporters. The campaign extended the reporting requirements typically associated with government contributions, including financial and narrative summaries, to include a much more detailed framework of reports designed to create a sense of ownership over the projects that individual donors support. This reporting system includes regular field updates, personalized end-of-project clearance certificates, and articles and photo journals of adopted minefields and beneficiary communities. While the donor feedback network that Adopt-A-Minefield has established is more time intensive to maintain than traditional reporting systems, the campaign's success has been based on its ability to engage and retain its donor base using a fundamentally different approach to fund-raising.

Building Partnerships

The model that Adopt-A-Minefield established has produced a shift in perceptions in a decade-long approach to funding and implementing mine clearance projects. For instance, the United Nations, which supports the coordination of much of the world's mine-related work through national mine action centers, entered into its first ever agreement with UNA-USA, a private organization, to finance the UN's demining operations. It was a departure for the United Nations, which has traditionally received most of its funding from governments. It also provided a unique and precedent-setting vehicle for the private sector to directly fund UN demining operations.[2] Within the UN system, the chief fiduciary and legal responsibility for Adopt-A-Minefield lies with the United Nations Development Programme (UNDP), which entered into the agreement with UNA-USA. UNDP in turn contracted the implementation of Adopt-A-Minefield to the United Nations Office for Project Services, which specializes in executing field projects. The establishment of this tripartite relationship has created a synergy that has not previously existed in the UN's approach to mine action.

The lessons learned from its first year of operation helped the Adopt-A-Minefield team and its UN partners refine the implementation of their five-country programs—Afghanistan, Bosnia and Herzegovina, Cambodia, Croatia, and Mozambique. For instance, the process of nominating minefields for adoption and providing donors with personalized updates required the national mine action centers in these countries to change some of the ways in which they conduct business. As an example, the mine action centers now carve up large, contiguous areas of land into smaller, more manageable units. A 300,000 m^2 piece of land would likely be divided into ten units of 30,000 m^2 each. Each of these units is included in the Adopt-A-Minefield portfolio. Guidelines prescribe the roles and functions of each party and they provide assistance in how to streamline the site nomination and reporting process and how to effectively manage donor funds. The model varies from country to country to take into account differing cultural and business approaches to mine action.

The early challenge for Adopt-A-Minefield was to persuade its mine action partners that their investment in this model would yield sufficient benefits among mine-affected communities. Five years after the launch of Adopt-A-Minefield, the campaign has raised approximately $10 million for mine action programs. In 2000, Adopt-A-Minefield was among the top ten donors for mine clearance in Afghanistan and Cambodia, representing a significant contribution toward these countries' mine action requirements. The established models have been so successful that in 2001 Adopt-A-Minefield began supporting clearance operations in Vietnam, and in 2002, the campaign established a survivor assistance initiative based on the original clearance model.[3]

Investing in the New Model

Adopt-A-Minefield has caused many individuals and organizations to look at mine action in a different way. Chief among these are two of the campaign's earliest supporters, the U.S. Department of State and the Better World Fund, the former representing the public sector and the latter the private sector. It is indicative of the unique role that Adopt-A-Minefield has played in shaping the public–private partnership paradigm that its two largest investors represent opposite ends of the public–private spectrum.

The Department of State's Office of Humanitarian Demining Programs has been among the primary sources of U.S. government funding for mine action projects over the past decade, disbursing over $700 million to more than forty mine-affected countries and providing substantial in-kind contributions since 1993. The Department of State has also invested significant funds in promoting private initiatives like Adopt-A-Minefield. In 1997, then-President Bill Clinton established the Office of Global Humanitarian Demining,[4] whose mandate has been to promote public–private partnerships in mine action. This office has harnessed the energies of the private sector and worked closely with governments and the international community to bring the landmine message to new audiences. Together, the Office of Humanitarian Demining Programs and the Office of Global Humanitarian Demining[5] recognized the potential of Adopt-A-Minefield to create a new standard for fund-raising and to involve the private sector in what had hitherto been a near-exclusive government undertaking. Their foresight and investment of time and money helped steer Adopt-A-Minefield to its current success.

The Better World Fund approached Adopt-A-Minefield from a different perspective. Philanthropist and entrepreneur, Ted Turner, established this organization in 1997 to support the United Nations and its many initiatives. He provided Adopt-A-Minefield with a challenge grant of twenty-five cents on the dollar, which has enabled the campaign to forward 100 percent of all mine clearance and survivor assistance funds raised to its implementing partners. The 25 percent match pays for internal program support costs. The marketing value of this arrangement has been significant and it has also helped Adopt-A-Minefield finance the establishment of three international Partner Campaigns in Canada, Sweden, and the United Kingdom. Each of these national programs raises funds for Adopt-A-Minefield from its own distinct donor base, effectively increasing the broad cross-section of support for the international campaign.

Managing the Donor Relationship

Private donors, whether individuals, businesses, or community groups, appreciate the "human face" of the projects they support. Financial accountability is as important to them as it is to government donors, but they also require detailed, personalized information about their adopted projects. Understanding this distinction is the first step in establishing a successful model for engaging civil society in funding aid programs like Adopt-A-Minefield. Recognizing the value of carefully monitoring funds received and tracing each dollar to a specific mine action project enhances a program's funding prospects. All donors have a vested interest in how their funds are used and each wants to know that their funds have been put to good use. In the case of Adopt-A-Minefield, donors can adopt entire minefields for $30,000 each or they can contribute smaller donations—as little as $10—that are pooled with other funds. From the perspective of the $10 contributor, their donation merits the same attention and care as a wealthier donor and Adopt-A-Minefield's donor feedback network has been built around this premise.

Of the $10 million raised to date, approximately 40 percent has been raised through grassroots campaigns and small individual gifts, 30 percent has been provided by high net worth individuals and family foundations, 25 percent by government, and 5 percent by business. In each instance, donors select minefields from a list provided to Adopt-A-Minefield by the national mine action centers through the United Nations. The types of sites vary considerably: agricultural land, grazing land, village centers, schools, pagodas, health centers, roads, irrigation canals, residential areas, buildings, power lines, and riverbanks. Knowing what type of land is being cleared and who the beneficiaries of this cleared land will be encourages donors to support Adopt-A-Minefield.

In addition to providing all its donors with site-specific information and updates, Adopt-A-Minefield also assists grassroots groups in organizing local fund-raising campaigns. This includes preparing targeted information packets, developing media strategies, and organizing speakers' tours of landmine experts from the public and private sectors to communities across the United States and overseas. Adopt-A-Minefield utilizes the Internet as a key source of information for its donors. Its Web site (www.landmines.org) was established in late 1999 as a clearinghouse for landmine-related information, a source of news about Adopt-A-Minefield and updates about adopted minefields. The importance of having a state-of-the-art Web site that educates the public and empowers donors in this technological age cannot be underestimated. It forms an integral component of any proactive cause-related marketing campaign.

The commitment that groups have displayed toward the landmine issue, and to Adopt-A-Minefield in particular, has been remarkable. Through bake sales and cocktail parties to lavish banquets and benefit concerts, well-organized groups have demonstrated that they can raise tens of thousands of dollars, and in some instances hundreds of thousands, in a relatively short period of time. What is more remarkable about these accomplishments, however, is that the average individual contribution to a typical $30,000 fund-raising campaign is between $20 and $50. The tens of thousands of individual donations to Adopt-A-Minefield represent a formidable base of donors to this program, as well as to the broader landmine community.

It is often said that the likeliest donor is a satisfied donor. Adopt-A-Minefield has many examples of this dictum, from schoolchildren to high-end corporate donors and philanthropists, and from community groups to government supporters who have returned to the campaign for multiple adoptions. One early high-end donor to Adopt-A-Minefield visited his site in Croatia and was so pleased with the way it had been cleared that he returned for a second, third, and fourth minefield adoption, each in a different country. It was the personal touch and frequent updates from the field about the status of his minefields that most endeared him to the campaign. Similarly, several grassroots coalitions have adopted two or more minefields each. One of these groups, the Adopt-A-Minefield Colorado Initiative, led a delegation of community representatives to visit one of their sites in Mozambique. They were able to capture the human and economic impact of landmines on their adopted community and share these stories with their fellow donors. In response, this statewide coalition of supporters continued to raise funds for Adopt-A-Minefield long after its first adoption was complete.

Adopt-A-Minefield has relied on its special donor appeal to carve out a unique niche for itself in the landmine community. Its broad-based fund-raising strategy relies on an extremely diverse group of traditional and nontraditional supporters. Furthermore, the Adopt-A-Minefield model complements the efforts of other landmine organizations, including advocacy groups like the International Campaign to Ban Landmines. In particular, because it is not an implementing agency, all funds raised by Adopt-A-Minefield are provided to other landmine organizations.

Although there are varying degrees of cooperation and competitiveness among aid organizations seeking funding from limited sources, Adopt-A-Minefield's philosophy is to work collaboratively with as many organizations as possible, including organizing joint fund-raisers. These activities further enhance the public–private partnerships that Adopt-A-Minefield considers to be the cornerstone of its success. Ultimately, mine-affected countries like Afghanistan benefit from these collaborative efforts.

Afghanistan: A Field Perspective

In early July 2001, I had the unique opportunity of visiting Afghanistan to undertake an assessment of the Adopt-A-Minefield program in the country. My visit was two months prior to the terrorist attacks of September 11, 2001, in the United States and the subsequent U.S.-led assault against the Al Qaeda terrorist network and the Taliban regime in Afghanistan. Significant changes have occurred in the country since this seminal event: the Taliban regime has been ousted, more than 2.3 million refugees and nearly 800,000 internally displaced persons have returned to their homes,[6] and the drought that has afflicted the country in recent years has subsided in many places. In spite of these positive changes, the intrinsic challenges that Afghanistan has faced in recent years remain and new challenges are appearing as the country emerges from decades of conflict and instability. Accordingly, the following observations about Afghanistan and the response of the Afghan government and the international landmine community to the landmine problem still apply.

The UN's Mine Action Programme for Afghanistan (MAPA) organized my visit to Afghanistan, including the cities of Kabul, Jalalabad, Herat, and Kandahar. This is the organization that nominates minefields for the Adopt-A-Minefield portfolio and that is responsible for overseeing the clearance of all Adopt-A-Minefield sites in Afghanistan. The visit offered me more than an opportunity to witness the landmine problem firsthand. It also presented me with a unique view of Afghanistan, its people and culture, and its political and security challenges.

I visited more than a dozen minefields throughout the country, met with several landmine survivors, became acquainted with the managers of the national mine action center and the regional mine action centers, and observed several demining organizations at work. It was an inspiring visit, which reaffirmed my opinion that the money that Adopt-A-

Minefield had raised for mine clearance operations in Afghanistan was being properly managed and was directly benefiting the communities it was intended to help.[7]

Afghanistan is a country that has suffered a systemic structural collapse over two decades of conflict. Essential services that we take for granted in our own societies, including health care, education, and basic infrastructure, are nonexistent in many parts of the country. Although large numbers of refugees and internally displaced persons have returned to their homes since the fall of the Taliban regime, millions more have not. In addition, much of Afghanistan continues to suffer from an ongoing drought. By early 2002, the United Nations and other international aid agencies were providing food and basic humanitarian services to 7.5 million Afghans, nearly one-third of the population.[8] The humanitarian demining effort in the country is an essential part of the services that the international community is providing.

UN Mine Action in Afghanistan

Millions of landmines and unexploded ordnance litter the Afghan landscape, severely impacting the lives of millions of Afghans. These remnants of war affect approximately 830 km^2 of land, including agricultural, grazing, and irrigation land; residential areas; roads; and even seemingly desolate mountainous areas. Approximately 400 km^2 is high-priority mined land and 50 km^2 is high-priority former battlefields, requiring urgent clearance so refugees and internally displaced persons can return safely to their homes and farms. Once cleared, local populations will be able to reconstruct their homes, return their agricultural and commercial land to productive use, and safely utilize roads and irrigation systems upon which their livelihoods depend.

The current ten-year national mine action strategy envisages all high-priority areas being cleared in five years, with remaining areas cleared in a further five-year period. These estimates assume that the Mine Action Programme for Afghanistan can sustain its current capacities and funding levels. MAPA also estimates that there are approximately 150 landmine casualties every month—about 50 percent less than a decade ago, yet still one of the highest rates in the world. The recent drop in mine casualties is directly related to the comprehensive approach that MAPA has taken in tackling the country's landmine problem, including the clearance and marking of mined areas and mine risk education programs.

The United Nations assumed responsibility for mine action in Afghanistan in 1989, after the withdrawal of Soviet forces, which had invaded Afghanistan a decade earlier. The UN's current objectives are to promote an integrated approach to the landmine issue, including developing a national capacity to address the landmine problem and eliminating the long-term threat of mines to the country. MAPA supports four specific activities: (1) minefield survey, mapping, marking, and clearance; (2) mine risk education (MRE); (3) training of national staff; and (4) advocacy to stigmatize the use of landmines and support a total ban on mines.

When the United Nations began its humanitarian activities in Afghanistan, it established five regional centers to facilitate the coordination and implementation of its work: the central, northern, southern, eastern, and western regions. Five regional mine action centers are headquartered in each of Afghanistan's five largest cities: Kabul, Mazar-i-Sharif, Kandahar, Jalalabad, and Herat. These mine action centers are responsible for overseeing the survey and clearance of mined areas in their regions. They work closely with the national mine action center in Kabul and with its implementing partners—those nongovernmental organizations that specialize in mine clearance, survey work, training, quality assurance, mine risk education, and survivor assistance.[9]

The MAPA staff and mine action workers throughout Afghanistan are a dedicated group of individuals whose efforts are respected by all Afghans, whether or not impacted by the landmine problem. In fact, in recent years the demining industry has not only helped make communities throughout Afghanistan safer, it has also been one of the largest employers in the country, indirectly supporting tens of thousands of Afghans.

It is because of the dedication and innovative approaches that the Afghan nongovernmental organizations, in particular, have brought to mine action in Afghanistan that the program has been such a success. As the oldest demining program in the world, Afghanistan's demining agenda is well respected among the international community. Most national mine action programs around the world are modeled to some degree on the Afghan example and owe their successes to the achievements of the Afghan mine action community. Many of the national and international managers of the Afghan program have lent their expertise to developing other national mine action programs and have become leaders in the international campaign to ban landmines.

The demining agenda has also played a critical role in advancing the general objectives of peace building and reconstruction in Afghanistan. By removing mines and unexploded ordnance from the ground and marking suspect areas, the demining community has helped foster a greater sense of personal and physical security and create a safer environment in which the government and the international aid community can undertake the important work of rehabilitating local economies. Although the security environment has been unsteady since September 11, 2001, the Mine Action Programme for Afghanistan has been able to continue its operations relatively unimpeded. Key mine action stakeholders are confident that the national mine action program will continue to achieve its objectives of rendering priority areas mine-safe over the next decade.

Background to Adopt-A-Minefield in Afghanistan

Afghanistan has been among the most popular and well-managed Adopt-A-Minefield programs at the country level. This is because of MAPA's reputation as one of the best coordinated and implemented mine clearance programs in the world. MAPA grasped the essential concepts of Adopt-A-Minefield from the beginning, providing site nominations and personalized reports in a timely and efficient manner.

Adopt-A-Minefield joined the UN's efforts to clear mines in Afghanistan in 1998. Since then, the campaign has funded the clearance of more than fifty minefields, which have been returned to their local communities. In the aftermath of the conflict in Afghanistan in late 2001, Adopt-A-Minefield established a new Adopt-A-Team model in the country, in which donor funds are linked to the activities of specific mine clearance teams rather than minefields. This model was more conducive to the security environment in Afghanistan at the time, enabling teams of deminers to move their operations to higher-priority areas as the need arose. The Adopt-A-Team concept continues to be implemented in Afghanistan. In the two years since the model was established, eight Afghan demining teams have collectively cleared over forty minefields.

The sites included in the Adopt-A-Minefield portfolio represent a cross-section of the projects that MAPA undertakes, both topographically and in terms of the types of clearance tools used. The areas cleared include dry, flat terrain, rugged and mountainous land, residential areas, and rocky hills overlooking magnificent vistas of the Afghan countryside. The diversity of the Afghan landscape is remarkable and the dangers inherent in clearing these areas are considerable. MAPA uses four main demining resources: manual clearance teams, mechanical clearance teams, mine detection dogs, and explosive ordnance disposal teams. The Afghan program's extensive use of dogs in its demining operations is noteworthy. Afghanistan has a majority of the world's mine detection dogs and most Adopt-A-Minefield sites are cleared with these dogs. MAPA incorporates a "toolbox" approach in its work, often combining two or more demining techniques to improve the efficiency of its clearance operations. Effective implementation of this approach also results in significant cost savings. In most of our site visits, I observed combinations of dog teams, manual clearance teams, and mechanical clearance teams, working side by side. Clearance operations in Afghanistan are a textbook example of how this integrated, toolbox approach to mine clearance works.

Data Reliability

The international landmine community has debated for many years the reliability of data in defining the scope of the landmine problem and identifying pragmatic responses to the challenges faced by mine-affected countries like Afghanistan. In the early years of mine action, there was a tendency to define the problem by the number of mines in the ground. This approach had two failings: First, estimating the number of mines is an imprecise science and the numbers quoted by various stakeholders varied widely.[10] Second, the number of mines does not reflect the actual impact of the mines on affected communities. The mere suspicion of an area being mined may keep an entire community from using otherwise arable land, whether there are in fact many or few mines present, if any at all. The current accepted methodology for defining the landmine problem is to assess the impact of mines rather than to quantify the number of mines. High-priority areas, such as those where the lives of people and livestock are immediately threatened by the presence of mines and where land has been rendered economically unproductive, are typically cleared first. More remote mine-affected regions, which do not necessarily impact large numbers of people and which are not economically significant, receive less priority in national mine action strategies and work plans.

Similarly, assessing the number of mine victims is a complex, inexact process. The accepted annual number of mine victims worldwide ranges from 15,000 to 20,000,[11] although until recently it has been as high as 26,000. In Afghanistan, estimates of mine victims have ranged from 150 to 300 a month. Part of the problem in determining the correct number relates to the remoteness and inaccessibility of many mine-affected communities. In addition, health officials face challenges in maintaining accurate records of landmine survivors who have received initial lifesaving treatment. This is because the stigma often associated with being disabled and the economic misfortune that befalls most landmine survivors can make it difficult for these people to obtain follow-up treatment.

The costs of clearance vary depending on the type of clearance activity, the terrain, and the country in which the operations take place.[12] The demining community has a relatively well-established means of determining costs based on these factors. Typically, manual clearance is the least expensive demining activity—as little as US$1 per square meter—mechanical clearance is the most expensive, and dog detection teams are in the midrange. An important point to note, however, is that assessing clearance costs is a more straightforward and reliable process than determining the number of landmines or mine victims in an affected area.

Data reliability issues have not hindered Adopt-A-Minefield's ability to raise funds for its mine clearance and survivor assistance programs. This is because the campaign's outreach activities emphasize the impact that mines have on adopted communities and landmine survivors. Adopt-A-Minefield gauges the benefits of individual contributions by measurable improvements in the quality of life and economic productivity of affected communities over the long term.

The Minefields

Of the many minefields that I visited in Afghanistan, a few stood out for the level of human misfortune that had befallen the affected communities. Our first site visit was to the village of Merza Khail in Logar Province, about an hour's drive from Kabul on a barren plain between the Hindu Kush Mountains. The area was being cleared by the Mine Detection and Dog Centre (MDC), recognized as one of the most advanced mine detection dog organizations in the world.

Merza Khail lies adjacent to a major north–south thoroughfare. Fifteen villages are situated to the east of this road. Soviet forces had used the road to travel between a nearby military base, which housed a rocket depot, and the Pakistan border. The Mujahedeen used the hills and mountains around Merza Khail as a base from which to launch attacks against the Soviets. They also used a landing strip about a mile from the village. The road was heavily mined by the Mujahedeen to deter the Soviets, affecting all the villages in the area. MDC had a five-week-long clearance plan, in which they expected to clear 117,523 m^2 of land—5 kilometers long and 25–30 meters wide. Mine Dog Group 7, or MDG7 as it is known, has a group leader who supervises two sections each of six deminers, two dogs with handlers, and one section leader. In the three weeks since starting their clearance operations, MDG7 had found 4 Italian-made TC6 antitank mines, 5 unexploded ordnance, and 2,650 metal fragments.

The village of Merza Khail comprises several compounds within a larger external wall. Before the Soviet occupation, eighty families of five or six people each lived in the village. At the time of my visit only twenty families remained, with most having left the area and settled as refugees in Pakistan. The conflict with the Soviet Union and, after its ouster, the Taliban rule in the 1990s had imposed significant changes on the community. Afghan society is based around the family and village structure, so changes to the family unit meant that the traditional system of family assistance and village life in Merza Khail had been radically altered.

Several children had been maimed and killed by mines in recent years and, as a result, they were confined to specific areas in and around their village. Niamatullah, the chief village elder, explained that his village had a home-based school for boys, not girls, which incorporates mine risk education into its curriculum. Deminers working in the area also provided mine risk education training sessions two times a week to the village children and men. This effort to increase local awareness of the landmine problem was part of a countrywide effort in Afghanistan to integrate MRE into the activities of demining organizations. Because of the Taliban prohibition on women receiving any form of education, the mine action community in Afghanistan had also established female MRE teams based in the cities that traveled to the villages to instruct women on the dangers of mines. The reality is that under the Taliban, women were rarely permitted to venture out of their homes or villages, so the immediate threat of mine injuries was significantly less to them than it was to men and children.

A Glimpse into the Soviet Occupation: The Village of Surkhab

Following our visit to Merza Khail, we drove to the village of Surkhab, along a shelled road with large, deep artillery craters. The sites that had been scheduled for clearance lie along both sides of the road. Before the drought, the entire region was fertile agricultural and grazing land. During my visit it was a massive, dry lake bed. Most of the area was littered with landmines, particularly antitank mines laid by the Mujahedeen to protect their positions against advancing Soviet troops. The mines prevented any cultivation of those few areas of agricultural land that had not been too severely affected by the drought. There had also been several accidents along the road, including children injured while playing with mines and unexploded ordnance. The net effect of the drought and landmine problem on the village of Surkhab was that three-quarters of the ninety families in the village had left. Most of the refugees wanted to return to their village, but were unable to do so until their land had been cleared of mines.

I met several men and older children in an orchard outside the perimeter of the village. The villagers had led relatively peaceful lives until 1980, when the Soviets attacked and occupied Surkhab for six days and nights. They used the main road along the villages of Surkhab and Merza Khail as a strategic garrison, as it led to the Pakistan border to the south and the military base to the north and east, toward Kabul. Although all the villages in the valley were attacked, Surkhab suffered particularly badly. The Soviets conducted repeated aerial bombings of the village because it was home to several Mujahedeen fighters. At one point, the Soviets raided the village for five continuous hours, shooting a dozen men, women, and children, and taking all the animals.

Following this incident, most of the villagers abandoned their homes, heading for the hills above or fleeing the valley for Pakistan. Tragically, four villagers, all Mujahedeen, remained behind. They were captured by Soviet forces and locked in the village mosque, a simple room, which was set ablaze. Three died and one was severely injured. Their fellow villagers witnessed the incident through binoculars. The three victims are martyrs to the Afghan jihad, or holy war, against the Soviet Union. The mosque in which they died is now a mausoleum to Tela Mohamed, Berget, and Lal Gul. The one survivor, Hazart Gul, now lives as a refugee in Iran.

Za Zai, the village elder who told me this story, said that village life was forever changed by this incident. By the late 1990s, most of the villagers who lived in refugee camps during the Soviet occupation of Afghanistan had established lives in Afghan communities in Pakistan. Surkhab received no food or other assistance from aid agencies. The remaining villagers worked primarily as laborers in Pakistan and Iran to support their families. The average laborer in Afghanistan earned US$0.80 a day; in Pakistan, they earned over US$1 a day. This is still less than the US$4 a day required to feed a family of eight to ten people, but with multiple family members working, most villagers just managed to survive.[13]

It was clear that the mines had to be removed from Surkhab before the villagers could live off their land. The villagers all hoped that the next year would be better—that the drought would end, the mines would be removed, and their families and neighbors could return home to a safe living environment. The regional mine action center in Kabul had surveyed the area and identified 160,000 m^2 of land that had to be cleared to accommodate the needs of the entire village. In the process of surveying the land, the deminers found one antitank mine by the side of the road. As a result, the villagers were more vigilant than ever, they welcomed mine risk education teams to their village and they carefully monitored the movements of their children. When asked what they thought their future prospects were, the villagers all said "It is up to Allah."

The Dara-i-Pashaye Valley

One of the enduring challenges that Adopt-A-Minefield faces is conveying an accurate depiction of the landmine problem to its donors. There are so many physical characteristics of minefields, differing types of terrain, and varying climatic conditions in which to undertake clearance operations. The village of Pashaye, in the Dara-i-Pashaye Valley, a two-hour drive from Kabul, typifies the ever-present dangers that villagers and deminers alike face.

The village is home to about one thousand families, a large village by Afghan standards. Steep, rocky hills that have traditionally been used as grazing land overlook the valley. During the Soviet occupation, the army targeted the village relentlessly, killing more than one hundred villagers. To repel Mujahedeen attacks, the Soviets mined huge sections of the hills, including the village cemetery. They eventually mined much of the agricultural land as well.

The Dara-i-Pashaye Valley was one of the most fertile areas I visited during my Afghan travels. It was green, agriculturally productive, and not affected by the drought that had devastated so much of Afghanistan. Afghan Technical Consultants (ATC), the country's largest demining organization, had cleared much of the agricultural land, which had been returned to the villagers. They were now hard at work clearing the rocky hills above the village.

On the day of my visit, ATC found three antipersonnel landmines. As I sat in my vantage point halfway up the hill, I observed more than twenty deminers sweeping the ground with their metal detectors, occasionally crouching down to clear the earth around a suspected mined area. The deminers faced two big problems: the hills were steep and dangerous, and the soil itself was hard and contained stones of high metallic content. The metallic substance slowed down the clearance process considerably because it triggered false alarms, each one requiring the deminers to manually check the ground for mines. It was the most perilous minefield I had ever observed being cleared. At the end of our visit, the deminers stopped their work and cautiously walked down the hill. The three mines were then detonated in quick succession.

There is a sad footnote to this story. Several days after my visit, I received news that one of the ATC deminers had slipped while unearthing a mine in the same hills above Pashaye. The deminer lost part of his leg. Until this accident, MAPA had not suffered any demining casualties in 2001, a significant drop from the eleven accidents in 2000.

The Residential Minefields of Herat and Kandahar

While in Herat, I visited the village of Deza, one of several villages on the outskirts of the city that had been heavily mined during the Soviet occupation. Deza is located next to an old Soviet munitions depot, which the Mujahedeen had blown up during the war. The ensuing fire burned for three days and nights. In all, fourteen people were injured and eight killed. The explosions also destroyed many homes. Years after this incident, the villagers of Deza and four nearby villages continued to suffer from the presence of mines. There had been several mine accidents and much of the land was unusable.

During recent clearance operations, deminers had found more than 300 unexploded ordnance and 48 antipersonnel landmines in the area immediately adjacent to the munitions depot. As I walked through the village, debris including old burned-out tanks was strewn everywhere. Red stones and red flags marked those areas where mines had been found, some as close as five or ten meters from homes. Several children greeted me during my visit and although they played in areas that had been cleared by the deminers, it was evident that as long as some of this land remained mined, there was an accident waiting to happen.

The final stop on my Afghan journey was Kandahar, home of the Taliban. This regional capital has a long and turbulent history. Years of fighting have left it with the dubious distinction of being the most heavily mined city in Afghanistan, as I discovered during my two-day visit. All residential neighborhoods and agricultural fields that I visited bore the scars of earlier conflicts. The landmine problem was not limited to Kandahar, however. The rural areas of the southern region of Afghanistan were equally affected.

An hour's drive from Kandahar is the village of Haji Basher, a former Soviet military base along the main transit route to Pakistan. Haji Basher was so strategically important to the Soviets that they laid a large mine belt around the entire village. Although most of the villagers no longer live in Haji Basher, Kuchi (nomad) tribes regularly travel through the area. Because of the large numbers of mines, the accident rate was very high. There had been fifteen accidents in this area, including three deminers, five Kuchis and villagers, and several animals. While walking through the "safe lanes" carved out of the mine belt, I found the remains of a camel that had been killed by a mine a year earlier. Because of the high-density nature of the minefield in and around Haji Basher, mine detection dogs did not work well in this terrain and the local demining organizations did not have suitable machines to clear the land. The entire area was being cleared manually. At the time of my visit, eight different tasks had been surveyed and it was expected to take several more months to complete the project.

One of the final Adopt-A-Minefield sites I visited was the village of Surpoza, along the main thoroughfare through Kandahar. Surpoza is also part of Kandahar's mine belt and was heavily contaminated with landmines during the Soviet occupation. Today, Surpoza has been cleared of mines and three residential compounds have been built on the former mined land. The residents have also cultivated large agricultural fields next to their homes. During my visit I met several friendly, playful children who lived in one of the new compounds. They were the direct beneficiaries of the cleared land. Meeting them highlighted the importance of telling the story of all landmine survivors, whether injured or displaced, or otherwise affected by mines. Through these accounts, donors who may not otherwise be able to visit their adopted minefields can obtain some sense of the impact that their support has had on others.

Strengthening Public–Private Partnerships

One of my lasting impressions of Afghanistan is that although the country is beleaguered and the situation often grim, the Afghan people display great fortitude in the face of all their difficulties. Theirs is a very proud can-do attitude and they are unfailingly grateful for any help they receive. I met a number of committed UN employees and brave and resolute deminers during my visit. Afghans are very fond of proverbs and seem to have one for every situation. One such commonly repeated proverb states: "A person who saves one life saves a society." This proverb sums up the efforts of everyone in the international landmine community. There exists today a broader representation of parties involved in mine action than a decade ago—an extensive network of individuals, civic organizations, businesses, and governments along the public–private spectrum. As the role of the private sector continues to expand, so do the opportunities to address the landmine problem in a more comprehensive and sustainable manner.

Financial accountability and tangible results in the field have always been important benchmarks for governments that fund aid projects. The participation of civil society as major funders of such initiatives has added an entirely new level of personalized accountability. Individual donors not only want to know where their money goes and that it has been wisely spent, but they also want to know who the beneficiaries are of the aid projects they support. This new approach to donor accountability improves transparency, enhances certain aspects of the implementation of such projects, and ultimately expands funding opportunities.

At a time when government funding has been reduced and dispersed over a wider range of issues than in the past, public–private partnerships offer an important source of new funding. They also encourage innovative ways of looking at old problems. Private individuals, businesses, and civil society—working through programs like Adopt-A-Minefield—stand to benefit significantly more than in the past because of their more inclusive involvement in the projects they support. Governments, international organizations, and other implementing partners benefit from a new source of experience, funding, and insight. Most important, individual beneficiaries of privately funded aid projects are enriched by a whole new universe of partners who are concerned about their individual well-being.

Civil society and governments reached a historic achievement with the signing of the Mine Ban Treaty in 1997. Since then, the landmine community has achieved further successes through the ever-expanding partnerships forged between the public and the private sectors. Perceptions of the landmine issue have changed and the business models used to address the problem in mine-affected countries have evolved. As the international community tackles the landmine problem in an increasingly coordinated and integrated manner, public–private partnerships have assumed greater importance in funding mine action projects and streamlining the business of landmines. At the end of the day, everyone stands to benefit from this enhanced, personalized approach to mine action.

Notes

1. As of October 23, 2003, 141 countries have ratified or acceded to the Mine Ban Treaty and a further 9 countries had signed but not yet ratified the treaty. See the International Campaign to Ban Landmines Web site: http://www.icbl.org/.

2. Adopt-A-Minefield clearance funds are channeled through the United Nations to national and international demining nongovernmental organizations and companies.

3. Adopt-A-Minefield has provided grants to survivor assistance organizations in six countries: Afghanistan, Angola, Bosnia and Herzegovina, Cambodia, Laos, and Vietnam.

4. In 2001, this office was renamed the Office of Mine Action Initiatives and Partnerships.

5. In September 2003, the Offices of Humanitarian Demining Programs and Mine Action Initiatives and Partnerships merged to form the new Office of Weapons Removal and Abatement.

6. United Nations High Commissioner for Refugees, "Afghanistan Humanitarian Update No. 68," August 15, 2003, available at http://www.unhcr.ch/cgi-bin/texis/vtx/afghan.

7. By September 2003, Adopt-A-Minefield had raised more than US$2 million for mine clearance operations and survivor assistance programs in Afghanistan.

8. In the two-year period from March 2003 to March 2005, the World Food Programme plans to feed 9.3 million Afghans.

9. In 2002, the Afghan government established the Consultative Group on Mine Action, within the National Development Budget Framework, which is responsible for priority setting and planning. Participants in the Consultative Group include national and local mine action authorities, nongovernmental organizations, relevant government ministries, UN agencies, and donor representatives.

10. The estimated number of mines worldwide, for instance, has varied from a few tens of millions of mines to over 100 million mines.

11. International Campaign to Ban Landmines, *Landmine Monitor Report 2003: Toward a Mine-Free World*, August 2003, available at http://www.icbl.org/lm/2003/.

12. Market conditions and labor costs in different countries will affect clearance costs.

13. Although unconfirmed, it is likely that several of the villagers from Surkhab have returned home since the end of the conflict in Afghanistan in early 2002, and that others have remained in Pakistan and Iran.

13

Landmines Prolong Conflicts and Impede Socioeconomic Development

NAY HTUN

L ANDMINES ARE USED AS A WEAPON TO MAIM COMBATANTS. UNFORTUNATELY, they also disable and incapacitate a large number of noncombatants and continue to do so after the cessation of fighting. Landmines are said to "fight on" long after the hostilities they parallel have ceased to take place. Almost all people injured by landmines suffer lifelong disabilities. Not only are individuals affected, but so too are their families, communities, and countries. Very often, the person maimed is the head of the household and the main wage earner for the family. When this person is disabled, the tragic consequences affect the whole family as well.

Many, if not all, aspects of a family and community existence are overshadowed by the tragedy. When a large percentage of people are disabled, the ability of a country to be able to recover from the war is very much handicapped. The country is already devastated by the hostilities, with its socioeconomic system wrecked. The resettlement of refugees and displaced families is hindered: delivery of humanitarian and development assistance is severely curtailed; agriculture and livestock production is greatly affected; economic recovery is difficult and resuming a normal existence is almost impossible.

The lack of livelihoods and employment opportunities exacerbates the sense of exclusion by those disabled by landmines. Poverty, fueled

169

by resentment, actual and perceived stigmatization, and the feeling of hopelessness, prolongs social tensions.

While the peace process has stopped physical conflicts, due to the depravation, both social and economic, hostilities continue to simmer and can readily boil over again. Hence, in reality, conflict viewed in the broader societal context continues on other fronts. Sustained and lasting peace is not possible without repair to the social fabric, reinvigorating the enabling economic base, and rehabilitating the ecological system such as the land, forests, rivers, and lakes. These are not only critical life-support systems but are also the major source of and means for sustenance, livelihoods, and food for the people.

The healing process for the human being and the human environment, as well as the ceasing of hatred and animosity cannot begin in earnest when there are large numbers of landmines still remaining in a country. The impacts of landmines extend far beyond and after its immediate purpose.

The Need for Integrated Mine Clearance Operations

The survey, mapping, clearance of mined areas, and victim assistance programs should be carried out as expeditiously as possible and as soon as possible. Often, and sadly, these are not feasible for many reasons, including continued sporadic fighting, political uncertainties, and, woefully, lack of funding. When "peace" is deemed to have taken place, the media coverage decreases and international concerns and interests move to other areas of conflict. The political will, internally and internationally, wanes.

Humanitarian aid, necessary and most laudable, is normally targeted to providing immediate lifesaving necessities, such as food, medicine, blankets, and shelter. Very little funds are budgeted and available for getting the social and ecological capitals rehabilitated and the economic base, particularly at the village level, restarted. The gap in the continuum, which has been long debated in the United Nations, of humanitarian assistance, reconstruction, rehabilitation, and development continues to exist.

The compartmentalized mandates, sectored functions, and specialized operations by development assistance organizations coupled with weak national institutions at the central and especially at the provisional levels pose a challenge for an integrated approach. Furthermore, the budgets of the donors are also segmented and not readily amenable to fund and support integrated humanitarian and development operations in concert with demining operations.

The 1997 international landmine treaty negotiated in Ottawa, formally titled the "Convention on the Prohibition of the Use, Stockpiling,

Production and Transfer of Anti-Personnel Mines and on Their Destruction," is a very important instrument to publicize the tragic legacy of landmines and to mobilize concerted international efforts to ban them. The affected countries need assistance to develop their capacities to meet the reporting systems related to this treaty. Hopefully, the imperative needed to foster an integrated approach will also be realized.

Some Examples of Integrated Mine Clearance

Afghanistan

Afghanistan is one of the most mine-infested and UXO-affected (unexploded ordnance) countries in the world. It is also where the United Nations in 1989 first became involved in creating a comprehensive mine action program. By December 1997, the UN Mine Action Programme for Afghanistan had technically surveyed and marked 189 square kilometers of contaminated land, cleared 132 square kilometers of high-priority land and 120 square kilometers of former battlefield, destroyed 161,000 mines and 549,000 items of unexploded ordnances. The program provided mine awareness briefings for approximately four million people.

The program directly funded five projects implementing mine awareness activities and used a variety of techniques; many specially designed for children. The Afghanistan program was a highly specialized and comprehensive response, but despite all these efforts, in 1997 more than 750 square miles of contaminated land remained, 323 square kilometers of which were high-priority areas. In the Kabul area alone, there were more than ten civilians a week involved in a mine accident.

In parallel with the UN Mine Action Programme for Afghanistan, the UN Development Programme (UNDP) implemented the Poverty Eradication and Community Empowerment (P.E.A.C.E) Initiative. This was a multisectoral community-focused area development program, with its projects planned in close consultation and collaboration with the demining work. For the P.E.A.C.E Initiative, the UNDP provided about US$12 million to US$15 million a year, which was, and is, a minuscule amount when compared with what is needed to alleviate the sufferings and poverty borne by the people. It is useful to observe that throughout the mid- to late 1990s, the P.E.A.C.E projects were implemented in over 85 percent of the country, and the vast majority of the project staff was Afghans.

Mines and UXO, unfortunately, continue to be a major problem in the country. New areas are being contaminated by UXO and when ammunition depots are hit, unexploded ordnance spread over a large area. It is estimated that at least 60 percent of mine- and UXO-contaminated areas environ schools, public buildings, roads, bridges, and irrigation systems. The people are denied safe access to these areas for farming, grazing, schooling, and other social economic activities crucial for rehabilitation, reconstruction, and development of the country.

An assessment by the Asian Development Bank, the World Bank, and the UNDP, published in January 2002, shows that mine action by the United Nations and nongovernmental organizations (NGOs) in Afghanistan is very cost-effective, in economic terms alone, even without estimating the social benefits:

- One U.S. dollar spent results in US$4.60 in economic returns.
- One square kilometer of land cleared yields US$2,000 for grazing.
- Fifty kilometers of cleared roads provide some US$250,000 in economic benefits.[1]

Mine clearance has enabled the return of approximately 1.5 million refugees and internally displaced persons.

The recently established Afghan Campaign to Ban Land Mines in partnership with the Mine Action Center, UNICEF, and over sixty NGOs and other partners to develop a new advocacy strategy will help increase considerably awareness and actions nationally and internationally.

Cambodia

The Supreme National Council of Cambodia created the Cambodian Mine Action Center (CMAC) in 1992. At the highest level of government, directed through the CMAC, there is recognition that the problem of landmines impacts across the entire spectrum of socioeconomic development.

In parallel with and augmenting the UNDP-coordinated CMAC activities is the UNDP Cambodia Area Rehabilitation and Regeneration Program. The range of activities included microsavings and microcredit schemes, vocational training, livelihood and income generation opportunities, provision of basic education and health, rural roads construction, water supply and sanitation, and the integration and strengthening of the role of women in social, health, and economic development. Over 95 percent of those who joined the microsaving and microcredit schemes were women. There was hardly any bad debt.

Cambodia is also one of the most mined countries in the world, with an estimated six to seven million mines, almost one per person. More than 40,000 Cambodians have lost limbs, a very high ratio of 1 in 250 citizens. Each month, more than two hundred persons continue to loose their limbs. The country probably has one of the highest rates of amputees in the world.

By 1999, CMAC had cleared 152 minefields and destroyed 72,511 antipersonnel mines, 877 antitank mines, and 428,769 pieces of unexploded ordnance. A two-year verification project registered an additional 2,500 square kilometers for mine clearance and released 1,074 square kilometers deemed fit for resettlement and where area rehabilitation and reconstruction can commence.

CMAC's mobile mine awareness project reached almost 400,000 individuals in over seven hundred villages throughout Cambodia. Plans were in place to expand awareness sixfold. The project was designed to reduce the rate of injury at the community level, taking into account the geographic and social environment of individual villages. Newspapers and television and radio programs, as well as Mine Awareness Day, were all brought to bear, warning Cambodians, especially children, of the inherent dangers posed by landmines and unexploded ordnance in their community.

The CMAC is considered one of the most developed national mine action centers in the world. However, it continues to face institutional and capacity development challenges, as well as predictable multiyear funding requirements as it expands and becomes more involved in new demining techniques.

A currently ongoing survey has thus far indicated that landmines and UXO contaminate almost half the villages in the northwestern parts of the country, a coverage much higher than expected. This is also a region where refugees and internally displaced persons were recently resettled.

Lao People's Democratic Republic

From 1964 through 1973, Lao was subjected to one of the most severe aerial bombing attacks: more than two million tons of bombs and an incalculable millions of antipersonnel bombs were dropped on this country of fewer than four million people. UXO adversely affects at least twelve of the country's seventeen provinces, with more than 11,000 accidents reported since the bombing was stopped in 1973. The accident rate remains constant, with an additional two hundred cases reported every year. Children and youth account for almost half the accidents. Since 85 percent of the Laotian population is involved in agriculture, adults and youth are in the highest risk group.

The UXO/mines-contaminated provinces are also the poorest of the poor villages. In early 1996, the government established the Lao National Unexploded Ordnance Program, with substantial support of the UNDP. The major objective is to reduce the number of civilian casualties and increase the amount of land available for food production and other development activities.

The Community Awareness Strategy launched in 1997 included posters, curriculum inserts, and radio programs and traveling puppet shows to warn people, particularly children, of the danger of UXO and landmines. The program compiles and coordinates landmine contamination data including the socioeconomic and development costs associated with minefields. Due to this strategy, the death toll has now dropped to about one hundred per year. With increasing population, an almost 70 percent increase within the past twenty-five years to a current figure of around 5.3 million, the need for and pressure on arable land is increasing. As the country is mountainous, the need to free up mine-contaminated lands is imperative to meet the food security, employment requirements, poverty reduction, and human and economic development aspirations of the country.

Some Reflections

Political will is necessary for mine clearance operations to be successful. Without this, it is difficult to plan and implement successful programs. A country that is emerging from a brutal war, with its infrastructure destroyed; its social, economic, and political systems ravaged; and the ecological resource base compromised, does not have the necessary financial and human resources to fund integrated programs. Donor assistance is urgently needed.

All landmines decommissioning programs are carried out under exceptional circumstances. The donor community needs to be more flexible in funding mine clearance programs. While strict financial accountability is necessary, there is much room for streamlining and simplifying procedures as well as reporting requirements. Furthermore, the continuous pleas by recipient countries for the donor community to harmonize their accounting and reporting requirements are never more pertinent and critical than for demining programs.

Equally important is the need for predictable multiyear funding. When this is uncertain, there is very little incentives for the government and people just emerging from the ravages of war and conflicts, whose immediate and urgent priority is to survive, conceptualize, plan, and implement sustainable development policies, strategies, programs, and projects.

A sensitive and contentious issue pertains to the criteria used to accord priorities for determining areas for mine clearance. An equally important and related issue is the methodologies and procedures used for releasing and allocating the cleared land. How should land use and ownership be determined? And who decides? The separation of regulatory, management, and operation functions would be a step in the right direction.

In sum, governance is the key. If the process is not responsive, open, inclusive, and transparent and seen to be fair and equitable, there will be much resentment, tension, and hostilities in the community, thereby perpetuating conflicts. This will pose a significant hurdle to a country and its people's aspirations for social and economic opportunities, as well as to peace.

There is a need to increase and strengthen the role of women in integrated demining operations. Social and economic reconstruction and rehabilitation policies and projects design, planning, and implementation will be more relevant to the needs and priorities of the family and community.

There are opportunities for improvement in victim assistance programs. Besides the need for immediate medical care, trauma counseling is very weak or most often nonexistent. In addition, more is needed in victim assistance programs, with projects such as skill training and reintegration into the community.

Mine clearance is a long and ongoing operation. While at the initial phase, international expertise is needed, this assistance should also include a dedicated and planned local training and capacity-building component. The country must have ownership of the task and have the capacity and capability to undertake it sooner rather than later.

Systematic exchange of information and experience between the various operations in a country as well as between countries need to be increased and improved. Innovative and instructive training manuals and awareness materials targeted at the village and community are available with all mine clearance operations. While many of these are prepared in the local language, they are often communicated with pictograms, which are readily understood universally. Mine clearance funding should include a budget line for the compilation, adaptation, translation, and production of relevant and successfully used materials, including audiovisuals.

The survey, identification, verification, and registration of landmines and unexploded ordnance will be significantly speeded up and enhanced by using better and more advanced technologies, such as remote sensing. This tool will help efficiently map a larger geographical area much faster. When used in conjunction with area planning for socioeconomic development and ecological resource reclamation and regeneration, the planning, design, and reconstruction would be more optimized.

Mine clearance policies and operations need to be an integral part of the country's overall development policies and plans. National decision makers and opinion leaders need to be made aware of the social, economic, and ecological costs as well as the corresponding benefits, many of which cannot be quantified, if mines and unexploded ordnance are not cleared and cleared appropriately. Those who are maimed are largely at their prime and are in the most productive years of their lives. No country can afford to have this most important resource—human beings—reduced and, tragically, often wasted.

Sustainable development is a concept, policy, and strategy adopted by almost all countries. This will be difficult to attain when there are still landmines remaining potent and posing a constant threat in the country.

Cooperation

Integrated mine action programs, including victims assistance work, provide a very good framework for cooperation between and among the government, nongovernmental and community-based organizations, the private sector, and the international community toward the shared goal of alleviating suffering and providing opportunities and hope. It is important that all countries ratify the Ottawa Treaty. More support should be given to the International Trust Fund for Demining and Mine Victims Assistance. While international assistance and cooperation are needed, national governments should also allocate more funds in their national budgets to underscore its commitment and will to clean up this scourge for the future of its country and citizens, particularly children.

An innovative program is the United Nations Association of the USA's Adopt-A-Minefield, which is in partnership with a number of other organizations. The campaign seeks national and international sponsors to adopt a minefield, identified by the United Nations, for clearance. Sponsorship of a minefield is typically in the range of US$25,000 to US$40,000, but can be as little as US$5, which is then pooled with other contributions. Every dollar raised is forwarded to the United Nations for mine clearance. This program and campaign is also implemented in the United Kingdom and Canada and should be replicated in more countries.

Conclusion

The pain, suffering, and death caused by landmines and UXO are immediate and evident. The tragedy has evoked very laudable international awareness and responses. However, there are also long-term consequences, such as environmental pollution, that can cause suffering and death. These problems often occur silently, are not immediately evident, occur over prolonged periods, and have equally significant social and economic effects. The overall impacts on the well-being and welfare of the people are similar. Contamination of water supply sources and land by pollutants, especially persistent organic products and hazardous wastes, have been correctly described as "time bombs" akin to planting of landmines and dropping of UXO. Continued reporting of the dumping of hazardous wastes in developing countries should be considered as an act of hostility. Hopefully, national and international mine awareness programs and clearance operations will help raise increased concerns with regard to these environmental time bombs and help foster increased cooperation and action.

While the political and military debates continue on the banning of landmines, there is the urgent and humane need to clear contaminated areas. The economic benefits alone for mine clearance are also considerable and compelling.

Landmines prolong conflicts, especially societal conflicts, by delaying and impeding rehabilitation and reconstruction of the basic and necessary constituents needed by a person and the community to begin the process of recovery. Sustained social and economic development is difficult, if not impossible, if there are landmines. Without this imperative foundation to support and strengthen the peace process, disputes and conflicts simmer and erupt, undermining peace. The vicious spiraling perpetuates, and without sustained peace, there cannot be sustained development, providing the healing balm of opportunities and benefits for a better quality of life and standard of living for the victims and their families, with the security of freedom from fear and freedom from want.

Note

1. Asian Development Bank, the United Nations Development Programme, and the World Bank, "Afghanistan: Preliminary Needs Assessment for Recovery and Reconstruction," January 2002, available at http://www.aims.org.af/.

14

The Victim Assistance Provision of the Mine Ban Treaty

GLENNA L. FAK

The 80 million or so landmines that lie hidden today in the fields, forests and roads of approximately 80 countries, and the 250 million stockpiled around the world waiting to be deployed . . . comprise one of the greatest public health hazards of our time—a modern, man-made epidemic.

—Her Majesty Queen Noor

APPROXIMATELY 15,000 TO 20,000 PEOPLE ARE INJURED BY OR LOSE THEIR lives to landmines/unexploded ordnance (UXO) each year.[1] Of the reported landmine casualties, an estimated 70 percent are civilian[2] and one-third are children.[3] Currently, there are an estimated 300,000 landmine survivors spread throughout eighty countries. Their rehabilitation costs will total close to $3 billion.[4] In Cambodia, Angola, and Afghanistan, landmine survivor statistics are horrifying. For instance, 1 in every 236 Cambodians and 1 in every 334 Angolans has lost a limb to a landmine accident.[5] One out of every fifty people living in Afghanistan has suffered some type of landmine injury.[6]

In the early 1990s and prior, nongovernmental organizations (NGOs) were being hindered from assisting mine victims and providing aid to restore countries that had been ravaged by war because antipersonnel landmines (APLs) were scattered throughout the lands.[7] NGOs claimed landmines were one of the main obstructions to achieving their work because "landmines exacerbated regional conflicts, hindered post-conflict reconstruction, seriously undermined infrastructure, and denied land to civilian use, thereby leading to extreme pressures on existing land."[8] The serious threat landmines posed to humanity led to an international treaty banning this weapon. The term *victim assistance* was created during the movement to abolish antipersonnel landmines. The term resulted from communication between the International Campaign to Ban Landmines, NGOs, governments, and the UN community and it encompasses a wide variety of ideas and activities, whose purpose is to aid in the complete rehabilitation of the landmine survivor and his or her family and community.[9] As a comprehensive ban on APLs gained momentum around the world, it became clear that focusing solely on banning the weapon would not suffice in alleviating the devastation wrought by landmines. Thus, the Landmine Survivors Network, a nonprofit organization founded by and for landmine survivors, and mine survivors around the world pushed for the inclusion of a clause to assist other survivors in attaining the physical, psychological, social, and economic rehabilitation needed to gain independence and become productive and contributing members of society.[10] Due to the victim assistance provision, which was included in the Mine Ban Treaty at the time of its drafting, the rehabilitation and reintegration of landmine survivors is now part of international law.

Types of Assistance and Ways to Reintegrate

> We know from the courage and energy of . . . victims that rehabilitation is possible, and that landmine survivors can play vitally important roles in their societies if only they are given the opportunity.
> —Secretary-General Kofi Annan

Once the landmine survivor situation in a given country has been correctly evaluated and the needs and limitations of a particular area are known, priorities must be established.[11] There is no systematic way of assessing the needs of various injured people in multiple countries throughout the world; therefore, each situation has to be assessed individually. By enhancing or creating services—immediate medical treatment, long-term medical treatment, physical rehabilitation, psychological and social reintegration programs, vocational and economic reintegration programs, education, awareness, laws protecting the disabled, and access—reintegration will be much more likely, as will the chance of becoming a self-sustaining and productive member of society who can provide for oneself and one's family and community.

Immediate Medical Treatment

Immediate access to medical treatment entails teaching medical personnel, who live in mine-affected countries, rudimentary first aid practices to be used in urgent situations.[12] First aid is an essential measure and must be administered in order to lengthen a mine survivor's chance of attaining medical treatment at a health facility. By learning first aid, the people in the local community are competently prepared to deal with painful injuries resulting from, but not limited to, landmines.[13] Generally, these measures can best be acquired through grassroots training programs that are both effective and cost-efficient.[14]

Although it is seldom practiced when implementing first aid, a blood transfusion may become essential if the survivor has lost a massive amount of blood.[15] Blood for transfusion comes from friends, family members, and community members; however, appropriate measures must be taken to test the blood for diseases such as hepatitis and HIV.[16] Not only is it important for a survivor to receive a blood transfusion during emergency care or upon arrival at a health facility, but it is also very important to administer antibiotics to the individual at one of these stages in order to help combat the start of a serious infection. Six hours after an injury is sustained, a wound becomes susceptible to infection.[17] Infection can become of a critical nature in a very short amount of time; so the sooner the antibiotics are administered, the safer the mine survivor will be.[18]

For a mine-affected community to have access to immediate care, it has to take the initiative and invest in the infrastructure of the community.[19] Unfortunately, according to the 2000 edition of the *Landmine Monitor Report*, less than 30 percent of the mine-affected countries and regions, which reported mine incidents for the period 1999–2000, were equipped to deal with emergency medical care. Less than 20 percent of these countries/areas had immediate medical assistance available, and in the outstanding countries, information regarding the existence or lack thereof was not disclosed.[20] Although immediate medical treatment is often difficult to provide, this type of treatment has to be enhanced in order for mine survivors to receive professional attention.

Long-Term Medical Treatment

Long-term medical care begins at the arrival and check-in of the injured person at the hospital. If possible, the mine survivor is asked to give information pertaining to how, when, and where their injury was sustained, which can be used to assist squads trained in mine clearance.[21] Individuals who have suffered mine-related injuries need to have their wounds washed immediately, if at all possible, so an accurate assessment of the damage can be made. Cleaning the patient is also performed to avoid further damage through the spread of infection.[22]

To ensure a patient has access to adequate long-term medical attention, hospitals must be equipped with the necessary supplies (i.e., appropriate technology, operating tools, and medical supplies) to meet basic standards. A staff of professionals, including trained surgeons and other skilled health personnel, is required to ensure that the unique injuries sustained by mine survivors are tended to appropriately;[23] however, specialty surgeons are rarely required.[24] By making sure hospitals are sufficiently endowed to care for mine survivors, the treatment of other injured people will ultimately be enhanced.

Physical Rehabilitation

Physical rehabilitation includes making available the appropriate services for long-term care, which in turn will allow survivors to become self-sufficient and independent. Amputation is a common result of a landmine accident; thus, many landmine survivors require prostheses, assistive devices, and access to local maintenance and restoration in case these devices break down. The limb loss survivor needs to be involved in the entire prosthetic-fitting process because the type of injury, how it has affected the person's remaining limb, and how it affects the individual and his or her daily activities has to be taken into account. It is also very important for prosthetic technology, which has been donated to a specific country, to be in line with the needs of the country.

> The solution should fit the problem, not vice versa. . . . Not just technology, but production of technology should be in the hands of the end-users. Prosthetics and wheel chair workshops . . . ensure that the equipment is actually suitable to the country and that what is needed is provided. They also provide jobs, skills, and a sense of self worth to those doing it.[25]

Resources have to be allotted to train physiotherapists as both pre- and postprosthetic physiotherapy are essential in ensuring the correct operation of assistive mechanisms and in keeping the limb loss survivors from sustaining any more discomfort or damage.[26] Landmine amputees need to maintain a wide range of motion in their injured limb; but at the same time, they have to be extremely careful when maintaining flexibility so they do not sustain any additional injuries or aggravate the one(s) they already have. Limb loss survivors should not engage in physiotherapy until the injuries have been closed; however, as soon as this occurs it is essential for the individual to engage in a wide range of movement. The remaining part of the limb must be healthy if the individual wants to wear a prosthetic limb.[27]

Generally, it takes four to five weeks for a mine survivor to recover from surgery. Once the survivor has stabilized, his or her injuries have been repaired, and the swelling of the limb has subsided, the landmine amputee is ready to be sized for a prosthetic limb. Being fitted with a prosthesis is an integral part of successful rehabilitation.[28] Without it, it is not only hard for the survivor to gain full use of other body parts,[29] it is also hard for the individual to recover the self-respect and self-esteem that was lost when the mine tore through the survivor's body.

Psychological and Social Reintegration

Although physical rehabilitation somewhat aids in the psychological rehabilitation of the survivor, additional steps need to be taken to further this type of rehabilitation as the trauma of becoming a landmine casualty is often overwhelming.[30] Local communities must encourage support groups to provide psychological and social support as they educate populations about the special requirements of people with disabilities and the means available to assist the disabled citizenry, including individuals who have survived landmine accidents. To benefit landmine survivors to the utmost, psychological support needs to be based at the local level and incorporate a range of social service providers. The families of landmine survivors are instrumental in their recovery and thus should be given the appropriate instruction and encouragement to help in the rehabilitation of wounded family members.[31]

Once a landmine survivor is fully and successfully rehabilitated, he or she can then serve as a compassionate and considerate ally to those who are undergoing rehabilitation. Peer support has been shown to have positive effects on landmine casualties both in the initial phase and in the long term. Funds should be appropriated to train mine survivors and other individuals and to encourage the implementation of local-level assistance programs in postconflict countries, especially where psychological encouragement programs are nonexistent.[32]

Much attention needs to be paid to this type of rehabilitation and there needs to be a substantial increase in the amount of resources allotted because psychological and social assistance are generally not provided for by the government. As with other types of assistance, if services are available they are generally located in metropolitan regions, not in the rural areas that have the highest incidence of landmine casualties. Finally, psychological rehabilitation, like immediate and long-term medical care and physical rehabilitation, is generally more accessible for military personnel than it is for the civilian population.[33]

Vocational and Economic Reintegration: Incorporating the Local Population

For victim assistance to be truly successful, people with disabilities must have a job and an income to enhance their well-being and self-respect.[34] Economic reintegration is also necessary for landmine survivors to provide for their families and to give back to their communities. To enhance the financial position and the self-sufficiency of the disabled populace in mine-torn areas, it is necessary for social service support programs to: teach the disabled citizenry, encourage the establishment of local communications and transportation systems, and generate numerous types of employment. The economic status of mine survivors strongly correlates with the political strength and economic condition in the area in which they live, so it is necessary to enhance community development in order to increase the economic status of landmine survivors.[35] According to the *1998–1999 Report on the Canadian Landmine Fund*, programs to assist mine survivors are now incorporating job opportunities in both the manufacture of artificial limbs and in the treatment of survivors. This definitely has a positive effect on their self-esteem and economic status and allows them to give back to their communities.[36] By enhancing the abilities of local donors, health personnel, and instructors and by incorporating the local population, survivors are being assisted in a sustainable way.

Public and private lending institutions are encouraged to empower, through social and financial support, previously established systems instead of developing new or similar ones. This will lead to the enhancement of community infrastructure and to the improvement of the types of treatment mine survivors, their families, and the communities in which they live will receive.[37] Currently, socioeconomic programs are generally not developed in mine-torn countries and if such assistance does exist, then, as with the previous types of assistance, it is usually located in the metropolitan area. Governments are typically not involved in this aspect of rehabilitation and any type of socioeconomic program implementation is generally left to NGOs.[38]

Educating, Raising Awareness, and Protecting the Rights of People with Disabilities

Education of the general public about the abilities of people with disabilities is essential if landmine survivors are to attain complete reintegration.

Not only is it the duty of each country to develop the appropriate legislation to ensure survivors have an adequate level of medical attention, but also countries must make sure they have the appropriate measures in place to guard survivors from discrimination and stigmatization. By establishing laws for the disabled citizenry, landmine survivors will be protected from incurring additional pain and suffering and will be in a better position to obtain assistance from their countries.[39]

It is the government's responsibility to increase community awareness of and to educate the general population about the necessities of the disabled population and to oppose the stigmatization of people with disabilities. A campaign to promote the skills, talents, and other capabilities of the disabled and to ensure the accessibility of treatment programs is an excellent way to attain this, and it can be best provided at the local level with the inclusion of the disabled populace.[40] Unfortunately though, less than half of the countries that experienced a landmine injury or fatality during the period 1999–2000 had an official policy or law on disability.[41] Even if policies to protect people with disabilities from discrimination are present, they are generally very difficult to enforce, making it challenging for survivors to reintegrate.[42]

Access

People with disabilities, including landmine survivors, should be treated in the same way as other citizens; thus, they should have access to a wide range of services and assistance to ensure their comprehensive rehabilitation. "Access includes: the elimination of physical obstacles to mobility; ensuring access to buildings and public places; availability of first aid; emergency and continuing medical care; physical rehabilitation; employment opportunities; education and training; religious practice; sports and recreation; safe land and tenure of land; and information and communication about available services."[43] By ensuring people with disabilities have an equal opportunity to engage in all realms of life, complete rehabilitation and reintegration will be much more probable.

Countries can offer survivors access to assistance through bilateral and multilateral relationships or by providing their own victim assistance programs. Countries do not have to actually initiate or develop projects specifically targeted to the needs of mine survivors; instead, they can encourage awareness and campaign for the rights of the disabled. This type of assistance can be very effective and cost-efficient for those countries that do not possess an adequate amount of resources or funds. States Parties, which do not have the means to assist their victims, may ask another State Party to assist them. Thus, "States Parties can ask, or be asked, for survivor assistance."[44]

Conclusion: Prognosis for the Future

We must end the carnage caused by anti-personnel land mines, the hidden killers that murder and maim more than 25,000 people a year. . . . Our children deserve to walk the Earth in safety.

—Former President Bill Clinton

Landmines pose a serious threat to dozens of countries and millions of people around the world, yet they and their survivors remain largely ignored. The countries in which large numbers of landmine survivors reside are best characterized as having a very poor social and economic infrastructure. Although it is extremely difficult for countries to provide appropriate care and rehabilitation for landmine survivors, it is the duty of each country to do so. Assistance can be provided in a number of ways, including through bilateral and multilateral exchanges or by campaigning for support for the rights of people with disabilities. There are certain types of assistance countries can provide for their mine survivors that are inexpensive; however, other types of assistance can be very expensive, which means the enhancement of data collection capabilities is a must in order to increase the amount of funding allotted to victim assistance programs.

Hundreds of thousands of landmine survivors worldwide are in desperate need of immediate and long-term medical treatment and sustained physical, psychological, and social care. Formal policies regarding the treatment of the disabled must be implemented in order to protect those with disabilities from discriminatory acts. Policies must also ensure they have access to treatment or they will be subjected to further discomfort. For victim assistance programs to be successful and sustainable, victim assistance has to entail a wide variety of programs, a broad range of actors, and the incorporation of mine victims and other people with disabilities in the decision-making process.

The Mine Ban Treaty banned an inhumane and indiscriminate weapon from the world's arsenal, but just as importantly the treaty took into account the individuals affected by the weapon, requiring countries to provide for the care and rehabilitation of their mine survivors. Through the victim assistance provision, mine survivors have a chance to rehabilitate, reintegrate, and lead self-sustaining and productive lives. There is much progress to be made to ensure all survivors have access to complete rehabilitation; however, the Mine Ban Treaty has served as a "model" global humanitarian treaty and is likely to do so in the future.

Notes

1. This number accounts for landmine casualties, those individuals who have been both injured and killed, by "antipersonnel mines, antivehicle mines, improvised explosive devices and unexploded ordnance." See International Campaign to Ban Landmines (ICBL), *Landmine Monitor Report 2002: Toward a Mine-Free World* (New York: Human Rights Watch, 2002), 40.

2. The number of reported casualties in 2001 was 7,987. ICBL, *Landmine Monitor Report 2002*, 40.

3. Holly Burkhalter, "The Mine Ban Treaty," *Foreign Policy in Focus* 5, no. 21 (July 2000): 1; and Holly Burkhalter, "Landmines: Time for a Ban," *Lancet* 350, no. 9070 (July 5, 1997): 63–64—both available at Ebscohost (accessed June 2, 2001).

4. ICBL, "Executive Summary," *Landmine Monitor Report: Toward a Mine Free World*, (New York: Human Rights Watch, 1999), 22.

5. James Cobey and Barbara Ayotte, "Tools to Measure Landmine Incidents and Injuries," *Lancet* 355, no. 9214 (April 29, 2000): 1549–1550—available at Ebscohost (accessed June 2, 2001); and Nils Arne Kastberg, "Plenary Speaker," *Surviving the Scourge of Landmines* (Washington, DC: Landmine Survivors Network, 1998), 13.

6. Cobey and Ayotte, "Tools," 1549–1550; and Kastberg, "Plenany Speaker," 13. In comparison with the United States, 1 out of every 22,000 Americans is a landmine survivor. See The Arms Project of Human Rights Watch and Physicians for Human Rights (HRW and PHR), *Landmines: A Deadly Legacy* (New York: Human Rights Watch, 1993), 126–127.

7. Jody Williams and Steve Goose, "The International Campaign to Ban Landmines," in *To Walk without Fear: The Global Movement to Ban Landmines*, ed. Maxwell A. Cameron, Robert J. Lawson, and Brian W. Tomlin (Oxford: Oxford University Press, 1998), 21, 22.

8. Kenneth Rutherford, "Banning Landmines," *International Politics* 37, no. 4 (December 2000), 459.

9. Working Group on Victim Assistance of the International Campaign to Ban Landmines and Standing Committee of Experts on Victim Assistance, Socioeconomic Reintegration, and Mine Awareness, "Portfolio of Victim Assistance Programs," 2002, available at http://www.landminevap.org/; and Jerry White and Ken Rutherford, "The Role of the Landmine Survivors Network," in *To Walk without Fear: The Global Movement to Ban Landmines*, ed. Maxwell A. Cameron, Robert J. Lawson, and Brian W. Tomlin (Oxford: Oxford University Press, 1998), 104.

10. White and Rutherford, "Role," 100, 101; See also Raquel Willerman's chapter in this volume.

11. For example, in an area where the number of new mine survivors is prevalent and mine survivors are flooding the hospitals, immediate medical care takes precedence. However, in an area where the war is over, immediate medical attention is no longer the main priority and long-term care becomes the most important aspect of rehabilitation. See Robin Coupland, *Assistance for the Victims of Anti-Personnel Mines: Needs, Constraints, and Strategy* (Geneva: International Committee of the Red Cross, October 1997), 25.

12. "Out of 100 mine casualties . . . half will die in pain and fear from obstruction of airways or blood loss before reaching the hospital, simply because no one in these rural areas had first aid training." See Hans Husum, "Plenary Speakers," in Landmine Survivors Network, *Surviving the Scourge of Landmines* (Washington, DC: Landmine Survivors Network, 1998), 16.

13. Coupland, *Assistance*, 10, 14.

14. Husum, "Plenary Speakers," 15.

15. Mine survivors need the largest amount of blood for transfusions, especially individuals who have lost a limb. For instance, "110 units of blood are needed for [every one hundred] mine victims" whereas amputees require 350 units per one hundred survivors. These numbers can be compared with the fifty units of blood required for people wounded by bullets or shrapnel. See Chris Giannou, "Emergency Medical Care," in Landmine Survivors Network, *Surviving the Scourge of Landmines* (Washington, DC: Landmine Survivors Network, 1998), 18; and Coupland, *Assistance*, 14.

16. Coupland, *Assistance*, 14. Both the shortage of blood and the inability of health professionals to safely rule out donors who may carry a disease (because of inadequate and unsanitary health facility conditions) means that many mine survivors will not have the chance at living they deserve. Also, due to cultural differences it may be harder to attain blood donations in some countries versus others. For instance, in Afghanistan the giving of blood by male donors is seen as "diminishing one's masculinity." See International Physicians for the Prevention of Nuclear War (IPPNW), *Landmines: A Global Health Crisis* (Cambridge, MA: IPPNW, 1997), 11.

17. According to the International Committee of the Red Cross (ICRC) surgical database, "Only 25% [of landmine victims] arrive within six hours of injury; 15% travel for more than three days to reach the hospital" (quoted in Coupland, *Assistance*, 6).

18. HRW and PHR, *Landmines: A Deadly Legacy*, 123, 124.

19. ICBL Working Group on Victim Assistance (ICBLWGVA), *Guidelines for the Care and Rehabilitation of Survivors* (Oslo: International Campaign to Ban Landmines, 1998), 2; and HRW and PHR, *Landmines: A Deadly Legacy*, 123, 124.

20. ICBL, *Landmine Monitor Report 2000: Toward a Mine-Free World* (New York: Human Rights Watch, 2000), 28, 29.

21. Coupland, *Assistance*, 11.

22. IPPNW, *Landmines: A Global Health Crisis*, 12.

23. ICBLWGVA, *Guidelines*, 2. In the most heavily mined countries, hospitals lack adequate equipment and personnel and personnel oftentimes lack the necessary training. See IPPNW, *Landmines: A Global Health Crisis*, 10.

24. Coupland, *Assistance*, 11.

25. Mereso Agina and Anne Capelle, "Administering and Allocating Funds: Framework for Allocation: Needs and Aspirations of People Affected," in Mines Action Canada, *Goodbye Landmines, Hello Life: Report on NGO Activities and Forum* (Ottawa: Mines Action Canada), 40.

26. Ibid., 47.

27. Coupland, *Assistance*, 12. Consideration must also be paid to the treatment of landmine-sustained injuries, aside from limb loss; therefore, medical professionals need to be appropriately trained. Such injuries include, but are not limited to, loss of sight, loss of hearing, and loss of partial or complete movement. See ICBLWGVA, *Guidelines*, 3.

28. Military personnel have a better chance of attaining prosthetic limbs than do civilians. It is estimated that only 10–20 percent of civilian limb loss survivors wear a prosthesis. See HRW and PHR, *Landmines: A Deadly Legacy*, 130.

29. It is speculated that if a mine survivor who requires a below-the-knee prostheses is not fitted with an artificial limb, that person can only do 25 percent of what they could normally do because both hands are being used to get around. See IPPNW, *Landmines: A Global Health Crisis*, 15.

30. Ibid., 21; and Seddig Weera, "War and Children," Department of Foreign Affairs and International Trade (DFAIT), *An Agenda for Mine Action* (Ottawa: Department of Foreign Affairs and International Trade, 1997), 33.

31. ICBLWGVA, *Guidelines*, 3.

32. Ibid., 3, 4.

33. This is a cause for concern since the civilian population makes up the majority of landmine survivors. See HRW and PHR, *Landmines: A Deadly Legacy*, 124.

34. Joshua Malinga, "Indigenous NGO Perspective: Job Creation and Advocacy," in DFAIT, *An Agenda for Mine Action* (Ottawa: Department of Foreign Affairs and International Trade, 1997), 34.

35. ICBLWGVA, *Guidelines*, 4.

36. DFAIT, *Seeds of Terror/Seed of Hope: 1998–1999 Report on the Canadian Landmine Fund* (Ottawa: Department of Foreign Affairs and International Trade, 1999), 23; and Sonia Mirabel Minero, "Local Rehabilitation from the Non-Governmental Organization Perspective," in DFAIT, *An Agenda for Mine Action* (Ottawa: Department of Foreign Affairs and International

Trade, 1999), 27. The ICRC has made it a habit to employ mine survivors in their regional prosthetics manufacturing centers. This benefits the survivor and it also ensures the long-term success of the program once the ICRC leaves. See Coupland, *Assistance*, 19.

37. ICBLWGVA, *Guidelines*, 4, 5.

38. ICBL, *Landmine Monitor Report 2000*, 31.

39. Ibid., 28; and Kenneth Rutherford, "State Legal Obligations to Landmine Victim Assistance," *Journal of International Law and Policy* 6, no. 3 (Fall 2001): 89–90.

40. ICBLWGVA, *Guidelines*, 5; and Rutherford, "State Legal Obligations," 90.

41. ICBL, *Landmine Monitor Report 2000*, 28.

42. Ibid., 28.

43. ICBLWGVA, *Guidelines*, 5. Unfortunately, in the majority of countries riddled with mines, less than 10 percent of the disabled citizenry has access to adequate health care and rehabilitative treatment. See Physicians for Human Rights, "Message on Behalf of ICBL Working Group on Victim Assistance," available at http://navigation.helper.realnames.com/framer/1/112/default. asp?realname=Physicians+for+Human+Rights&url=http%3A%2F% 2Fwww%2Ephrusa%2Eorg&frameid=1&providerid=112&uid=10271145 (accessed June 28, 2001).

41. Rutherford, "State Legal Obligations," 85.

15

The Environmental Impacts
of Landmines

CLAUDIO TORRES NACHÓN

THIS CHAPTER ADDRESSES SOME OF THE ENVIRONMENTAL ASPECTS AND impacts of antipersonnel landmines (APLs) in the global environment, with an emphasis on Africa and the Americas. The impact of landmines goes beyond the killing and maiming of civilians and military well after conflicts are over. Landmines affect many components of the global biosphere. While this chapter recognizes the broader spectrum of unexploded ordnance (UXO), my research was limited to antipersonnel landmines. According to article 2(1) of the Convention on the Prohibition of the Use, Stockpiling, Production and Transfer of Anti-Personnel Mines and on Their Destruction (1997 Mine Ban Treaty), an "Anti-personnel mine" is a mine designed to be exploded by the presence, proximity, or contact of a person and that will incapacitate, injure, or kill one or more persons.[1] Mines designed to be detonated by the presence, proximity, or contact of a vehicle as opposed to a person, that are equipped with anti-handling devices, are not considered antipersonnel mines as a result of being so equipped.[2] Historically, landmines have been widely used in a number of conflicts in many regions of the world since the end of World War II. According to Geoffrey Best, "[I]t may be said that mines became for the 1970's and 1980's what napalm had been for the 1950's and 1960's; the weapon whose careless and indiscriminate uses have inflicted the most cruel and extensive injuries on civilians. . . . [I]n scale and persistence, mines make up a giant problem and scandal."[3] Africa in particular has been severely contaminated with such indiscriminate explosive devices, although other regions of the world such as central and Southeast Asia and Central and South America have been heavily mined as well. Among the many problems attached to the use of landmines are those related to its impact on the natural environment and its components. Being silent, indiscriminate, patient killers, landmines remain active long after conflicts have ended. Its victims are not limited to human beings; landmines have killed and maimed large numbers of wildlife and domestic species worldwide. In that logic, landmines set in motion a series of events leading to environmental degradation in the forms of soil degradation, deforestation, pollution of water resources with heavy metals, and possibly altering entire species' populations by degrading habitats and altering food chains. In other matters, landmines turn already difficult tasks for conservation into almost impossible missions, as is the case of APL contamination of natural protected areas. More generally, taking into consideration the prevalent socioeconomic conditions of most of the countries seriously affected by landmines, it can be said that APLs represent a tremendous challenge for both international organizations and local governments. It has been widely recognized that "AP [antipersonnel] mines have long–lasting social, economic, and environmental implications."[4]

Unfortunately, the environmental aspects of landmines have not been studied in detail. Preference has understandably been given to channeling most available funds to humanitarian demining, victim assistance, and landmine awareness programs. Many sad stories can be told about the way landmines transform the lives of thousands of people, mostly civilians, in many cases children and elders, every year. In any case, a great effort by international organizations, nongovernmental organizations, and local governments has arisen over the past decade to eliminate this threat to humanity. Much is still to be done.

In my view, the international humanitarian landmine crisis should be understood as an ancillary element of the current global environmental crisis. In the following pages I will present and evaluate certain direct and indirect environmental impacts of landmines in an attempt to call on the attention of decision makers in humanitarian and environmental organizations to generate policy and priorities and allocate funds to conduct a complete global environmental impact assessment of landmines. Such an assessment would follow the recent advances of environmental organizations and agencies such as the Balkans Task Force of the United Nations Environment Programme/United Nations Centre for Human Settlements (UNEP/UNCHS) to assess environmental damages caused by the military conflict in Yugoslavia. Ideally, environmental assessments of war should depart from regional influence and concentrate on assessing environmental impacts of specific weapons, such as landmines.

By doing so, the movement for a universal ban on landmines would expand and strengthen greatly by calling the attention of international and local environmental groups. According to Phillip Weller of the Worldwide Fund for Nature (WWF), "[I]t is essential to conduct an environmental assessment of war activities. . . . Both the short term impacts and potential long term impacts need to be addressed. A successful reconstruction and redevelopment strategy requires that there be such assessment."[5] It is particularly important that organizations traditionally involved in conservation, such as the WWF, are actively aware of negative environmental impacts of armed conflict. Other groups have established specific programs, such as Green Cross International's Environmental Legacy of War Project, founded by Mikhail Gorbachev in 1993.

Factual Environmental Issues

The International Landmine Crisis and the Environment

APLs are an insidious characteristic of war, past or present, internal or international. After conflicts are over, APLs remain active, silently waiting for any step to detonate them. Former UN Secretary-General Boutros Boutros-Ghali noted, "After troops withdraw, land mines remain in the ground as brutal reminders that successful peace-building and development are still beyond the horizon."[6] Common estimates consider the number of landmines planted around the world total around 110 million. An even larger number are kept in stockpile, such number may exceed 250 million landmines.[7] An economic reality, a single landmine can cost anywhere from US$3 to US$75; in contrast, the cost of removing a single mine may range anywhere between US$350 to over US$1,000,[8] or even more, depending on the demining circumstances. It is not the same to clean up a flat, accessible minefield than to clean up a mined mountainous border. Even though landmines are now banned by international treaty and customary law, landmines are still openly available. A 1998 report on landmines in Senegal states that "one can find landmines, including near-undetectable plastic varieties, on sale in markets for around CFAfr1,500 ($2.75) each, next to the chickens and dried fish."[9] To some armies, the utility of landmines resides on its low price and availability, "[i]n practice, however, they are used to demoralize the adversary, terrify and control civilian populations, and overburden the adversary's support systems and resources."[10] Landmines then, are weapons of social terror.

According to the International Committee of the Red Cross (ICRC), some 24,000 people are killed or maimed by landmines every year.[11] In reality, no one knows for sure the exact figure or the exact spectrum of the problem. Many accidents involving landmines are never reported. Environmentally speaking, in Angola, for example, "humans are not the only victims of land mines. Dr. Foster . . . has personally seen a herd of cows blown up while crossing a road, and then parts of the cows raining down. They probably saved his life. He also knows of elephants and other wildlife being maimed or destroyed in this way."[12] According to Anna Richardson, "Thousands of animals such as antelopes and elephant fell prey to landmines, hunters and hungry soldiers during Angola's long and bitter war."[13] Although Angola is a signatory of the 1997 Mine Ban Treaty, landmines have continued to be used by both Angolan government and UNITA rebels;[14] such actions are severely condemned by the International Campaign to Ban Landmines and the international community.

As presented above, the international landmine crisis goes well beyond classical humanitarian, anthropocentric approaches. Its impact on the natural environment is ever growing and, unfortunately, not yet fully assessed. In general terms, environmental impacts of APLs can roughly be categorized as direct or indirect:

- *Direct.* By direct environmental impact I refer to those effects, alterations, and disruptions caused to the natural environment and/or its components at the moment and specific location of the blast of a landmine.
- *Indirect.* Indirect environmental impact of landmines are those effects, alterations, and disruptions that may take place at differentiated spatial and temporal schemes from an original location or explosion of a landmine.

From a temporal spectrum, indirect impacts may be continuous and/or delayed at a short, medium or long term. By continuous impacts I refer to those landmine-related physical-chemical effects that degrade, pollute, or transform in any ecologically sensitive perspective those environmental elements interacting with the device. That is, decomposition or corrosion of the landmine's case may produce a prolonged leaking of toxic heavy metals, such as mercury and lead, typically present in a landmine. Delayed impacts are those negatively affecting the environment and its components at a later time in a single, recognizable event. That is, certain methods of mine clearance may produce such impacts.

Short-term effects generally include the physical destruction of close range vegetation and killing/injuring of wildlife. Medium-term impacts may include deterioration of soil composition, preventing cultivation lands to return to levels of agricultural production prior to a landmine explosion. Long-term impacts include the persistence and bioaccumulation of certain toxic substances freed into the site of the blast, such as mercury and lead, both present on most landmines. It is open to discussion how to classify impacts that are especially difficult to assess and quantify. A probable influence on global warming by depletion and enhanced human pressure over natural carbon dioxide sinks as forests present an enormous task for scientists. As entire populations may not be able to return to their villages or cultivation lands, on occasion they are forced to find new land to settle. To better comprehend the issue, let us remember some basic principles of environmentalism: First, nature knows best; second, everything must go somewhere; and third, but not least, everything is connected to everything else. Therefore, even if such impact on global warming is minimal, thinking about it helps us to understand the effects of armed conflict on nature. When considering the wide array of environmental impacts it can be said that "landmines may be the most widespread, lethal, and long-lasting form of pollution we have yet encountered."[15]

Landmines in Africa

Since World War II, landmines have been extensively used in Africa during armed conflict. Wars of national liberation in southern Africa during the last quarter of the twentieth century left millions of landmines and other UXO, condemning future generations to suffer the burden of such insidious high-explosive devices. Intergenerational responsibility was not taken into consideration whatsoever. Although many regions of the world are heavily mined, "[i]t is generally accepted that Africa is the most heavily mined continent. Severely affected countries include Angola, Mozambique, Somalia (and Somaliland), Sudan, Eritrea, and Ethiopia. Others include Zimbabwe, Rwanda, Zambia, Chad, Namibia, Burundi, Uganda, DR Congo, Mauritania, Sierra Leone, Liberia, Senegal, Guinea-Bissau, Congo-Brazzaville, Djibouti, Malawi, Niger, South Africa and Swaziland."[16] Going into deeper detail, "Southern Africa is probably the most heavily mined region in the world, with Mozambique and Angola listed by the United Nations as among the most mine-contaminated countries.[17] According to Noel Stott, from the South African Campaign to Ban Landmines, "an estimated 20 million mines lie buried in the soils of southern Africa, many unmapped and unmarked."[18] Landmines were widely used by most factions to conflicts in both Angola and Mozambique. As mentioned above, reports of continued use of landmines in Angola, a signatory to the 1997 Mine Ban Treaty, darkens the hopes to universally ban the weapon in the region. For Alex Vines, a specialist on humanitarian demining in the region, "Southern Africa is the most mine affected region in the world."[19]

Social/Economic Dimensions of the Problem

Social and economic consequences of landmines are tremendous. They impose a multidimensional burden on the countries affected by landmines. In the words of UN Secretary-General Kofi Annan, "Not only do these abominable weapons lie buried in silence and in their millions, waiting to kill or maim innocent women and children; but the presence—or even the fear of the presence—of a single landmine can prevent the cultivation of an entire field, rob a village of its livelihood, place yet another obstacle on a country's road to reconstruction and development."[20] In many mine-infested countries, the return to a peaceful way of living faces tremendous challenges. Humanitarian demining costs are elevated and in most cases drain vital funds from other badly needed investments for reconstruction. As well, large surfaces of land cannot be cultivated. According to a report from the U.S. Department of State, "A more relevant measure of the problem, however, is not the number of landmines per country, but the number of square kilometers of productive land rendered unusable by the presence or suspected presence of landmines or other unexploded ordnance (UXO)."[21] In Libya, it is estimated that about 8.49 percent of its arable land is contaminated by landmines.[22] A larger surface may not be cultivated solely because of fear of landmines.

In other spheres, landmines are, in most cases, laid near vital infrastructure installations such as bridges, electrical towers, water and sewage treatment plants, hospitals, and roads. Unless landmines are removed and destroyed from all these sites, they "will pose huge ancillary social costs; create vast numbers of internally displaced persons (IDPs); impede economic recovery, prolonging the need for international assistance: prevent the delivery of government services; serve as physical obstacles to unity and reconstruction; create conditions for the spread of disease, as well as inflicting injuries, ending lives; and encourage continued militarization of post-conflict societies."[23] Therefore, uncleared landmines may affect pacification efforts and compromise the environmental and food security of mine-affected countries. Policymakers for funding of humanitarian demining assistance should, accordingly, consider at least the above-mentioned factors while deciding how to allocate funds in postconflict master recovery planning. Poor decision making may in fact prove disastrous and counterproductive in determined scenarios. As well, environmental and human settlements assessments may serve "as a management tool for the international community as an integrated part of the needs assessment requirements in the overall emergency humanitarian effort in war-torn areas."[24] A report of the First Meeting of the Standing Committee of Experts on Mine Clearance of the 1997 Mine Ban Treaty recognized that "simple measures of effectiveness of clearance—such as numbers of mines removed or destroyed, or the area of land cleared—had their uses but do not provide adequate measures of benefit to the communities affected or of impact on development. Hence there is a need for socio-economic indicators, which shall include humanitarian and environmental concerns."[25]

Landmines, Biodiversity, and Natural Protected Areas

In certain cases, "there is a repetitive geographical coincidence between mine-affected zones and biodiversity hotspots. Such coincidence is acutely present in diverse regions of the planet."[26] By degrading habitats, impacting population species, altering the food chain, and placing additional pressure on biodiversity hotspots, landmines pose a considerable risk to pristine ecosystems throughout the world. To make things worse, valuable income from wildlife tourism has been deteriorated as many natural protected areas, including national parks, are contaminated with landmines. The danger of landmines may extend to tourists as well. In Africa such incidence is strong, as shown in table 15.1.

Landmines have taken a deadly toll on biodiversity in Africa as well as other places of the planet (see table 15.2). Numerous wildlife and domestic animals casualties have been reported. Considering the difficulties to properly assess the exact number of fauna killed or maimed by landmines, it is not adventurous to consider those figures as a fraction of the actual direct impact of landmines on biodiversity. Indirect impacts on wildlife are even harder to assess. From North to South, testimonies account for the killing and suffering of fauna. In Libya, for example, "[m]inefields have claimed the lives of an estimated 75,000 camels, 36,250 sheep, 12,500 goats and 1,250 cattle."[27] In southern Africa, the situation is delicate as the region is host to a wide spectrum of biodiversity. In Zimbabwe, according to Lieutenant Colonel Martin Rupiya, "every village near Chiredzi has lost at least one animal to land mines. . . . In the Gonarezhou National Park, elephants and buffaloes have had to be killed after they were injured by land mines."[28] In neighboring Mozambique, "[m]ines reportedly have killed more than 100 elephants."[29]

Another avenue for direct impact on wildlife may be the intentional use of landmines as a technique for poaching wildlife. Landmine poaching presents the ultimate distortion of this insidious weapon. It is used as a simple and effective mechanism for killing wildlife. Cases of landmine poaching of highly endangered species such as tigers have been reported in Burma and other Southeast Asia locations. A single bowl of tiger penis soup, an alleged aphrodisiac delicacy, may cost up to US$500 in Japan. Returning to Africa, "people of the village of Mulondo in southern Angola

Table 15.1. Landmines, Biodiversity, and Natural Protected Areas in Africa

Country and 1997 Mine Ban Treaty Status	Landmines Planted	Species Diversity	Species At Risk	Natural Protected Areas Surface (km²)	Natural Protected Areas Total	Natural Protected Areas Surface in Hectares
Algeria (S)	1,300,000+	3,976+	169	2,381,741	19	11,919,288
Angola (S)	10,000,000+	7,667+	62	1,246,700	6	2,641,200
Chad (P)	50,000+	?	28	1,284,640	9	11,494,000
Egypt (NS)	23,000,000	2,776+	115	1,001,449	12	793,200
Ethiopia (S)	500,000+	8,707+	194	1,103,341	23	6,022,600
Liberia (P)	18,250	3,177+	33	111,370	1	129,230
Mauritania (S)	10,000+	?	19	1,029,920	4	1,746,000
Morocco (NS)	200,000	4,831+	221	409,200	10	362,120
Mozambique (P)	3,000,000	6,835+	125	798,800	1	2,000
Namibia (P)	50,000	4,097+	49	823,146	12	10,217,777
Rwanda (S)	100,000+	3,134+	22	26,338	2	327,000
Senegal (P)	?	2,962+	52	196,840	10	2,180,709
Somalia (NS)	1,000,000+	4,568+	80	637,140	1	180,000
South Africa (P)	?	24,945+	1,176	1,221,042	237	6,928,258
Sudan (S)	1,000,000+	4,399+	37	2,505,813	16	9,382,500
Zimbabwe (P)	2,200,000+	5,838	112	390,600	25	3,067,823

(P) = party; (S) = signatory; (NS) = nonsignatory

Sources: Data collected from World Conservation Monitoring Centre, *Biodiversity Data Sourcebook* (London: World Conservation Press 1994); International Campaign to Ban Landmines, *Landmine Monitor Report 1999*, May 1999, available at: http://www.icbl. org/lm/1999.

198

Table 15.2. Other Regions of the World

Country and 1997 Mine Ban Treaty Status	Landmines Planted	Species			Natural Protected Areas	
		Diversity	At Risk	Surface (km²)	Total	Surface in Hectares
ASIA						
Afghanistan (NS)	5,000,000+	5,076+	28	647,497	6	218,438
Cambodia (P)	10,000,000+	?	53	181,035	?	?
China (NS)	4,000,000+	53,258	509	9,596,961	463	58,066,563
Korea, Rep. of (NS)	1,000,000+	3,712+	94	98,488	28	693,798
Russia (NS)	540,000+	?	221	17,075,400	199	65,536,759
Sri Lanka (NS)	25,000+	4,968+	485	65,610	56	795,953
Thailand (P)	100,000+	13,810+	475	513,115	111	7,020,276
Vietnam (NS)	3,500,000+	9,494+	434	329,565	59	1,329,788
EUROPE						
Albania (P)	215,000+	3,473	69	28,748	11	34,000
CENTRAL AMERICA						
Costa Rica (P)	5,000+	14,630	492	51,022	29	638,564
Cuba (NS)	70,000+	10,295	847	114,524	53	892,757
Nicaragua (P)	70,000+	8,850	94	148,000	59	903,450
Panama (P)	5,000+	12,775	590	77,046	15	1,326,332
SOUTH AMERICA						
Bolivia (P)	80,000+	23,666	102	1,098,579	25	9,233,019
Colombia (S)	?	55,943+	477	1,138,914	79	9,358,011
Ecuador (P)	100,000+	26,705	487	283,561	15	11,113,893

(P) = party; (S) = signatory; (NS) = nonsignatory

Sources: Data collected from World Conservation Monitoring Centre, *Biodiversity Data Sourcebook* (London: World Conservation Press 1994); International Campaign to Ban Landmines, *Landmine Monitor Report 1999*, May 1999, available at: http://www.icbl. org/lm/1999.

took anti-tank mines from a mine-belt surrounding their village and planted them into the traditional elephant migration paths of the Mupa National Park. As elephants flee strictly straight ahead, the whole herd was massacred here."[30] There are as well unconfirmed reports of UNITA rebels use of landmines to kill elephants to procure their valuable ivory tusks to buy weapons.

From another perspective, it is necessary to reflect on the impact of landmines on domestic species. In impoverished, less-developed countries of Africa to own cattle means much as they serve many cultural, social, and economic values. Losing a cow means much more than losing a source of protein.

Landmines and Natural Protected Areas Management

To effectively manage a declared natural protected area is a difficult task under any circumstances. To do so in some mine-infested African regions has been proven extremely difficult at present conditions. The presence, or suspected presence, of landmines represents an obstacle to achieve in-situ conservation goals, as expressed in article 8 of the 1992 UN Convention on Biological Diversity.[31] A number of African mine-affected countries have ratified the convention, for example, Angola, Mozambique, Ethiopia, Egypt, Zimbabwe, Sudan, Eritrea, Rwanda, Senegal, and the Democratic Republic of the Congo. Unfortunately, many natural protected areas have become, or worst, have always been, "paper parks," that is, natural protected areas that exist mostly in name only[32] and where effective management is minimal or nonexistent. Such a situation presents a complicated panorama for those worried about effective implementation of multilateral environmental agreements in developing and less-developed countries as "more often than not such paper parks are under threat or are already experiencing damage."[33]

How to implement international environmental law? How to enforce national environmental legislation on protected areas in countries undergoing present, or past, armed conflict? How to advance conservation goals where already short national and international funds tend to go to other urgently needed social necessities? War is a beast of many faces constantly threatening environmental conservation. For many, war is reality, while environmental conservation is an ideal. In Ethiopia, according to Dr. Tsegay Wolde-Georgis, "most of the fighting is done in areas that are strategic, such as mountains, rivers and forests. Unfortunately, these are also the areas where wildlife lives. When there is fighting all animals are confused, scared and leave the area. Most of them either migrate to neighboring countries or die in the new inhospitable environment."[34] In a number of cases, natural protected areas in Africa have been mined during conflict. In

Rwanda, "areas which are being demined are parts of the Kagera National Park currently being used to resettle thousands of returning refugees from Uganda who fled anti-Tutsi pogroms by the majority Hutu population in the early 1960s."[35]

In Mozambique, Scott Nathanson, a Disarmament Campaign organizer, writes that elephants in the Gorongoza national game park "have been maimed because of anti-personnel landmines or killed because of anti-tank mines."[36] As well, according to Alda Salomao:

> Large areas of the country were affected by the armed conflicts and one of the major problems in addressing the landmines issue is that there are no accurate records as to the exact locations were these mines were planted. If one considers that one of the largest national parks, the "Parque da Gorongoza" was almost completely destroyed by military actions, it would not be unreasonable to conclude that it is possible that landmines were planted in the area. The animals that were protected in this park were indiscriminately hunted to feed the soldiers and mines might have been used for this purpose. This park is protected under the CITES convention and under the national legislation."[37]

Such a description of the situation in Mozambique illustrates how complex a task it is to restore, conserve, and manage natural protected areas affected by war and contaminated by landmines in the region. Mozambique's neighboring country suffers a similar situation:

> In Zimbabwe, . . . wildlife also suffer. The Hwange and Gonarezhou national game parks have reported many mine incidents involving wildlife and there have been several cases of buffalo wounded by landmines attacking people living near the game parks. Without fencing, there has been considerable triggering of mines in remote areas by game animals. Many hundreds of elephants were killed towards the end of the Rhodesian war by mines. An elephant would wander into the minefield and initiate an explosion, and once wounded it would stagger into other mines, setting off further explosions."[38]

Adding to the already tragic incidental killing of elephants by the hundreds, reportedly, landmines have been used by poachers to purposely kill elephants in Mupa National Park in Angola.[39] Sometimes in an effort to procure their valuable ivory tusks to buy new weapons.[40]

Even plans to improve transboundary parks have been negatively influenced by landmines in southern Africa. Fortunately, recent announcements have indicated the formal intention of Mozambique, South Africa, and Zimbabwe "to consolidate plans for what could become the biggest Transfrontier Conservation Area in the world. . . . The newly protected area will encompass roughly 100,000 square kilometers."[41] One of the objectives of the transfrontier project is to clear minefields spread around those areas.[42] According to a UN report, "Wildlife is threatened by mines because the planned Mozambican extension to the Kruger Park requires mine clearance. Elephants have been found maimed by AP [anitpersonnel] mines and killed by AT [antitank] mines."[43]

Landmines and Soil Pollution

Being planted on the surface of the land, or just beneath its surface, landmines most direct impact is to soil quality and composition. Soil may be affected by the explosion of the weapon or by leaking of toxic substances after a period of time in which it is affected by corrosion if it is made of metals, or by decomposition if it is made of wood or other degradable materials.

> Any of the three varieties of high-explosive weapons (blast, fragmentation, or general purpose) may be extremely dangerous (fatal) for soldiers and/or civilians and may also cause local disturbance of soil. The fragmentation effects can be more severe in some ecosystems than in others, especially in forests where fragments implanted in trees could open a way to invasion of micro-organisms. After a prolonged period, consequences of the corrosion of fragments and the release of various alloying elements, such as iron, manganese, chromium, zinc, copper, etc., start to show. Mercury is also appearing as pollutant after utilization of high-explosive weapons. In agricultural regions the toxic elements can easily penetrate the human food chain.[44]

Therefore, as toxic elements penetrate the soil, processes of bioaccumulation may start and reach humans in one way or another. As well, those toxins may rise to the atmosphere and travel long distances, finally polluting other habitats in distant regions of the world. This process of long-distance transboundary pollution of chemicals leaked by landmines has not been studied in detail. Again, it is necessary to produce accurate data on the amount of toxins released by landmines.

Landmines and Water Pollution

It is generally accepted that the use of landmines has been concentrated not only on the battlefield, but also in and around civilian populations and basic infrastructure. Sewage and water treatment facilities have been targeted in many African locations. As well, unconfirmed reports of use of landmines as a method for fishing in places such as the Tanganika Lake in Tanzania may suggest that such a technique could be in use elsewhere, polluting water with heavy metals and possibly altering chemical composition of sediments. Additionally, landmines may be removed from their original locations by heavy rain, floods, and other meteorological phenomena, traveling downstream to more stable bodies of water such as lagoons, lakes, and estuarine ecosystems.

Other Impacts

Landmines may cause a number of unregistered impacts on the environment and its components. Most of the reports on wildlife impacted by landmines tend to focus on certain charismatic species, that is, tigers, elephants, and camels. It would be a sensible gap not to give proper attention to other lesser-known species that may play a fundamental role on the food chain in a given habitat. By altering these populations, the existing equilibrium of these species and their habitats may be placed under additional pressure.[45]

An issue of controversy is the use of dogs and other animals for detecting landmines. Animal rights organizations have protested against the use of dogs for mine detection as they consider such practice cruel. According to Stephen Wells, "the Animal Legal Defense Fund strongly opposes the use of dogs to detect and explode mines. . . . Animals have no place in human wars."[46] On the other hand, some favor the use of dogs because of their accuracy and reliability. According to a Norwegian humanitarian deminer, "[D]ogs will be trained to detect mines left over from Angola's civil war because they are more efficient, faster and less expensive than electronic detectors."[47] In any case, animals are affected, either as intentional or incidental victims of landmines. As well, other species have been trained to conduct mine detection such as bees or, more recently, rats. On the other side, a more informal detection technique has been used in some mine-infested areas where humanitarian demining has not been conducted. Having to deal with landmines on their own, displaced villagers have used domestic animals such as pigs, sheep, or cattle as living, untrained detectors as the only alternative to return to farms, villages, and cultivation lands after conflict. The cost of such practice is significant because detection may equal the killing of the animal.

Final Policy Recommendations

My first and overall recommendation resides on the need for a global environmental impact assessment of landmines, Africa being the first region to be assessed. Be it for assessing its impact on wildlife or to evaluate atmospheric emissions by destruction of stockpiles, environmental impact assessments are essential to advance humanitarian demining in Africa and elsewhere as a prerequisite for redevelopment after war.

Second, specific attention should be paid to the advances of the Study on the Use of Socio-Economic Analysis in Planning and Evaluating Mine Action Programmes undertaken by the Geneva International Centre for Humanitarian Demining.[48] As it is to include environmental indicators, environmentalists should try to participate at every level possible in the development and follow-up of such study as it will serve as a cornerstone for humanitarian demining policymakers in the aftermath of the Second Meeting of the State Parties to the 1997 Mine Ban Treaty held in Geneva on September 2000.

Third, in countries where the 1997 Mine Ban Treaty has not been signed or ratified, it may prove effective to follow a strategy consisting of distributing this and other publications on environmental impacts of landmines to national environmental organizations in order to get them on board for advocacy goals for signature, ratification, and/or effective implementation of the 1997 Mine Ban Treaty. By doing so, environmental organizations may become part of national campaigns and use their influence to advance the goal of the universal ban of landmines.

Notes

1. The 1997 Mine Ban Treaty was opened for signature on December 3, 1997, and entered into force on March 1, 1999.

2. Ibid.

3. Geoffrey Best, *War and Law since 1945* (New York: Oxford University Press, 1994), 299.

4. Maxwell A. Cameron, Robert J. Lawson, and Brian W. Tomlin, "To Walk without Fear," in *To Walk without Fear: The Global Movement to Ban Landmines*, ed. Maxwell A. Cameron, Robert J. Lawson, and Brian W. Tomlin (Oxford: Oxford University Press, 1998), 5.

5. Interview with Philip Weller, December 3, 1999, regarding his "Landmines and the Environment." Weller is director for WWF's Danube Carpathian Programme and head of WWF's scientific delegation to assess environmental impacts of war in Yugoslavia. He can be reached by e-mail at Philip.Weller@wwf.at.

6. Boutros Boutros-Ghali, "The Land Mine Crisis: A Humanitarian Disaster," *Foreign Affairs* 8 (September/October 1994), 9.

7. International Campaign to Ban Landmines, *Landmine Monitor Report 1999*, May 1999, available at http://www.icbl.org/lm/1999/.

8. The Arms Project of Human Rights Watch and Physicians for Human Rights, *Landmines: A Deadly Legacy* (New York: Human Rights Watch and Physicians for Human Rights, 1993), 251.

9. Alioune Tine, "Landmines in Casamance: Against the March of History," *African Topics* 23–24 (May–July 1998), 22.

10. Cameron, Lawson, and Tomlin, "To Walk without Fear," 4.

11. International Committee of the Red Cross, *Landmines Must Be Stopped* (Geneva: ICRC, May 1998), 16.

12. See http://www.pgs.ca/pages/lm/stfoster.html.

13. See Anna Richardson, "War-Ravaged Angola Looks for Missing Wildlife," *Reuters,* Luanda, April 29 1998 (see http://members.aol.com/adrcnet/marmamnews/98042901.html).

14. International Campaign To Ban Landmines (ICBL), "Nations Refusing to Ban Landmines Meet Again," ICBL Press Release, Geneva, December 14, 1999, 3.

15. *Statement of the United Nations Secretary-General.* Assistance in Mine Clearance, 49th session, item 22 of the agenda A/49/357, September 6, 1994, 2.

16. ICBL., "Executive Summary," *Landmine Monitor 1999*, available at http://www.icbl.org/lm/1999/english/exec/Execweb1-06.htm#P787_110915.

17. Kristian Harpviken, "Landmines in Southern Africa: Regional Initiatives for Clearance and Control," *Contemporary Security Policy* 18, no.1 (April 1997). Cited in Cameron, Lawson, and Tomlin, *To Walk without Fear* (see note 4), 68, note 1.

18. Noel Stott, "The South African Campaign," in Cameron, Lawson, and Tomlin, *To Walk without Fear* (see note 4), 68.

19. Alex Vines, "The Crisis of Anti-Personnel Landmines," in Cameron, Lawson, and Tomlin, *To Walk without Fear* (see note 4), 125.

20. United Nations, *A Review of United Nations Activities in Mine Action* (New York: United Nations, April 1999), 3.

21. U.S. Department of State, *Hidden Killers: The Global Landmine Crisis* (Washington, DC: U.S. Department of State, Bureau of Political–Military Affairs, Office of Humanitarian Demining Programs, September 1998), 5.

22. A. H. Westing, SIPRI, and UNEP, "Appendix 8: Explosive Remnants of Conventional War: A Report to UNEP," in *Explosive Remnants of War: Mitigating the Environmental Effects*, ed. A. H. Westing, SIPRI, and UNEP, 117–136. (London: Taylor and Francis, 1985).

23. U.S. Department of State, *Hidden Killers*, 9.

24. Klaus Töpfer, Foreword to *The Kosovo Conflict: Consequences for the Environment and Human Settlements* (Geneva: UNEP–UNCHS, 1999), 3.

25. *Report of the First Meeting of the Standing Committee of Experts on Mine Clearance*, Summary and Action Points (Geneva: Geneva International Centre for Humanitarian Demining, September 13–15, 1999), 5.

26. Claudio Torres Nachón, "Environmental Aspects of the International Landmine Crisis and the 1997 Ottawa Convention" (an introduction to the Global Project on Environmental Aspects of Landmines of the Center for Environmental Law and Economic Integration of the South, A.C.), *DASSUR-Mexico 1999*, available at http://members.xoom.com/dassur/envir.html.

27. See http://www.un.org/Depts/Landmine/country/libyanar.htm.

28. See Adam M. Roberts et al., *Landmines: Animal Casualties of the Underground War*, available at http://fn2.freenet.edmonton.ab.ca/~puppydog/aa-art.htm.

29. Ibid.

30. See http://www.mgm.org/.

31. Convention on Biological Diversity, UN Document DPI/130/7, June 2, 1992, reprinted in 31 I.L.M. 818 (1992).

32. See Nigel Dudley et al., "Effectiveness of Forest Protected Areas" (paper presented at the IFF intersessional meeting on forest protected areas, San Juan, Puerto Rico, March 15–19, 1999).

33. Ibid., 1.

34. Interview with Dr. Tsegay Wolde-Georgis regarding his "Landmines," at the Ethiopian Embassy in the United States, November 29, 1999. Wolde-Georgis can be reached by e-mail at tsegay@Tidalwave.net.

35. *UN Country Report: Rwanda*, available at http://www.un.org/Depts/Landmine/country/rwanda.htm.

36. Scott Nathanson, quoted in Roberts, *Landmines: Animal Casualties of the Underground War*.

37. Interview with Alda Salomao regarding her "Environmental Impact of Landmines in Mozambique," November 16, 1999. Ms. Salomao is presently conducting graduate studies on international environmental law at the Washington College of Law, The American University in Washington, DC. She can be reached by e-mail at aldadriano@aol.com.

38. Human Rights Watch, "Still Killing: Landmines in Southern Africa," cited in Cameron, Lawson, and Tomlin, *To Walk without Fear* (see note 4), 130, note 43.

39. "Hunted Elephants," Dumbo Internet page of MGM Stiftung Menschen gegen Minen Web site (includes photograph): http://www.dsk.de/mgm; cited in Cameron, Lawson, and Tomlin, *To Walk without Fear* (see note 4), 130, note 45.

40. See *Report of the First Meeting of the Standing Committee of Experts on Mine Clearance*, 5.

41. See Environmental News Service, *World's Largest Transborder Conservation Area*, available at http://ens.lycos.com/ens/may2000/2000L-05-05-02.html.

42. Ibid.

43. See http://www.un.org/Depts/Landmine/country/mozambiq.htm.

44. Z. Orehovec, S. Music, L. Palinkas, S. Miko, M. Ristic, and S. Bokan, "Danger of Land Mines, Unexploded Shells, and Environmental Consequences of the Recent War on the Territory of the Republic of Croatia" (paper presented at the First International Conference on Addressing Environmental Consequences of War, Washington, DC, June 10–12, 1998), 1.

45. *Report of the First Meeting of the Standing Committee of Experts on Mine Clearance*, 5.

46. Interview with Stephen Wells regarding his "Landmines and Dogs," January 10, 2000. Wells is the director of education of the Animal Legal Defense Fund. He can be reached by e-mail at info@aldf.org.

47. See http://www.un.org/Depts/Landmine/country/angola.htm.

48. See the "Terms of Reference" for the study on the Geneva International Centre for Humanitarian Demining Web site at http://gichd.ch/docs/studies/index.htm.

16

A Necessary Evil?:
Reexamining the Military Utility
of Antipersonnel Landmines

TED GAULIN

Be on your guard against the capital fault of letting diplomacy get
ahead of military preparedness.

> —Sir Winston Churchill, "Letter to Sir Samuel Hoare,
> 25 August 1935"

Anti-personnel landmines as used by American forces . . . are not
only entirely legitimate and valuable weapons. They are weapons
that are absolutely essential to the way we fight and our ability to do
so successfully.

> —General Raymond Davis, Testimony before the Senate
> Foreign Relations Committee, February 3, 1998

Everything that is shot or thrown at you or dropped on you in war is
most unpleasant but, of all horrible devices, the most terrifying . . . is
the land mine.

> —Field Marshall Sir William Slim, *Unofficial History*

SOMEWHERE ON A DUSTY DESERT BATTLEFIELD A MOTORIZED INFANTRY BRIGADE
rumbled toward its objective. Its mission was to seize a key piece of
terrain from a smaller and considerably less modernized unit. Before
the battle, the brigade had used its sophisticated intelligence-gathering

assets to analyze the terrain and determine the location of the defender's tactical obstacles. Yet, this information proved of little use, for when the brigade advanced on the defender, its attack immediately faltered. It had great difficulty breaching enemy obstacles and succeeded only after a long delay and only after suffering heavy casualties. What obstacles had the defender arrayed? In some areas, nothing more than barbed wire and landmines. But these humble obstacles were enough to temporarily halt and seriously damage the U.S. Army's most advanced combat unit: Task Force 21.[1]

This battle took place in the Mohave Desert at the U.S. Army's National Training Center in 1997. It was part of the army's Advanced Warfighting Experiment, an exercise designed to assess future combat capabilities. While the difficulty encountered by the army's "brigade of the future" surprised some observers, the event actually underscored a trend long seen at army training centers, namely, that maneuver units often have difficulty in overcoming relatively low-tech countermeasures such as landmines.[2]

These events would have been less surprising to the military historian, who would know that concealed traps and victim-activated devices have been used to great advantage throughout history. In 52 B.C. for example, the Roman army was able to defeat a Gaulic force more than five times its size by fortifying its position with goads, caltrops, and other primitive landmines.[3]

Taken at face value these examples—one from an ancient battlefield, the other from tomorrow's—suggest that recent claims about the nonexistent or "marginal" military advantage offered by landmines may need to be reassessed.[4] But there are also other reasons for such a reappraisal. First, the overwhelming majority of active and retired military leaders in the United States have argued that these weapons are an important military asset.[5] Indeed, even those military officers who appear to have advocated a ban on this weapon have since clarified their positions, stating that there are some situations in which antipersonnel landmines are required, and that there are types of antipersonnel landmines that should be retained.[6] This outspoken unanimity is virtually unprecedented in the military community and can hardly be dismissed as an example of a habit-bound bureaucracy clinging to an outmoded weapon.

Second, American military officials are not alone. Most of the more than fifty other states that have not signed the Ottawa Treaty have also identified military security issues as the primary reason. This includes democracies as well as nondemocracies, and major military powers as well as those with few military assets.[7] This is even the case with countries that have experienced firsthand the residual effects of landmines—countries like Egypt, Finland, and Kuwait.[8] The position of these states suggests that antipersonnel landmines make an important contribution to military security.

Third, an extensive study of alternatives to antipersonnel landmines conducted by the U.S. National Research Council found that there are no existing weapons (and none likely to be available in the near future) that perform all of the functions currently performed by antipersonnel landmines.[9] If these weapons were truly of "dubious military utility,"[10] as some have asserted, they would be quite easily replaced.

With the foregoing in mind, this chapter undertakes a reevaluation of the military utility of antipersonnel landmines, with particular attention to the U.S. policy position. This chapter begins by describing the function of antipersonnel landmines on the battlefield. The next sections highlight the material and psychological contributions that antipersonnel landmines have played in combat over the past half century. Next, I look at the role of antipersonnel landmines in South Korea—since the security situation in Korea is intimately linked with the U.S. policy position. The chapter concludes by considering the likely utility of antipersonnel landmines to future war-fighting scenarios.

The Tactical Use of Landmines

Antipersonnel landmines serve a number of key functions on the battlefield, most of which are related to defensive operations. In the latter context, landmines channel enemy forces into specific areas where they are more vulnerable to direct and indirect fire. Landmines also protect friendly flanks—an area that strategists and tacticians have long considered the weakest point of defense. In both of these capacities, landmines provide advance warning of an attack and degrade an enemy advance through delays and by causing direct casualties, thus enhancing the effectiveness of other weapons. One detailed study concluded that landmines improve the effectiveness of other defensive weapons by a factor of up to 2.5.[11] Antipersonnel landmines are also critical to defensive operations in that they protect antitank mines from being disabled or quickly breached by enemy forces.

Recent developments in mine technology have allowed antipersonnel landmines to be used in support of offensive operations as well. Specifically, remotely delivered landmines can aid an attacking force by sealing off the escape routes of a retreating enemy. While less prevalent than defensive uses of landmines, this deep interdiction approach has been used with good effect in recent combat situations.

One high-profile report has concluded that landmines used in support of both offensive and defensive operations offer little military utility.

This finding is based on two specious conclusions: that antipersonnel landmines have never been decisive in war; and that they merely delay an enemy advance rather than stopping one.[12] Before describing when and how landmines have historically mattered, these conclusions merit brief consideration. First, it is doubtful that any single weapon—save perhaps the atomic bomb—has been decisive in war. The machine gun, for example, a weapon that so profoundly shaped World War I, was not decisive in the outcome of that war. Similar arguments could be made about broader categories of weapons. Air power, for example, was not decisive in World War II, Korea, or Vietnam and it is questionable whether it was decisive in the Persian Gulf.[13] Victory in war is based on a number of materiel, tactical, and strategic factors. To say that a single weapon has little utility because it has never been decisive in combat is intellectually deceptive.

Second, the assertion that landmines merely delay an enemy advance neglects the fundamental importance of timing on the battlefield.[14] It neglects the fact that delays, even short delays, have often had significant consequences. Three examples from three different eras illustrate this point. In May 1940, a series of small defensive battles staged by the British Expeditionary Force and elements of the French army in the villages of northern France over the course of a few days effectively delayed the advancing German army and bought time for the allies to organize an evacuation at the French port of Dunkirk. This evacuation saved the British army and is considered by many historians a crucial turning point in the war.[15] In the American Civil War, a one-day holding action by the Union Army's 1st Cavalry Division on the first day of the Battle of Gettysburg prevented a Confederate advance on the town and allowed time for Union reinforcements to arrive. Historian Stephen Starr suggests that this single action became the basis of a Union victory in this important battle.[16] Most dramatically, perhaps, during the Napoleonic Wars, a delay of the French army's attack by a matter of hours is said to have caused Napoléon's defeat at the Battle of Waterloo.[17]

In light of the foregoing, it would appear that to the extent landmines merely delay an enemy advance, they are in fact performing a vital military function. One of the chief ways that antipersonnel landmines enter into this calculus is the sense of fear they arouse among soldiers. Landmines act, according to one scholar, as a sort of "psychological warhead."[18] This notion is explored further in the next section.

The Psychological Effects of Landmines

In addition to directly delaying or degrading an enemy advance, the psychological effect of antipersonnel landmines is another important aspect of their military utility. In particular, landmines, which lie quietly waiting to exact their toll, arouse a grave sense of fear among soldiers. Indeed, they appear to be one of the most feared hazards of war. Consider this account by an American infantryman approaching the heavily mined Siegfried Line in World War II:

> By now I had gone through aerial bombing, artillery and mortar shelling, open combat, direct rifle and machine gun firing, night patrolling and ambush. Against all of these we had some kind of chance; against landmines we had none. The only defense was not to move at all.[19]

Another soldier fighting on the western front echoed a similar sentiment: "Nothing was more feared than mines, they were insidious, treacherous things hiding in deep grass and in the earth."[20] So great was the fear of landmines during World War II that some Allied soldiers preferred to remain standing under German artillery fire rather than ducking for cover and risk laying on a landmine.[21] This dread of landmines was also present among Allied soldiers that landed on D-Day. Historian Stephen Ambrose describes how an entire regiment came to a halt on Omaha Beach for several hours when a rumor spread among the troops that the Germans had deployed landmines that were undetectable.[22]

This psychological effect of landmines has been documented in scientific studies as well. Eugenia Kolasinski, for example, interviewed soldiers who had encountered landmines in situations other than training and found that this grave fear arises from the type of injury that antipersonnel landmines inflict, the certainty of being injured if the landmine detonates and the inability to fight back against mines—all attributes unique to this weapon system.[23]

This strong fear caused by landmines was in evidence during the Persian Gulf War. In a survey of forty-five newspaper articles published during Operation Desert Shield that considered the prospects for an Allied ground offensive, all but three identified Iraqi landmines as a serious hindrance to success. These minefields were variously described as "buried terror," "a perilous gantlet," and "death traps" and often linked to high Allied casualty estimates.[24] This acute concern with the threat posed by Iraqi minefields was not confined to the press and the public. In planning the Allied ground assault, American military leaders General Colin Powell, General Norman Schwarzkopf, and Secretary of Defense Richard Cheney decided against an amphibious assault on Kuwait precisely because of the preponderance of Iraqi landmines both in the water and on the beach.[25] There was widespread concern about enemy landmines at lower echelons as well where maneuver units spent literally thousands of hours conducting landmine training and breaching drills.[26]

The Soviet army was also apparently intimidated by antipersonnel landmines, for throughout the Cold War it identified Western mine-delivery and mine-emplacing equipment as one of the few targets that reconnaissance patrols were directed to attack, despite the risk of compromising their location.[27]

The psychological aspects of warfare are hardly new. Military thinkers like Napoléon, for example, understood that victory comes as much from upsetting the enemy's psychological outlook as through degrading his physical capability. In a contemporary context, antipersonnel landmines appear to provide an important tool for upsetting this disposition. By striking fear into the hearts of field commanders and soldiers these weapons undermine enemy morale and the cohesion of the command process. In some cases, they may even be a source of deterrence. Government officials in Latvia—a country with a long history of invasion and occupation—no doubt had this in mind when they referred to antipersonnel landmines as providing "psychological security" against potential aggressors.[28] Leaders in South Korea have made similar statements, arguing that antipersonnel landmines strongly discourage invasion from the north.[29] Since the political and military situation on the Korean peninsula is integral to U.S. policy on antipersonnel landmines, it is important to examine the military utility of landmines in this particular case.

The Value of Landmines in Korea

Much world attention has recently been drawn to the threat posed by North Korea. However, regional experts and military analysts have long been aware of the volatile situation on the Korean peninsula. Here, two countries face off against each other with the same apprehension and resolve as they did throughout the Cold War. Writing in the 1990s, one analyst called the Korea peninsula "the most dangerous place on earth"[30] and before the recent terrorist attacks on America, the U.S. Defense Intelligence Agency considered the threat posed by North Korea to be the country's primary security concern.[31] There are two characteristics of this confrontation that U.S. policymakers cite as reasons for retaining antipersonnel landmines: the formidable size and strength of the North Korean armed forces and the geography of the region.

North Korea has spent much of the past thirty years pouring 25 percent of their gross national product into building and maintaining a huge conventional military.[32] The result is that North Korea has the world's third largest army, with over one million active ground forces and nearly five million in the reserves. This massive force is arrayed against a combined South Korean and American force just over half its size—560,000 South Korean and 36,000 U.S. troops.[33] Equally important, much of the North's offensive capability is forward-deployed. Nearly 65 percent of its army units and 80 percent of its firepower are within seventy miles of the Demilitarized Zone (DMZ) that separates the two countries.[34] North Korea has been implementing an ambitious program to improve its ground-force posture even further.[35] Given their size, equipment, and morale, North Korea's armed forces are "considerably stronger than the Iraqi Republican Guard."[36]

A number of geographic factors are also relevant to the use of antipersonnel landmines in Korea. To begin with, Seoul, the capital of South Korea and the key objective of any North Korean invasion,[37] is only twenty-seven miles south of the DMZ. This presents defending forces with a distinct problem: what military strategists call a "shallow defensive zone." In practical terms, this means that very little ground can be ceded to the enemy before significant losses are incurred. To the 14 million residents of Seoul, the inability of the combined forces to defend this stretch of ground would be catastrophic. Another important geographic factor is the peninsula's mountainous landscape. This terrain restricts the movement of armored forces and would cause the North to employ dismounted infantry soldiers in any attack. The North, aware of this situation, is well prepared: more than seven-eighths of its army is composed of dismounted troops.[38]

While certainly not ensuring victory against North Korea, antipersonnel landmines help U.S. and South Korean forces cope with this strategic situation. First, antipersonnel landmines act as a force multiplier against the North's substantially larger forces. They do so by providing early warning of an enemy advance, by preventing the enemy from maneuvering freely along the front, and by producing direct casualties. Second, antipersonnel landmines, as part of an integrated barrier defense system, compensate for a lack of strategic depth by slowing an enemy advance and giving the combined forces a chance to mobilize and transition to a wartime posture. Third, antipersonnel landmines are absolutely essential to defense in Korea's rugged terrain. As previously stated, this terrain not only necessitates a dismounted assault but also gives a distinct advantage to the infantryman. According to one experienced observer, the opening stages of any future Korean conflict are likely to resemble the close-in fighting that characterized much of the last Korean War.[39] In this light, non-self-destructing antipersonnel landmines would provide critical force protection, defending friendly flanks against enemy maneuvers and preserving unit positions during close combat—just as they did for General Bernard Trainor's unit in 1952.[40] But the mixed landmine system (antipersonnel/antitank) would also be important as a North Korean dismounted assault would have the dual mission of penetrating and destroying defending forces, as well as clearing the valleys to make way for North Korean armored units.[41]

These observations are not purely theoretical: an extensive study by the Army Concepts and Analysis Agency found that a defense of Korea without landmines would increase allied personnel and weapons losses by 10 percent.[42] In raw numbers, such losses might amount to the death of 6,000 American troops and 50,000 South Korean troops.[43] The study concluded that risks associated with such a strategy were "unacceptable."[44] Importantly, the combat functions served by landmines in Korea are not easily replicated by other weapon systems. Two of the key drawbacks common to all landmine alternatives examined in the aforementioned National Research Council study, are that these potential substitutes cannot be used in close proximity to friendly forces and they are not effective against dismounted assaults.[45] In this respect, simply replacing antipersonnel landmines with more tactical air support, for example, is an option that involves considerable risk.

Of course, the foregoing analysis is based on the assumption that North Korea is still seriously contemplating an invasion of South Korea. This assumption seems well founded given the accounts of high-ranking North Korean defectors;[46] the offensive posture of its armed forces;[47] its frequent incursions into the DMZ;[48] its threats to withdraw from the 1953 armistice that suspended the Korean War;[49] and its declaration that preemption—that is, the ability to strike first—is not the sole prerogative of the United States.[50]

However, some analysts have questioned the North's interest in and ability to overrun the peninsula. Tony Ohe, for example, asserts that economic conditions in the North have deprived it of critical resources necessary to conduct offensive operations.[51] Since the North's offensive capabilities are implicated in any discussion of landmines, it is worth briefly considering this issue.

It is certainly true that North Korea has suffered severe economic setbacks with the loss of support from its Cold War allies, a serious famine and extensive fuel shortages. However, one must question the impact that such developments have had on its military readiness.[52] Pyongyang has pursued a strict "military-first" policy in which all of the country's resources—financial, technological, and material—are diverted to the armed forces.[53] This policy has allowed the North to stockpile a ninety-day war-fighting supply of oil.[54] It has also allowed the North to conduct more training exercises than in the past. And it has allowed them to upgrade their military hardware.[55] In fact, when asked to assess the readiness of North Korea's armed forces, the Combined Forces Command (CFC) commander General Thomas Schwartz declared that they are "bigger, better, closer and deadlier" than they have ever been.[56] These observations—by a man who is particularly well positioned to evaluate the North's capabilities—suggest that the United States and South Korea should underestimate the strength of North Korea's armed forces at their own peril. They also call into question the assertion that recent economic problems have deprived the North of offensive capabilities.

Whether the North will act on these capabilities is uncertain, what is more certain is that antipersonnel landmines contribute significantly to the defense of South Korea.[57] The North's capability of and doctrinal bias toward massive infantry attacks, the South's lack of strategic depth, and the peninsula's restrictive terrain create a situation in which defense is strongly enhanced by antipersonnel landmines. They act as a force multiplier and provide force protection. In the words of General John Tilelli, former commander in chief of the CFC and U.S. Forces Korea:

> [Antipersonnel landmines], both the non-self-destructing and self-destructing types, are absolutely vital to the success of UNC/CFC's mission to deter North Korean aggression and defend the Republic of Korea.[58]

Finally, the contribution of landmines to security on the Korean Peninsula may be even more critical given recent world developments. During 2003, the United States had to face the possibility of fighting two wars at the same time: Iraq and North Korea. In the case of a two-front war, the U.S. strategy would have been to defeat Iraq first and then shift its attention to North Korea.[59] Military experts such as Anthony Cordesman believe that this would make U.S. and South Korean forces fight with less manpower, firepower, and intelligence assets than strategists have planned for.[60] In these circumstances, the multiple functions performed by landmines—warning, delaying, force protection, and force multiplication—become even more crucial.

The Value of Landmines in the Post–Cold War Era

To recap the argument so far: landmines have been a very useful weapon in past military campaigns and they appear to contribute significantly to the defense of Korea. What role, if any, do they play beyond the thirty-eighth parallel? To answer this question requires consideration of the structure of American forces and the nature of the threat that these forces are likely to encounter in future war-fighting scenarios.

Since the close of the Cold War, there has been a substantial reorganization in the American military. To begin with, there has been a dramatic reduction in the force structure. The military is only two-thirds the size it was during the Cold War. Second, it has significantly fewer forward-deployed troops than in recent decades. As a result of the latter, U.S. military doctrine now emphasizes quick force projection—that is, the ability to rapidly deploy combat power to distant regions around the globe.

Both aspects of this post–Cold War reorganization create a situation that is well served by antipersonnel landmines. The effectiveness of a smaller army will be greatly enhanced by the economy of force attributes provided by antipersonnel landmines, allowing fewer forces to continue to defend large areas. In addition, the army's new force projection orientation means that many forces will be deployed without the traditional heavy assets to ensure their survival. Antipersonnel landmines can provide security for these forces, which may have to fight a considerably larger opponent during the initial phase of deployment.[61]

In the wake of 9/11, there has also been a considerable reorientation among defense analysts in terms of the nature of the threats our armed forces will be required to deal with. According to a number of experts, the need now is to cope with unconventional threats—so-called asymmetrical threats—in which we cannot expect to fight from large fixed bases. Dealing with these threats will involve small, autonomous ground forces operating in hostile areas.[62] Again, these light forces must be prepared to fight outnumbered and often without traditional protective assets like air support and artillery. In this tactical scenario, the passive defenses provided by landmines could be very important.

The lessons from Operation Enduring Freedom in Afghanistan are instructive in this regard. While the United States established large bases at Bagram and Kandahar, the key and most damaging assaults against Al Qaeda were conducted by special forces units operating out of forward bases in the Pakistani border region. These forces regularly employed self-deactivating landmines and mixed antitank systems to augment their defense.[63] Special operations forces working behind Iraqi lines used landmines in a similar capacity during the Persian Gulf War, and it appears likely that such force structures will play an important role in any U.S. attempt to disarm Iraq of weapons of mass destruction.[64]

Thus, to the extent that evolving and future military concepts involve small discrete units operating in hostile terrain or over a wide battlefield, landmines will continue to perform an important military function. How the United States reconciles the utility provided by these weapons—a utility not readily performed by other weapon systems—with some of the humanitarian concerns raised throughout this volume is beyond the scope of this chapter. Suffice it to say that justifying their prohibition to an increasingly casualty-sensitive society will be a serious challenge.

Notes

1. Daniel Krueger, "Obstacles to Maneuver," *Military Review* 79, no. 6 (1999): 5–11.

2. Ibid.

3. Mike Croll, *The History of Landmines* (Barnsley, UK: Leo Cooper, 1998), 1–5.

4. The U.S. Campaign to Ban Landmines recently stated that landmines have "no military value." See Ken Rutherford, "The Evolving Arms Control Agenda: Implications of the Role of NGOs in Banning Antipersonnel Landmines," *World Politics* 53, no. 1 (2000): 94. Richard Matthew and Ken Rutherford argue that they have a "marginal" military utility (see their "Banning Landmines in the American Century," *International Journal of World Peace* 16, no. 2 1999).

5. One example of this is a letter to the U.S. Senate dated July 10, 1997, signed by sixteen four-star generals, including every member of the Joint Chiefs of Staff and all of the regional Commanders in Chief. Another example of this is the letter to President Bill Clinton dated July 21, 1997, signed by twenty-four of the country's most respected retired military leaders.

6. General David Jones, chairman of the Joint Chiefs of Staff during the Carter administration, said that antipersonnel landmines were necessary to the defense of South Korea. See Philip Shenon, "Clinton to Act on Banning Many Types of Mines," *New York Times*, May 16, 1996. General Norman Schwarzkopf (Ret.), commander of Allied forces during the Gulf War, has suggested that self-destructing landmines are "a capability we can use." See Tom Bowman, "Tug of War over Landmine Issue," *Baltimore Sun*, September 8, 1997.

7. According to *Landmine Monitor 2000*, almost half of nonsignatory governments specifically identify security concerns as the primary reason for not signing the treaty. See Human Rights Watch, *Landmine Monitor Report 2000* (New York: Human Rights Watch, 2000).

8. Croll, *The History of Landmines*, 135.

9. National Research Council, *Alternative Technologies to Replace Antipersonnel Landmines* (Washington, DC: National Academy Press, 2001), 34.

10. Rutherford, "The Evolving Arms Control Agenda," 76.

11. C. E. Sloan, *Mine Warfare on Land* (London: Brassey's, 1986), 113.

12. International Committee of the Red Cross, *Anti-Personnel Landmines: Friend or Foe?*; available at http://www.icrc.org/ (accessed November 21, 2001).

13. With regard to airpower in the Persian Gulf War, see Daryl Press, "The Myth of Air Power in the Persian Gulf War and the Future of Warfare," *International Security* 26, no. 2 (2001): 5–44.

14. Military thinkers have long recognized this importance; in the words of prominent military analyst Basil Liddell Hart, "the time factor rules war." See his *Thoughts on War* (London: Faber and Faber, 1944), 62.

15. According to Walter Lord (*The Miracle of Dunkirk* [New York: Viking, 1982]), defending forces "took a merciless beating, but their sacrifice enabled two French divisions and untold numbers of the BEF to reach the coast" (72). For Dunkirk as a pivotal turning point in the war, see page 275.

16. Stephen Starr, *The Union Cavalry in the Civil War* (Baton Rouge: Louisiana State University Press, 1985), 422–430.

17. Christopher Hibbert, *Waterloo* (London: Wordsworth, 1998).

18. William Greer and James Bartholomew, *Psychological Aspects of Mine Warfare* (Alexandria, VA: U.S. Center for Naval Analysis, 1982).

19. Stephen Ambrose, *Citizen Soldiers*, cited in John Troxell, "Landmines: Why the Korea Exception Should Be the Rule," *Parameters* (Spring 2000), 94.

20. Charles Whiting, *Sigfried: The Nazis' Last Stand* (New York: Stein and Day, 1982), 119.

21. Ibid.

22. Stephen Ambrose, *D-Day* (New York: Simon and Schuster, 1994), 462.

23. Eugenia Kolaskinski, *The Psychological Effects of Anti-Personnel Landmines* (West Point, NY: U.S. Military Academy, 1999).

24. The survey data was gathered from thirteen major English-language newspapers with different political orientations. It includes all articles published between August 1990 and February 1991 dealing with the prospective ground war. The newspapers consulted include the *Boston Globe*, the *Christian Science Monitor*, the *Los Angeles Times*, the *New York Times*, *Newsday*, the *St. Petersburg Times*, the *Seattle Times*, the *St. Louis Post Dispatch*, *USA Today*, and the *Washington Post* in the United States; the *Independent* and the *Observer* in the United Kingdom; and the *Toronto Star* in Canada. It does not include the considerably fewer articles that evaluated the threat posed by naval mines.

25. James Blackwell, *Thunder in the Desert* (New York: Bantam Books, 1991), 175.

26. Reflecting the level of concern in society about Iraqi landmines, one such training session was beamed directly into the homes of millions of American television viewers during a commercial break of Super Bowl XXVI.

27. Richard Simpkin, *Race to the Swift* (London: Brassey's, 1985), 110.

28. Human Rights Watch, *Landmine Monitor 2000*, 830.

29. In the words of former South Korean Deputy Defense Minister Lieutenant General Park Yong, "[T]he use of landmines is a very effective way of deter-

ring war." See Nicholas Kristof, "South Korea Extols Some of the Benefits of Landmines," *New York Times*, September 3, 1997.

30. Joseph Galloway and Bruce Auster, "The Most Dangerous Place on Earth," *U.S. News and World Report*, June 20, 1994.

31. David Reese, *The Prospects for North Korea's Survival* (New York: Oxford University Press, 1998), 64.

32. Kongdan Oh and Ralph Hassig, *North Korea: Through the Looking Glass* (Washington, DC: Brookings Institution Press, 2000), 105.

33. U.S. Department of Defense, *2000 Report to Congress: The Military Situation on the Korean Peninsula* (Washington, DC: U.S. Department of Defense, September 12, 2000).

34. Reese, *The Prospects for North Korea's Survival*, 66.

35. Steven Bradner, "North Korea's Strategy," in *Planning for a Peaceful Korea*, ed. Henry Sokolski (Carlisle, PA: Strategic Studies Institute, 2001), 35.

36. Taeho Kim, "Korean Security in a Post–Cold War Northeast Asia," *American Defense Annual* (Washington, DC: Brassey's, 1996), 197.

37. Oh and Hassig, *North Korea*, 110–111.

38. Ibid.

39. Troxell, "Landmines," 93; see also Galloway and Auster, "The Most Dangerous Place on Earth," 41.

40. Bernard Trainor, "Landmines Saved My Life," *New York Times*, March 18, 1996.

41. Troxell, "Landmines," 93.

42. U.S. Army Concepts and Analysis Agency, *Anti-Personnel Landmine Study* (Bethesda, MD: U.S. Army Concepts and Analysis Agency, May 1997).

43. These figures are extrapolated from Reese, *The Prospects for North Korea's Survival*.

44. Information briefing on the *Anti-Personnel Landmine Study*, U.S. Army Concepts and Analysis Agency, May 12, 1997.

45. National Research Council, *Alternative Technologies*.

46. "Sound the Alarm: Defector Says North Korea Is Preparing for War," *Economist* 26 (April 1997), 34.

47. Oh and Hassig, *North Korea*, 109.

48. These incursions nearly brought the two sides to war in 1996, but they are not the only form of military provocation used by the Democratic People's Republic of North Korea. North Korean patrol boats and submarines have been known to enter South Korean territorial waters; North Korean fighter

planes have crossed into South Korean airspace; and North Korea has conducted a number of unannounced long-range ballistic missile tests over Japan.

49. Richard Lloyd Parry, "Korean Armistice in Jeopardy after 50 Years of Peace," *Times* (London), February 19, 2003.

50. Jonathan Watts, "North Korea Threatens US with First Strike," *Guardian* (London), February 6, 2003.

51. See J. Antonio Ohe, chapter 17 in this volume.

52. According to military analyst Anthony Cordesman, "North Korea's immense economic problems have never halted the build up of its conventional forces." See his "Is There a Crisis in US and North Korean Relations? Yes, There Are Two!" *Center for Stategic and International Studies*, December 30, 2002; available at http://www.csis.org/features/cord_nkorea.pdf (accessed January 20, 2003).

53. Oh and Hassig, *North Korea*, 105; see also Michael Hirsh, "Kim Is the Key Danger," *Newsweek*, January 13, 2003, 30.

54. David Hackworth, "A War with No Winners," *Newsweek*, July 18, 1994, 24.

55. General Thomas Schwartz, *Testimony before the Senate Armed Services Committee*, March 27, 2001; available at www.senate.gov/~armed_services/statement/2001/010327ts/pdf (accessed October 12, 2002).

56. Ibid.

57. With regard to the likelihood of North Korean aggression, Victor Cha suggested in a recent article that given Pyongyang's international isolation, the regime could see it as completely rational to launch an attack on the South. See his "Hawk Engagement and Preventive Defense on the Korean Peninsula," *International Security* 27, no. 1 (2001): 46–78.

58. John Tilelli, *Statement before the House National Security Committee*, March 3, 1999; available at http://russia.shaps.hawaii.edu/security/990303 tilelli.html (accessed November 21, 2001).

59. Paul Richter, "Two War Strategy Faces Test," *Los Angeles Times*, February 13, 2003.

60. Cordesman, "Is There a Crisis in U.S. and North Korean Relations?"

61. These points were raised in a letter to the U.S. Senate signed by sixteen of the military's top generals. See http://www.centerforsecuritypolicy.org/index.jsp?section=papers&code=97-D_97at (accessed January 12, 2000).

62. Barry Posen, "The Struggle against Terrorism: Grand Strategy, Strategy, and Tactics," *International Security* 26, no. 3 (2001), 47–49.

63. This information is based on research I conducted in Afghanistan in the fall of 2002 and extensive discussions with special operations soldiers. These forces regularly employed the Modular Packed Mine System, which is a

man-portable, mixed-antipersonnel/antitank system, as well as other self-destructing antipersonnel landmines.

64. Dave Moniz, "How the War against Iraq Could Unfold," *USA Today*, February 21, 2003; and Thomas Ricks, "Special Operations Units Already in Iraq," *Washington Post*, February 13, 2003.

17

Are Landmines Still Needed to Defend South Korea?: A Mine Use Case Study

J. Antonio Ohe

The nation which forgets its defenders will be itself forgotten.
—Calvin Coolidge, Vice Presidential Nomination Speech

IN 1998, PRESIDENT BILL CLINTON SIGNED PRESIDENTIAL DECISION DIRECTIVE 64, which directed the Department of Defense (DOD) to end its commitment to antipersonnel landmines (APLs) outside of Korea by 2003 and within Korea by 2006. But an examination of the DOD's efforts to end the reliance on APLs in Korea calls into question the DOD's commitment to the Presidential Directive. The DOD has continued to rely on a misdirected study it commissioned from the National Research Council (NRC). This chapter, though thorough, fails to transcend current applications of alternative technologies, looking instead solely at physical replacements for APLs. U.S. efforts to end APL use have been hampered by misguided research for alternative technologies to APLs, and an overwhelming failure to consider doctrinal alternatives to those currently established in South Korea, which rely heavily on the use of APLs as the first level of defense against an attack by North Korea.

There are two means of pursuing alternatives to APLs. The first method is to search for a specific replacement for the physical characteristics of landmines; in this case, a weapon that would warn of an initial strike as well as slow or deter the aggression of North Korean ground forces, as considered in the report the DOD commissioned from the NRC. The second method is a search for alternatives to the goals and purposes of landmines; in Korea, this means reconsidering strategy and tactics instead of simply searching for technological alternatives to replace APLs. Although U.S. efforts have been directed at the first, the second method would be more appropriate. This chapter will look at the current military situation in Korea, the current defense plan established to defend South Korea, and the strength and potential threat of the North Korean military forces. An analysis of current weapons will establish the availability to deploy tactical alternatives to APLs in Korea. I will assess the DOD's commitment to employing alternatives to APLs—physical, strategic, and tactical—on the Korean peninsula, and suggest some reasons why true alternatives and not just substitutes to APLs are vital to meeting Presidential Decision Directive 64.

The case of Korea is the basis for the U.S. stance on the International Treaty to Ban Landmines. It is the Korean situation that U.S. officials have cited again and again in their refusal to sign this treaty, arguing that South Korea is indefensible without APLs. In conclusion, I will argue that APLs are not actually necessary to the defense of South Korea and that, as a result, the refusal of the United States to sign the Landmine Treaty on the grounds of military necessity is faulty.

U.S. Policy Considerations

It is common to issue the dates for directives in order of priority or likely ability to accomplish them. The directive issued by President Clinton in 1998 clearly states that the DOD should focus on eliminating APL use outside of Korea (by 2003) before making the change within Korea itself (by 2006). There has been opposition to the United States replacement of APLs. The *Alternative Technologies to Replace Antipersonnel Landmines 2001* report from the National Research Council is the latest to come to the conclusion that the United States cannot currently replace landmines due to practical needs.[1] Although this is a thorough and in-depth report, it is constrained by requirements placed on it by the DOD. It does look at alternatives that are available today, but it does not look for untraditional applications of the technology. Instead, the report mainly focuses on finding physical replacements for APLs. Such a focus ignores the potential evolution in the doctrine under which landmines are employed that could occur if untraditional approaches were used in the examination of "alternative" solutions. The DOD should be challenged to exceed traditional analysis and incorporate technological advances that would allow for distant monitoring through aerial and satellite means as well as electrical sensors that do not contain lethal capabilities.

Unfortunately, as a DOD contractor, the NRC was required to follow the DOD's guidelines, overlooking some of the intriguing paths to the objectives of landmines that could utilize projected armament and power. Furthermore, real-time power should be incorporated into defensive capabilities as well. The quest to eliminate APLs will not put U.S. soldiers at a disadvantage; U.S. concerns with fratricide prevention on today's rapidly moving and highly technical battlefield is not incompatible with its humanitarian concerns. The United States has planned and equipped its military with the ability to move quickly and freely throughout the battlefield. The deployment of APLs constricts such movement, limiting soldiers' abilities, and is thus more likely to produce friendly force casualties. It is therefore a benefit to both the soldiers in the field and U.S. humanitarian efforts that the DOD should be guided to shift its reliance away from APLs.

The Case of Korea

Though there are millions of mines emplaced in the Korean Demilitarized Zone, the DOD does not feel there are yet enough to secure South Korea in the event of invasion by North Korea. Currently, there are approximately 2.2 million South Korean–owned antitank and antipersonnel landmines emplaced along the 1,000 square kilometers of the DMZ, which measures 4 kilometers (2.5 miles) deep and 250 kilometers (155 miles) wide. Many were emplaced directly following the Korean War in 1953. On September 17, 1997, the White House released a fact sheet stating:

> Anti-personnel landmines play a crucial role in the defense of Korea and the city of Seoul, which is just 27 miles from the Demilitarized Zone (DMZ) and which has a population in excess of 10 million inhabitants. Across the DMZ are nearly 1 million North Korean forces. These forces are well-prepared and could come across the border at any time, with little warning.[2]

The South Korea defense plan calls for deploying approximately one million additional landmines between the DMZ and Seoul in an event of aggression by North Korea.[3] Such mines would serve to "delay and disrupt

the attack long enough for the U.S. to bring in air power and other reinforcements with the objective of halting the attack and preventing the
enormous loss of life that would result if North Korean forces were to
overrun Seoul."[4] It is also believed such mines would be distributed north
of the DMZ to slow and canalize North Korean Forces (NKF) reinforce-
ment. It was believed that such mines would come from U.S. reserves,
which number well over one million landmines. The future use of landmines by the United States, then, depends on the North Korean aggression against South Korea. Thus, any discussion of the use of landmines in
Korea necessarily involves consideration of the actual threat posed by
North Korea.

North Korean Force Analysis

An analysis of the NKF leaves mixed interpretations of the threat they
represent. They are currently the fifth largest military force in the world
and maintain the world's third largest army. Although that seems quite
powerful, the army's size is meaningless if it is not effective. For example,
one must ask how effective an army can be if its soldiers are pushing
tanks on empty stomachs. North Korea's grain production does not meet
its national demand. As a result of this dire situation, North Korea is the
largest recipient of U.S. aid in Asia.[5] When a country lacks the ability to
sufficiently feed its troops, its military's functioning capacity must be
called into question.

Approximately 65–70 percent of North Korea's air force consists of
outdated fighter aircraft that are vintage early 1950 to 1970 (Mig 17s,
Mig 19s, and Mig 21s). It is said that their updated Mig 29 aircraft are
left in disrepair.[6] In their background note on North Korea, the U.S. State
Department asserts that "its air force has twice the number of aircraft as
the South, but, except for a few advanced fighters, the North's air force is
obsolete."[7] Moreover, the continuing undesirable economic conditions in
North Korea have left it with barely enough fuel to fly for training. In analyzing the North's air force, Army Captain Jeff House, intelligence officer assigned to the J-2 staff of the United States Forces Korea said,
"Never mind the North's air force, which can boast of quantity but not
quality. American and South Korean fighter-bombers would have to take
out surface-to-air missile sites, but would quickly neutralize enemy air."[8]

Although the NKF may be short on food and fuel, it does possess
the ability to inflict severe projected damage with artillery forces and
rocket systems. It is believed that the NKF can sustain a firing rate of
500,000 rounds an hour for several hours. However, the effectiveness of
these units in the face of U.S. counterfire radar and artillery is unknown.

Additionally, it is believed that the threat from NKF missiles would be severely reduced by the developments in the PATRIOT missile systems and its deployment to South Korea.

The North Korean tanks may outnumber the U.S./South Korea force, but these tanks too are outdated. The U.S. and South Korean tanks not only outmaneuver the NKF's older Soviet-style tanks, they also outrange and outpower them. The newer tracking and targeting technology utilized in U.S. tanks will allow the United States to acquire and destroy North Korean troops before they can engage U.S. tanks. The tank ammunition utilized by the United States is also superior to that used by the NKF, which allows the United States to maintain an even greater edge.

However, the rough terrain in Korea makes armored warfare different and more challenging than open-terrain combat. The landscape on the Korean peninsula consists of high mountain ranges and low restrictive valleys. In many cases, the maximum firing range of tanks may not be reached because of the terrain restrictions. It will be U.S. advanced target acquisition technology and highly mobile tanks that will "outgun" the NKF. Against this technology, combined with unmanned aerial reconnaissance drones, intelligence-gathering planes, and satellite surveillance, the NKF will find it difficult to advance. The end result of a conflict between North Korea's larger force and the more advanced armies of the combined U.S. and South Korean forces would leave North Korea in defeat. This belief is supported by Secretary of Defense William J. Perry's comments to the Council on Korean Security Studies:

> Several times each year we conduct major exercises to test our powerful combined capabilities. Though these exercises are purely defensive in nature, they send a clear message, a message that any attack against South Korea would be met by overwhelming forces. This is not only a powerful force, it is a force at high level of readiness.[9]

Any attack then, would be met with uncompromising force and would end in the certain defeat of North Korea. The United States believes this to be true and, more importantly, North Korea believes it, and that has led to the deterrence of war now for more then forty-five years.

Landmines and North Korea

The DOD has confidence that we will win any potential conflict in Korea. General Thomas A. Schwartz, commander in chief United Nations Command/Combined Forces Command and commander of United States Forces Korea, stated on March 27, 2001, before the Armed Services

Committee that "our combined forces can fight and win today if called upon. Our power, might, and daily readiness are unparalleled."[10] The combined forces in Korea are prepared to fight. Among its ranks are some of the most highly trained soldiers in the world. These soldiers complete several major exercises each year. They also continually practice not only their wartime profession but also alerts that simulate a North Korean invasion. U.S. forces could fight with little notice if it were necessary. There would not be any delay in their meeting aggression on the Korean peninsula.

The DOD believes that victory is possible without APLs. However, as a result of not using APLs, the DOD has calculated that more then 10,000 individuals would be killed in and around Seoul. The DOD does not believe the combined forces would have enough time to react to a sudden and swift attack from North Korea without APLs. Contrary to that, the Institute of Defense Analysis (IDA) published a report in 1994 on the Korean defense plan, stating that there would not be a substantial difference in success or protection with or without the use of APLs.[11] The DOD refuses to accept the IDA scenarios. Regardless, based upon my examinations of empirical evidence, I believe the effectiveness of landmines has been overestimated. History and North Korean doctrine demonstrate that landmines will not cause the delays and canalizing for which they were intended. Instead, North Korea might use rollers, brute force, and simple manpower to quickly push through a minefield. Although these suicidal tactics are not customary to Western-style war fighting, it has been seen in other doctrines. One such doctrine is the Japanese kamikaze fighter. Given war paradigms other than that under which the United States operates, the true effectiveness of landmines may be much lower than the DOD anticipates. As a former commander of the United States Forces Korea, Lieutenant General James Hollingsworth stated:

> There is indeed a military utility to APLs . . . but in the case of U.S. Forces in Korea it is minimal, and in some ways even offset by the difficulty our own APLs pose to our brand of mobile warfare. . . . Not only civilians, but U.S. armed forces will benefit from a ban on landmines. U.S. forces in Korea are no exception. . . . To be blunt, if we are relying on these weapons to defend the Korean peninsula, we are in big trouble. . . . North Korean's mechanized assault can be destroyed well north of Seoul without the use of U.S. APLs. I never counted on our APLs to make much of a difference.[12]

Fifteen retired military generals have recognized the limited military utility of APLs and sided with the ban on landmines. These generals include the former chairman of the Joint Chiefs of Staff, General David Jones; General H. Norman Schwarzkopf, commander of Operation Desert

Storm; Lieutenant General Dewitt C. Smith Jr., former commander, U.S Army War College; Lieutenant General Dave Palmer, former commander, U.S. Military Academy, West Point. They wrote President Clinton urging him to ban landmines.[13] As these experienced officers noted, there are more effective ways to counter the North Korean threat than APLs.

Alternatives to Antipersonnel Landmines in Korea

As I examine Korea, it should be kept in mind the key reason the DOD claims it needs APLs: to slow and canalize the advancing force to allow enough time for its forces to react. The DOD's main goal is to protect Seoul, only twenty-five miles from the DMZ, from damage and invasion. Army FM 20-32 of May 1998 states the following as the concepts of use for landmines:

- Produce vulnerability on enemy maneuver that can be exploited by friendly forces.
- Cause the enemy to piecemeal his forces.
- Interfere with enemy command and control (C2).
- Inflict damage to enemy personnel and equipment.
- Exploit the capabilities of other weapon systems by delaying enemy forces in an engagement area (EA).
- Protect friendly forces from enemy maneuver and infiltration.[14]

These are clear objectives. It is easier to find ways to reproduce these objectives in a familiar location such as Korea where the United States has been for almost fifty years than it would be to reproduce them in an unfamiliar location. Since the United States has been in Korea for almost fifty years, it is not only likely that every choke point, bridge, valley, and vulnerable point has been noted, but the DOD has recorded exact grid coordinates, worked up firing plans, and performed reconnaissance (either ground or aerial) on each location. It is also likely that in preparation for war, the DOD has had numerous experts researching every inch of land along the DMZ as well as the entire peninsula in search of means to exploit all enemy forces and find opportunistic locations for its own force multipliers. With all of these advantages and information, and I cannot stress this enough, it should be easier, not harder, to find alternatives to APLs in Korea.

Since all the landmines currently emplaced in South Korea are under the ownership and responsibility of South Korea, not the United States, they will not be of concern to this chapter. Instead, my concern lies with finding an alternative to the APLs that would be used in the defense plan in the event of North Korean aggression. There are two methods that can be followed to formulate such alternatives. The first is to find a "deploy-and-forget" system similar to APLs. This is a system that once deployed, it no longer requires monitoring or upkeep. This is the method on which the DOD has mainly focused. However, it is the unattended minefields that cause indiscriminate killing and injuries of noncombatants; so, this method is truly not an appropriate alternative. Closer to meeting the goals of the Presidential Directive, the second method is to utilize a system that contains two parts: an advance warning system and projected power for the distant destruction of enemy forces.

The DOD claims it will have very little warning of any aggression from North Korea and that, therefore, landmines are needed to increase the time available for reaction. Although 70 percent of the NKF are within one hundred miles of the DMZ, they are not lined up along it ready for an invasion. It will take some time for them to move and prepare an appropriate force. With today's surveillance technology, it is difficult to believe that this preparation could not be detected. Current satellite capabilities can picture a three-foot-by-three-foot area on the ground. Spy planes are able to monitor and detect the movement of ground troops, vehicles, and airplanes. Unmanned aerial drones are also an effective means of obtaining advance warning of a pending attack. If the security of the Korean peninsula is of such importance, it would be expected that some of these devices would be deployed in the region. If these methods are not enough, the Joint Surveillance Target Attack Radar System (Joint STARS) that was deployed in Operation Desert Storm can provide any further required intelligence. Joint STARS is a wide-area surveillance system capable of providing real-time information. It can monitor railhead activities, assembly areas, lines of communications (including communications for convoy activities or staging areas), movement of threat units from garrison locations to field sites, airfield activities, and displacement of artillery units.[15] With a complete Joint STARS system deployed to Korea, the United States should have ample advance notice of any intended attack from North Korea. To provide even further target acquisition, an AN/GSQ187 Remote Battlefield Sensor System (REMBASS) or the Improved Remote Battlefield Sensor System (IREMBASS) can be employed in naturally occurring or existing man-made canalizing points dear the DMZ. REMBASS is capable of detecting enemy forces and their exact location in real time. REMBASS supports offensive, defensive, rear-area, and special operations such as military operations on urbanized terrain, rear security, and border surveillance.[16]

Today's military forces no longer use the tactics of employing ground forces first in a battle. Currently, the United States first employs a precision air and missile campaign to gain air superiority and destroy key targets. This is combined with extensive satellite and aerial reconnaissance to gain intelligence. Only after that will ground force movements begin. This tactic was demonstrated in Operation Desert Storm, Bosnia, Kosovo, and Afghanistan. This tactic has proven effective and there does not seem to be a compelling reason to employ anything else in Korea. In fact, currently the United States has several effective weapons platforms that can kill or stop both armor and personnel from extended ranges. All of which are either in Korea now or can be deployed there; these systems include Multi Launch Rocket Systems, the Remote Anti-armor Mine System, and Sense and Destroy Armor Munitions, among many others.[17] The combined force of these systems could stop North Korean aggression without the use of additional APLs.

Utility of Antipersonnel Landmines

Antipersonnel landmines have been used by military forces for generations. Ted Gaulin effectively outlined their use in the previous chapter. He argues that landmines still maintain a military utility. I do not entirely disagree with his claims of utility. I do, however, find it necessary to point out that it is not the utility of APLs that is being called into question but instead their safety and humanitarian concerns that demand an alternative. Even military commanders are now recognizing and acting on these concerns. The General Accounting Office report titled *Military Operations, Information on U.S. Use of Land Mines in the Persian Gulf War* states:

> Numerous issues included in service and DOD Gulf War lessons-learned, after-action, and other reports concerned the safety and utility of conventional submunition U.S. land mines. Fratricide and battlefield mobility were cited often as important overall concerns associated with both available and used U.S. land mines and nonlandmine submunitions. These concerns led to the reluctance of some U.S. commanders to use land mines in areas that U.S. and allied forces might have to traverse.[18]

These commanders were concerned about fratricide caused by higher-than-anticipated dud rates and unreported, unrecorded, or unmarked minefields. These commanders' actions demonstrate the need for alternatives to APLs not only on the basis of protecting U.S. soldiers, but also for humanitarian concerns. If they can overlook the utility of APLs for safety reasons, why can't the DOD?

Conclusion

It is clear from the previous sections that APLs are unnecessary, and perhaps even undesirable, in the defense of South Korea. Such a conclusion is a strong one in that it invalidates the refusal of the United States to sign the International Treaty to Ban Landmines on the grounds that it must have access to APLs stores in order to protect South Korea. There is currently no other barrier to a U.S. signature of the treaty, other than the reluctance of the DOD. The reluctance of the DOD to abandon use of APLs is also apparent in its unwillingness to even pursue the action of Presidential Decision Directive 64. Right now, the DOD does not appear to be on course to meet either the 2003 or the 2006 deadline of this directive. In summation, I emphasize the importance of decision makers within the DOD to move beyond APL and APL-like technology to meet defense and deterrence objectives. As I have noted, appropriate alternatives already exist, or are quite close to development, but the DOD appears reluctant to adopt them. Though U.S. support is not vital, the lack of support provided by the United States for the Landmine Treaty is a great disappointment to the international community, and may be a barrier to the inclusion of all countries as signers. However, landmine activists should take hope from the preceding analysis, as it provides an opening for increased pressure on the DOD and the U.S. government to discontinue their employment of APLs.

Notes

1. National Research Council, *Alternative Technologies to Replace Antipersonnel Landmines* (Washington, DC: National Academy Press, 2001).

2. The White House, "US Requirement for Landmines in Korea," September 17, 1997.

3. Rachel Stohl, "Landmines Remain Issue in Korea," *Defense Monitor* 29, no. 5 (2000): 1–4.

4. The White House, "U.S. Requirement for Landmines in Kores," September 17, 1997.

5. Asian Pacific Media Network; available at http://www.asiamedia.ucla.edu/deadline/northkorea/articles/manning.htm (accessed May 12, 2001).

6. Center for Defense Information, *Asian Military Situation*; available at http://www.cdi.org/issues/Asia/asianmil.html (accessed May 5, 2001); and Center for Defense Information, "Democratic People's Republic of Korea," *Asian Military Situation*; available at http://www.cdi.org/issues/Asia/DPRKMILI.html (accessed May 5, 2001).

7. U.S. Department of State, Bureau of East Asian and Pacific Affairs, *Background Brief: North Korea* (Washington, DC: U.S. Department of State, October 2000).

8. Douglas J Gillert, "With an Eye on the North," *American Forces Press Service*, November 6, 1996.

9. William J. Perry, "Alliance Forged in War, Tempered by Regional Challenges," *Defense Issues* 10, no. 100 (1995): 1–3.

10. *Statement of General Thomas A. Schwartz, Commander in Chief United Nations Command/Combined Forces Command & Commander, United States Forces Korea, before the Senate Armed Service Committee*, March 27, 2001.

11. Stephen D. Biddle, Julia Klare, and Jaeson Rosenfeld, *The Military Utility of Landmines: Implications for Arms Control* (Washington, DC: Institute for Defense Analysis, 1994).

12. Demilitarization for Democracy, *Exploding the Landmines in Korea Myth*, foreword by Lieutenant General James Hollingsworth (Washington, DC: Demilitarization for Democracy, August 1997).

13. "Letter to President Bill Clinton," *New York Times*, April 3, 1996.

14. U.S. Army (1998), FM 20-32, Mine/Countermine Operations.

15. U.S. Army (1995), FM 34-25-1, Joint Surveillance Target Attack Radar System.

16. U.S. Army (1990), FM 34-10-1, Tactics, Techniques, and Procedures for the Remotely Monitored Battlefield Sensor Systems.

17. Sources include the Vietnam Veterans of America Foundation (http://www.vvaf.org); the Federation of American Scientists, Military Analysis Network (http://www.fas.org/man/); and the Committee on Alternative Technologies to Replace Antipersonnel Landmines, Commission on Engineering and Technical Systems, Office of International Affairs, National Research Council, *Alternative Technologies to Replace Antipersonnel Landmines* (Washington, DC: National Academies Press, 2001).

18. U.S. General Accounting Office, *Military Operations, Information on U.S. Use of Land Mines in the Persian Gulf War* (report to the Honorable Lane Evans, House of Representatives, GAO-02-1003) (Washington, DC: U.S. General Accounting Office, September 2002).

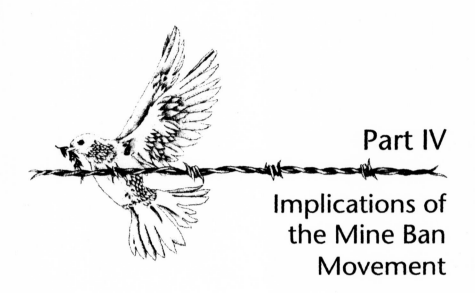

Part IV

Implications of the Mine Ban Movement

18

The Campaign to Ban Antipersonnel Landmines: Potential Lessons

STEPHEN GOOSE AND JODY WILLIAMS

THE INTERNATIONAL CAMPAIGN TO BAN LANDMINES (ICBL) WAS FORMALLY launched by six nongovernmental organizations (NGOs) in October 1992. It galvanized world opinion against antipersonnel landmines to such a degree that within five years a clear and simple ban treaty had been negotiated. Signed by 122 nations in December 1997, the treaty became binding international law more quickly than any such agreement in history. The treaty has, for the first time, comprehensively prohibited a widely used conventional weapon.

In the late 1980s, a number of NGOs had begun to recognize that the tens of millions of landmines contaminating dozens of countries around the world posed a humanitarian crisis. Human rights organizations, children's groups, development organizations, refugee organizations, and medical and humanitarian relief groups were having to make significant adjustments in their field programs to address the impact of landmines on the people they were trying to help. It became very clear that the only way to eliminate the problem was to eliminate the weapon.

This chapter is adapted from articles written by Stephen Goose for the October 2000 Montreal International Forum and Jody Williams for the *Harvard International Review.*

The NGO community did not wait for leaders to appoint themselves; they recognized a critical problem and initiated an effort to address it. These organizations had expertise on a wide range of issues related to landmines, and they worked diligently to gather field-based information that supported their demands for a global ban on the weapon.

As the ICBL effort was getting off the ground, the changing global situation helped set favorable conditions for talks on the use of conventional weapons. The end of the Cold War and shifting centers of power made it possible to approach issues of war and peace in ways other than simply trying to avoid a nuclear holocaust. Organizations and individuals began to look at how conflicts had actually played out during the Cold War and what weapons and methods of warfare had produced the most significant impact on the lives of civilians. In addition, possible responses by governments to issues of global concern were no longer as constrained as during the Cold War, when the two major powers dominated diplomacy.

The process that brought about the Mine Ban Treaty has added a new dimension to diplomacy, and its success has generated hope for its wider applicability. In awarding the 1997 Nobel Peace Prize to the International Campaign to Ban Landmines and its coordinator, Jody Williams, the Nobel Committee stated that the ICBL "started a process which in the space of a few years changed a ban on antipersonnel mines from a vision to a feasible reality."[1] The committee highlighted the ICBL's role in bringing about the 1997 Mine Ban Treaty.[2]

But, the Nobel Committee went on to note that the campaign had been able to "express and mediate a broad range of popular commitment in an unprecedented way. With the governments of several small and medium-sized countries taking the issue up . . . this work has grown into a convincing example of an effective policy for peace." It concluded, "As a model for similar processes in the future, it could prove to be of decisive importance to the international effort for disarmament and peace."[3]

Six years later, one might ask, can the mine ban movement indeed serve as an example or a model for other efforts by elements of civil society to bring about change on the global scene? It seems apparent that it has already done so at least in some respects with issues such as child soldiers, small arms, the International Criminal Court, and "human security." Here, we will focus on key factors that have led to the success of the movement, in an effort to identify some potential lessons to be learned from the landmine campaign. This is not an attempt to retrace the still rather brief history of the global movement to ban antipersonnel landmines or the ICBL, nor is it an elaboration on the key role of civil society, especially the ICBL, in the mine ban effort.[4] It should also be recognized that it is somewhat odd to draw lessons from an ongoing process and campaign.

Several overarching and interrelated lessons emerge from the mine ban movement. First, it is possible for NGOs to put an issue—even one with international security implications—on the international agenda, provoke urgent actions by governments and others, and serve as the ongoing driving force behind change. Civil society can indeed wield great power in the post–Cold War world. Second, it is possible to achieve rapid success internationally through common and coordinated action by NGOs, like-minded governments, and other key actors such as UN agencies and the International Committee of the Red Cross (ICRC). It is through concerted action that change is most likely to be effected. Third, it is possible for small- and medium-size countries, acting in concert with civil society, to provide global leadership and achieve major diplomatic results, even in the face of opposition from bigger powers. Fourth, it is possible to work outside of traditional diplomatic forums, practices, and methods and still achieve success multilaterally. In further elaborating lessons learned, it may be useful to consider them in two different clusters: those regarding international campaigning and those regarding the "new diplomacy."

Lessons Regarding Campaigning, Coalition Building, and Organizing

International Context and Timing Matter

The changing global situation in the late 1980s and early 1990s was a critical factor in the development of the ban movement. The end of the Cold War made it possible for governments and NGOs to look at war and peace issues differently. Many governments were no longer as constrained in their possible responses to issues of global humanitarian and security concern. Many NGOs were looking for new issues in which to become engaged. Increased attention was being devoted to conventional, as opposed to nuclear, weapons at the same time that the impact of antipersonnel landmines was reaching a crescendo, due to widespread and increasing use from the mid-1960s forward.

Provide Expertise and Documentation

One key to ICBL success was the fact that the movement grew out of fieldwork in mine-affected communities. The founding members of the ICBL were NGOs engaged in clearing mines, putting prosthetics on victims, and documenting the impact of mines on civilians. Governments immediately recognized that the NGOs had unmatched expertise to contribute on the subject.

Members of the ICBL carried out a concerted research agenda, and endeavored to publish informational materials extensively and distribute them widely to governments as well as the public. NGOs provided comprehensive materials on the impact of landmines around the world, on global mine production, trade, stocks, and use, as well as sophisticated legal analysis, including draft treaties and treaty provisions. These were powerful tools for advocacy.

Articulate Your Goals and Message Clearly and Simply

Every issue is complicated, but the importance of clear, concise, and consistent articulation of goals and messages cannot be overstated. This is true not only with respect to the overarching goals of a campaign, coalition, or movement, but also for each phase, conference, or event.

Focus on Human Costs

The landmine campaign has kept the international focus on the humanitarian aspects of the issue, not the arms control or security aspects. This has been crucial not only in influencing public opinion, but also in influencing governments. One aspect of this has been the ICBL effort to encourage government officials dealing with development and aid issues to take the lead in, or at least be part of, diplomatic delegations, rather than those dealing with military or disarmament issues.

Maintain a Flexible Structure

Those involved in the campaign are convinced that its loose structure has been a major strength. It is a coalition of independent NGOs that are free to make their own determinations about the best way to contribute to the common goals. Over time, it has largely become a coalition of national campaigns, along with a number of major individual NGOs. ICBL members have met regularly to strategize and plan joint actions, but each NGO and national campaign has been free to carry out whatever aspects of the work best fit its individual mandate, political culture, and circumstances.

Indeed, the ICBL was not even a legally registered entity until after it received the Nobel Peace Prize at the end of 1997. There has never been a secretariat or central office of the ICBL, and until 1998, no "ICBL" employees or joint ICBL budget. Various NGOs in essence seconded (and provided funding for) individuals to work on the campaign. There are now two people funded by a joint ICBL budget (a coordinator and a resource director). This lack of centralization was a conscious decision—each NGO has to find a way to participate in making the campaign work;

this helps ensure that the ICBL belongs to all of its members, and that these members have to be active in the process to achieve the campaign's goals. There is no bureaucratic structure that either dictates to members how they should contribute to the campaign, or does the work for them.

Be Inclusive

The ICBL has always ascribed to the big-tent theory. To become a member, it was only necessary to inform the coordinator that you shared and endorsed the campaign's call for a total ban on antipersonnel mines, as well as increased resources for mine clearance and victim assistance programs. No dues, no requirements, no restrictions.

Be Diverse

The mines campaign had built-in diversity almost from the start; indeed, it largely came about because so many different countries, as well as so many different fields, sectors, and interest groups, were affected. There are now some 1,400 organizations from more than ninety countries involved in the ICBL. The campaign has also sought to reflect this diversity in its leadership. Though founded by three U.S. and three European organizations, the current Coordination Committee includes NGOs or national ban campaigns from Africa, east Asia, south Asia, and South America, as well as the United States and Europe. It includes representatives from several mine-affected states, organizations involved in mine clearance, and victim assistance programs, as well as human rights, humanitarian aid, and religious organizations. There have, on occasion, been tensions in the campaign about the need for greater diversity and/or more structured diversity within the leadership. The general principle has been that leadership positions should only go to those willing and able to bear the burden of the work, not just be names on letterhead.

Speak with One Voice

There are benefits beyond sheer numbers when one can speak as a coalition on behalf of many, instead of individually. For example, even when pursuing similar objectives as NGOs, governments have traditionally been reluctant to deal with NGOs as partners, or to permit their meaningful participation in diplomatic meetings, in no small part because of the fear of being overwhelmed by numbers and diverse views. In that respect, the ability of the ICBL to serve as a banner for nearly every NGO working on the issue, and to speak authoritatively with one voice, served the movement very well. The ICBL has been able to have a seat at the table, with virtually the same status as states, during the Ottawa Process diplomatic meetings, whereas that would not have been possible for a larger number of NGOs.

Need for Leadership and Committed Workers

Successful coalitions will naturally be large and diverse. But experience shows that most coalitions operate on the extensive work of a committed and dedicated few, supported by the many. Most organizations cannot devote full-time staff to coalition efforts, but it is essential that there be a core of people working full time. With diverse coalitions, strong, effective leadership from a handful of organizations and individuals is essential. This applies equally to NGOs and governments.

Communication Is Key

Clear and consistent communication is an irreplaceable element of success. In the early days of the campaign, individual members gained strength by being able to speak with authority about what was happening everywhere to eliminate the problem. Sharing the successes and failures of the work empowered all organizations and lessened the possibility of isolation of any one. Because of strong communication, the ICBL often has known of developments before governments, which made the ICBL a focal point of information for governments and NGOs alike.

The importance of e-mail to the success of the campaign has often been noted, and often overstated. Certainly, the ease and speed of communication as a result of technological developments have had a great impact on the ability of civil society from diverse cultures to dialogue and formulate global political strategies, but e-mail alone has not "moved the movement." From the beginning, ICBL leaders recognized that in order to hold together NGOs of such diverse interest, organizations would have to feel an immediate and important part of developing the work of the campaign. In the early years of the ICBL, this was achieved by extensive use of the fax and regular mailings to campaign members of documents and informational updates. It was fax and telephone communication upon which the ICBL relied for much of its almost daily communications until 1996. Since then, e-mail has permitted the ICBL to carry out its priority of frequent and timely internal communication to a greater degree than ever before.

As important—and many might contend more so—as fax, phone, and e-mail to link together the huge coalition has been networking through travel and the building of personal relationships—both within the campaign and between campaigners and various government representatives.

Indeed, e-mail has been used relatively little for communications outside of the campaign, and the much-remarked-on close cooperation between governments and NGOs during the Ottawa Process was more the result of face-to-face meetings than anything else.

Know How to Organize

The typical members of many coalitions, including research and advocacy organizations, and even grassroots-oriented organizations, often do not have skills and expertise in large-scale organizing. Issue expertise does little good without organizing expertise when it comes to campaigning. The ICBL has produced educational materials on how to organize national campaigns, prepare for major conferences, and interact with the media, as well as other aspects of international campaigning work. Creative engagement of the public has also been a crucial element of success.

Always Have an Action Plan and Deadlines

The Ottawa Process that led to the Mine Ban Treaty and its aftermath can be characterized as an ongoing series of diplomatic and NGO international, regional, and national conferences and meetings. While it is easy, and perhaps usually correct, to criticize costly get-togethers, in the case of the mine ban movement, such conferences and meetings had been carefully planned with concrete objectives in mind: one meeting building on another, and, most importantly, an action plan emerging in which various actors took responsibility for specific tasks to move the ban forward. Deadlines are essential to spurring action: negotiate the treaty by December 1997, get the forty ratifications needed for entry into force within one year, accede by the Second Meeting of States Parties, and so on. ICBL meetings also usually included campaign capacity-building workshops and training sessions.

Utilize All Forums to Promote Your Message

Though it seems obvious, few realize how many opportunities there are internationally to put an issue on the agenda and get language in final statements and declarations and resolutions. It takes considerable effort to do this, first to identify, but of course especially to do the necessary advocacy.

Always Follow Up

It has been remarked that there are plenty of good treaties, conventions, and international laws in existence; the problem is implementation. The same is true of coalition work. There are always plenty of good ideas about what needs to be done. The difficulty is implementing those ideas. Follow-up and follow-through are what make the difference. Jody Williams is fond of telling audiences, "Words without action are meaningless."

Lessons Regarding the "New Diplomacy"

The key elements of the "new diplomacy" model fostered by the ban campaign include operating outside the UN system (when necessary), extensive and meaningful NGO participation, leadership from middle and smaller states, rejection of consensus rules, and geographic diversity (avoidance of regional blocs). It also features a focus on norm building, with emphasis on the moral norm driven by humanitarian concerns.

Partnership Pays

Perhaps the key factor in the success of the ban movement has been the close and effective cooperation between NGOs (primarily through the ICBL), governments, the ICRC, and UN agencies, especially UNICEF. This cooperation has been at the strategic and tactical level, and continues to this day. The first formal diplomatic conference of the ban process, held in Ottawa in October 1996, is a good example. In the six months leading up to the conference, Canadian diplomats and the ICBL consulted frequently on nearly every aspect of the conference, including how best to ensure maximum attendance by governments. The ICBL was given a seat at the table as a full participant in the conference, while those governments unwilling yet to declare themselves pro-ban sat in the back as observers. Campaigners were actively involved in drafting the precise language of both the final declaration and the action plan. At the end of the conference, Foreign Minister Lloyd Axworthy stunned delegates, but not the ICBL, by announcing that Canada would hold a treaty signing conference by the end of 1997.

Build a Core Group of Like-Minded Governments

After being in an adversarial relationship with nearly every government from 1992 to 1995, an increasing number of governments began to endorse an immediate ban. The campaign called on individual governments to come together in a self-identifying pro-ban bloc at the beginning of 1996, and they rapidly did so. Historically, NGOs and governments have too often seen each other as adversaries, not colleagues, and at first some in the NGO community worried that governments were going to "hijack" the process in order to undermine a ban. But a relationship of trust among a relatively small "core group" of governments (most notably Canada, Norway, Austria, and South Africa) and ICBL leadership quickly developed and has been maintained. This core group was geographically diverse, committed, and willing to provide leadership in the face of opposition from bigger states. The extraordinary dedication, energy, and talent of key governments and key individuals within those governments were absolutely vital in the success of the ban movement.

NGOs Need to Be Inside Too

Obviously, a crucial role for NGOs is mobilizing public opinion. But the mine ban movement has demonstrated that extensive involvement of NGOs in what are traditionally thought of as diplomatic activities is also crucial to ensuring rapid and effective change. The ICBL played a major role in the actual drafting of the ban treaty, from its earliest stages. The ICBL was given a formal seat at the table in all of the diplomatic meetings leading up to the negotiations, and then during the negotiations as well. Not just plenary sessions, but all working meetings were open to the ICBL. Many government representatives have since commented that the presence and input of the ICBL and the ICRC made a huge difference in the Oslo outcome. This prominent and official role for the ICBL has continued during the treaty intersessional work (with its Standing Committees of Experts Meetings) and during the annual meetings of States Parties.

Nontraditional Diplomacy Can Work

The Ottawa Process that led to the Mine Ban Treaty largely grew out of the failure of the UN-sponsored negotiations in 1995–1996 on the Landmines Protocol to the 1980 Convention on Conventional Weapons (CCW). The pro-ban governments decided to pursue a "fast-track" approach, outside of the CCW, the United Nations, and the Conference on Disarmament. The members of the Ottawa Process were self-identifying. Core group governments Austria, Germany, and Belgium hosted what were in essence preparatory meetings, followed by negotiations hosted by Norway and a treaty signing conference hosted by Canada. Though done outside the formal UN structure, the Ottawa Process was strongly supported by various UN agencies, and especially by Secretary-General Kofi Annan. The secretary-general now serves as the depositary of the convention.

Say No to Consensus

From the start of the Ottawa Process, the core group governments made clear that this was not to be a repeat of the Landmine Protocol negotiations where any one country could thwart the will of others. While always striving for consensus, the Ottawa Process stressed the concept of like-minded, in essence saying, if you are not like-minded regarding a total ban, do not participate. During the Oslo negotiations, the Rules of Procedure rejected the consensus approach, and while a vote never occurred, the fact that it took a two-thirds majority to make changes to the text contributed to the demise of several severely weakening amendments sought by the United States and others.

Promote Regional Diversity and Solidarity without Blocs

Both the campaign and core group governments worked hard to ensure geographic diversity within the ban movement, and to promote a sense of ownership of the issue among regional organizations, especially the Organization of African Unity. This strategy paid off well. But parallel to that, it is important that the traditional diplomatic alignments never came into play; there were no "Western Group" or other regional meetings.

As noted, all of these lessons will not be applicable in all cases, will be difficult to carry out in some cases, and could be counterproductive in others. Some have noted how the mine ban campaign had certain "advantages"—its focus on a single weapon, an easy-to-grasp message, its highly emotional content. Perhaps even more important, the weapon is obviously not vital militarily, nor important economically. But the difficulties encountered should also not be underestimated. There was virtually uniform opposition from governments at first, due to the widespread deployment of mines, considered by most as common and acceptable as bullets, an integral part of in-place defenses and war plans, training, and doctrine. About 125 nations had stockpiles of antipersonnel mines; mines had been used in 88 countries. They were considered a cheap, low-tech, and reliable substitute for manpower, but were also the focus for future research and development for richer nations. These were long odds to overcome.

There is now also the reality that those who oppose the ban treaty and the process leading to it are also learning lessons, in order to ensure that the model is not repeated.[5] It is clear that many governments still do not feel comfortable with increased citizen involvement in defining national and international security and in seeking new ways to resolve global problems. For some, the ICBL and its partnership with governments has resulted in a threatening process in which small and middle powers can work together with civil society and address humanitarian concerns with breathtaking speed, despite reservations by bigger states. In this context, the continued success of the landmine campaign is critical and has broader implications than the removal of an indiscriminate weapon. When the campaign succeeds, the model succeeds.

Notes

1. *Statement by the Nobel Committee*, October 10, 1997.

2. Formally, the Convention on the Prohibition of the Use, Stockpiling, Production and Transfer of Anti-Personnel Mines and on Their Destruction. It was negotiated in Oslo, Norway, in September 1997, and opened for signature in Ottawa, Canada, on December 3, 1997. As of August 2000, it had been signed by 138 nations, and ratified by 101.

3. *Statement by the Nobel Committee.*

4. The best source for this is: Maxwell A. Cameron, Robert J. Lawson, and Brian W. Tomlin, eds., *To Walk without Fear: The Global Movement to Ban Landmines* (Oxford: Oxford University Press, 1998).

5. In July 2001, at negotiations at the United Nations to try to curb the proliferation of small arms and light weapons, the Bush administration attacked the model created by the ICBL. John Bolton, the U.S. representative told the countries and nongovernmental organizations and agencies assembled there that the United States does "not support the promotion of international advocacy activity by international or nongovernmental organizations, particularly when those political or policy views advocated are not consistent with the views of *all* member states. What individual governments do in this regard is for them to decide, but we do not regard the international governmental support of particular political viewpoints to be consistent with democratic principles. Accordingly," he concluded, "the provisions of the draft Program that contemplate such activity should be modified or eliminated" (emphasis added; see Jody Williams, "'Democracy' and the Bush Administration"; available at http://www.icbl.org/amb/williams/democracy_bush.html).

19

The Campaign to Ban
Antipersonnel Landmines and
Global Civil Society

PAUL WAPNER

MANY SCHOLARS OF INTERNATIONAL RELATIONS DIVIDE THE GLOBAL system into three differentiated but related domains of politics. First, there is the state system, which refers to nation-states and the relations between them. Politics here involves states wielding power over each other, cooperating to realize collective goals, and assuming certain identities due to structural constraints. Key to this domain is that states possess authoritative power within their territories. This enables them to shape widespread thought and behavior within their respective domains and to act legitimately in international affairs. Second, there is the world economy, which refers to businesses and the structures of the world capitalist system. Politics here entails economic power conditioning relations between, and the behavior of, states, firms, and ordinary individuals. The central insight is that the practices of production, exchange, and consumption of goods and services significantly shape social and political life. That is, the world economy itself acts as a mechanism of governance-influencing behavior throughout the world. Finally, there is global civil society, which is made up of nonstate actors that operate transnationally. Politics here involves nonstate actors changing the way states, firms, and citizens think about and act in the world. It includes a type of transnational politics by which nongovernmental organizations (NGOs) work to shift the standards of good conduct, laws, and economic dynamics in multiple countries. In each case, the emphasis is on how a given set of actors or structures influences world affairs.

This chapter focuses on global civil society. It seeks to understand what we can learn about this domain of world politics from the transnational campaign to ban antipersonnel landmines. Since at least the 1970s, there have been NGO efforts to demine areas of the world. In the early 1990s, many of these efforts joined forces seeking a worldwide ban on the production, use, and transfer of antipersonnel landmines. The main NGO actors were part of a coalition, known as the International Campaign to Ban Landmines (ICBL), and their efforts helped secure the Mine Ban Treaty (MBT) that was signed in 1997 in Ottawa, Canada. The MBT, which, as of October 2003, was ratified by 141 countries and signed or acceded to by 11 others, seeks formally to outlaw the production, use, and transfer of antipersonnel landmines throughout the world.

As almost every chapter in this book attests, the MBT would never have been considered, let alone signed, if it had not been for the ICBL and other active NGOs. NGOs built widespread public sentiment against antipersonnel landmines, convinced a number of corporations to voluntarily stop producing these weapons, and pressured governments to take up the issue and pursue international legal measures to ban formally the production and use of such weapons. NGOs were fundamental to the MBT. As Richard Matthew puts it, "One could not possibly explain the MBT without mentioning the activities of the NSAs [nonstate actors]. There would be no story to tell, no process to explain."[1]

To the degree that NGOs constitute global civil society, the campaign to ban landmines stands as a paradigmatic case for studying the role and political effectiveness of this third domain of politics. What can we learn about global civil society by reflecting on the ICBL and the MBT? What do these reflections tell us about this domain of world politics and its relations to the other realms? What can be gleaned about the claims theorists make on behalf of global civil society from the antilandmines campaign? As I hope to show, the landmines issue can provide important insight into the workings of global civil society. It represents a highly successful, large-scale effort by numerous NGOs to shift state, corporate, and citizen behavior around the world. Today, the number of landmines being deployed is outpaced by the number being removed, casualty rates have declined significantly since the ban, and the vast majority of countries known to have antipersonnel landmines producers have taken official steps to halt production and sale of these weapons.[2] To the degree that NGOs have been fundamentally responsible for this turn of events–which is undisputable–the landmines campaign represents one of the clearest cases yet of NGO effectiveness on the global scene and thus the role of global civil society in world politics.

While I wish to use the landmines campaign to reflect on global civil society in general, I want to do so with a particular intention in mind. Over the past few years, a number of scholars have questioned key elements of the idea of global civil society; some have even questioned the entire concept itself. In the following, I use the landmines campaign to address these criticisms. My hope is that in doing so we can learn something about the character of global civil society itself. The criticisms fall into three categories. They question, respectively, just how "global," "civil," or "societal" this thing called "global civil society" really is. This chapter proceeds by addressing each of these points of criticism in turn. By using the landmines campaign, it seeks to illustrate the complexities involved with the idea of global civil society but also to demonstrate the analytical utility of the concept for understanding world politics.

Global or Western Civil Society?

Global civil society refers to the growing societal dimension of world affairs. Communication and transportation technologies have enabled people more easily to share information, organize themselves, and express their aspirations across state boundaries outside the rubric of states and the world economy. Social movements, churches, unions, political parties, and clubs of all sorts are now increasingly transnational in character, and this points to a growing level of societal interdependence or, put differently, a social dimension to globalization. Most theorists of international relations focus on the activities of politically motivated NGOs when considering global civil society and, as John Boli and George Thomas demonstrate, the number of these organizations has skyrocketed over the past few decades.[3]

One of the key questions about this realm of collective life is just how global it is. Critics often point out that there are vast pockets of the world that have been left out of the communication and transportation revolutions, and thus are not plugged into the technological "superhighway," made up of air travel, the Internet, reliable telephone service, and the like. People living in these areas lack the experience of communicating and forming relationships with those outside their particular locale to say nothing of those who live in other countries. Thus, critics claim that it is truly a misnomer to say there is something "global" about transnational civil society. At best, while it may cross the borders of all states it certainly does not extend to the hinterlands of all countries. Consequently, there is nothing genuinely global about intersocietal relations.

Other critics go even further in their concerns. Some question not simply if civil society extends everywhere but also challenge the globalist character often attributed to the idea. In other words, some critics question whether *global* civil society is simply a trope to universalize what is really a Western experience and a globalizing force that emanates primarily from the West. Global civil society, for these people, is really Westernization, and thus a repackaged form of colonialism. The most active and effective NGOs tend to be Western and the lines of communication and cooperation tend to flow from the West to the rest. Global civil society, then, is not something all peoples participate in—to say nothing of them participating equally. It is simply the sociocultural realm at the international level through which Western societies are able to assert their hegemony.

These criticisms raise serious questions about the overall character of transnational social life and the analytical utility of the term *global civil society*. This is especially the case with the latter one. To assess its veracity, we can turn now to look explicitly at the case of the antilandmines campaign. How Western has the effort been to ban landmines? Have NGO activities emanated primarily from the West? How much of a presence have non-Western NGOs had in the campaign? In short, how global has the NGO campaign been?

The ICBL was spearheaded in 1991 by two Western NGOs: the Vietnam Veterans Foundation of America (VVAF), based in the United States, and Medico International, based in Germany. Within a year these organizations joined forces with four other Western-based NGOs and began a concerted and coordinated effort to ban landmines. Within seven years the organization grew to include one thousand NGOs from seventy countries with a strong presence from non-Western countries.

Notwithstanding the participation of non-Western NGOs, at first blush it would appear that a Western imprint was part of the ICBL from the beginning and, given the vast financial and political disparities between Western and non-Western NGOs in general, it might look as though the ICBL was destined to always be a Western creation and effort. While this may be part of what has been going on, there are reasons to question it as the complete story. The VVAF and Medico International started the ICBL intentionally as a coalition. Small, local organizations operating in places such as Cambodia and Guinea-Bissau, for example, had been working for decades to demine their countries and the ICBL was set up partly to advance these groups' efforts. Indeed, original members of ICBL's first Steering Committee (now called the Coordination Committee) included NGOs from Afghanistan, Cambodia, Kenya, and South Africa. In 1998, the committee expanded to include members from Latin America as well as additional groups from Asia and Africa. The committee works to coordinate activities and communication between NGOs throughout the world. An early presence and active participation in the committee by non-Western NGOs suggests that the ICBL was more than a Western project.

Inclusion on the Steering Committee suggests collaboration but one can easily imagine the lines of power still operating in one direction. There is, however, evidence to complicate this picture. As Kenneth Rutherford makes clear, the ICBL has been pursuing a number of strategies in a host of countries that would not have been successful without an extreme sensitivity to the sociopolitical and sociocultural contexts of individual countries and much leeway for local NGOs to pursue their own political strategies.[4] Once all members agreed to the aim of a ban on landmines—as opposed simply to demining efforts or assistance to mine victims—individual NGOs were relatively autonomous to design appropriate strategies for public outreach and governmental access. Put differently, national NGOs had to customize the landmine ban message to their own states. This was in keeping with a fundamental, organizational tenet of the ICBL, namely, to remain decentralized in terms of tactics and nationally appropriate strategies.

One sees the decentralized character of the ICBL in its effort to engage rebel groups, insurgents, and other nongovernmental armed combatants that use landmines and whose members suffer the consequences. The ICBL has long recognized that one of the driving forces behind landmines was their use by militant groups. A number of years ago, the ICBL launched a campaign to try to bring such organizations into discussions and convince them that, however attractive the use of landmines may be in the short run, in the long run it harms an organization's goals rather than advances them. The ICBL left the exact explanation of this and the task of dialogue with such groups up to local NGOs. This proved wise. For example, the Pakistan Campaign to Ban Landmines and the Afghan Campaign to Ban Landmines, both of which are staffed by local people but financed with international funds, worked to convince the Taliban that antipersonnel landmines were un-Islamic. In 1998, the Taliban issued a statement to this effect and both campaigns reported no subsequent use of mines by the Taliban (though the opposition Northern Alliance continued to deploy mines within Afghanistan through 2001[5]). It is also worth noting that Afghanistan acceded to the Mine Ban Treaty in September 2002.[6]

Similarly, the Philippines Campaign to Ban Landmines has been working with the Filipino government and the Moro-Islamic Liberation and the Revolutionary Proletarian Army to renounce the use of landmines. While the record is mixed in terms of a complete abandonment of landmines by all sides, it is clear that the deal was broached and is being brokered largely by Filipino NGOs with some help from transnational NGOs.

Finally, the ICBL has worked against a Western character by holding many of its meetings in non-Western countries and trying to bring non-Western participating NGOs to such gatherings. It has held meetings, for example, in Lebanon, Mozambique, Egypt, and Korea. To push the point further, it is useful to note that many non-Western states were among the first signers of the Ottawa Treaty. These included Algeria, Angola, Burundi, Indonesia and Guyana. To say this does not mean that these countries or their NGOs had a significant impact on the negotiations but it does suggest that non-Western NGOs must have played an important role in the political dynamics before the Ottawa Treaty was opened for signature.

All of this does not prove that the ICBL and other associated NGOs sidestep the challenges of keeping transnational coordination nonhegemonic. As mentioned, in a world of extreme disparities between the West and the rest, it is difficult to cultivate transnational relations between equal partners. Nonetheless, the NGO campaign to ban landmines appears to have done a relatively good job avoiding complete capture by Western groups and Western ideas. While probably not completely a two-way dialogue, a combination of ICBL's membership, intention, organizational structure, and practical activities suggest that it was far from a Western imperialist project. As such, it implies that there is, indeed, something "global" about transcivil relations; there is some justification for using the term *global* civil society.

Civil or Self-Interested Society?

The idea of civil society at the domestic level emerged in the West with the rise of the liberal state. The liberal state has long recognized that human beings possess rights to engage in citizen-to-citizen relationships independent of state prerogatives and directives. While this right enabled people to pursue common enterprises and develop social trust among themselves, it also facilitated the ability of people to organize themselves in opposition to, and direct their energies toward, the state in the form of public pressure and accountability. Civil society, as such, then, has traditionally been associated with a distinction between state and citizen practices, with an emphasis on the latter holding the state accountable for its actions.

The idea of global civil society retains this same flavor. States are key actors in world affairs and the interactions between them largely dictate the character of world politics. NGOs emerge and undertake actions across state boundaries partially to hold states accountable. They organize public sentiment and pressure multiple states to take such sentiment seriously.

While not active in every part of the world, as mentioned, NGOs provide a modicum of public presence at the global level, and this is what many take to be a key element in the phrase, global *civil* society.

While many might agree that NGOs work to hold states accountable, there are some serious questions about the accountability of NGOs themselves. Who elects NGOs? Who designates them as global spokespersons for world society? How can NGOs really express the global interest as opposed to the interests of a specific group of people? What mechanisms of accountability are available, and who is able to exercise them, to restrict NGO activities?

Critics often raise these questions to point out the lack of NGO accountability. While many NGOs perform admirable work, there are plenty that pursue goals many of us would find abhorrent. Moreover, even those with whom we share political aims are not beyond criticism and deserve public scrutiny. This is especially the case given the extraordinary rise of NGOs over the past few decades. NGOs have grown in number, size, and strength such that the budgets of the largest organizations, such as the World Wildlife Fund or Amnesty International, rival those of small states and certainly those of many international agencies. What is to prevent this power from being used in an arbitrary fashion? What is to stop "might making right" in the NGO world? Is there any element of accountability for NGOs?

Before looking to the landmines campaign to examine these questions, it is useful to address the problem of accountability in the abstract. One of the key challenges in political thought since at least the modern era has been the issue of legitimate political power. Thomas Hobbes, John Locke, Jean-Jacques Rousseau, and others continually reflected on how to constitute and maintain legitimate political power. Almost all of these thinkers proposed some form of constitutional or institutional constraint.[7] At the domestic level, many states have effected such constraints in the form of liberal, democratic polities. Liberal, democratic polities distribute power within the government to enable constitutional checks on the arbitrary use of power, and key officeholders are voted into power through largely democratic means. Accountability is thus folded into the system insofar as leaders lack full freedom to pursue their own agendas, can be removed from office, and face elections every few years when they must make an accounting to their constituents. At the international level, legitimacy is bestowed upon those states that meet certain minimum requirements of approval. For instance, all legitimate states must be accepted by the United Nations General Assembly, a process that involves a legal commitment to the principles of the UN Charter and the Universal Declaration of Human Rights.[8] Legitimacy is further won on a bilateral basis through the exchange of ambassadors and interstate legal agreements.

NGOs enjoy none of these mechanisms of accountability. The leaders of many NGOs are not elected and, if they are, the electorate consists only of members. Additionally, there are no external, institutional limits on NGOs. Many NGOs may have boards of directors or councils of advisers but often these are made up of like-minded people whose views rarely differ from those they are overseeing. Outside groups or individuals at large have no say on the workings of NGOs. Finally, while there are processes of accreditation for NGOs to participate in certain international fora—such as the United Nations Economic and Social Council accreditation for UN participation—there are no universal standards of legitimacy. NGOs can emerge and engage in political activity independent of recognition from other NGOs or actors. As P. J. Simmons observes, "Hailed as exemplars of grassroots democracy in action, many NGOs are, in fact, decidedly undemocratic and unaccountable to the people they claim to represent."[9] Given this, how should one think about NGO accountability?

Perhaps the best way to do so, initially, is to reverse the question and ask about the accountability of states. Yes, there are domestic and international mechanisms to constrain state actions, but how well do these actually provide accountability? At the domestic level, the story is complex. First, while there are many liberal regimes that have constitutional checks on power and allow citizens to vote (and thus elect and remove public officials), there are many nondemocratic polities that make no bones about ruling independently of any widespread collective interest. Warlord regimes, theocracies, and kleptocracies exist throughout the world and, while many are transitioning to democracies, many are not. The presence of nondemocratic regimes raises skepticism about states in general being held accountable to their citizens.

Furthermore, there is room for skepticism among even democratic states. As many democratic theorists have pointed out, there are different levels of democracy. All democratic states are representative forms of government where people elect others to govern on their behalf. The democratic state, in a representative context, has the constant challenge of governing in the so-called public interest. Indeed, all theories of the state explain as much. For example, Marxist notions of the state point out that, although citizens vote for their representatives, the interests of capital (and, for some theorists, capitalists) always win out. That is, people may vote to try to influence politicians but the structure of the system always privileges certain interests over others. To be sure, there is an element of accountability in such a perspective; the only problem is that the state is accountable to only a select group of citizens or interests, and these tend to be of the wealthiest and, not coincidentally, politically most powerful.[10]

Pluralistic theories of the state provide a more attractive explanation of democratic accountability but even these orientations highlight problems. According to pluralistic notions of democracy, citizens organize themselves into various interest groups and these groups compete for the ear of the government. The government, as such, plays the role of a referee that tries to balance competing interests rather than an actor with its own agenda. State action consists in implementing the wishes of the strongest voices. The virtue of the pluralist state is that no single group or class can consistently win out in all issue areas because the various political resources it takes to do so cannot be captured by one group. That is, no group can speak consistently with the strongest voice in all issue areas.[11] There are, of course, a number of problems with the pluralist model in terms of accountability. The most obvious is that it assumes, erroneously, that all people have equal access to mechanisms for expressing their interests. It assumes that Exxon and family farmers, for example, are on equal footing to influence the government.[12] What is accountability, even from a pluralist perspective, in states with dramatic differentials in income and political power? And which states do not have such differentials?

Finally, Weberian notions of the state, that see it as autonomous from society and thus able to make decisions on its own, also point out problems of state accountability. The Weberian state is made up of bureaucratic institutions that have their own interests separate from classes or interest groups in society. The state, as a set of bureaucratic institutions, advances certain policies that reflect given institutional interests.[13] One could, of course, debate the merits of such interests and argue that in well-functioning democracies these interests reflect the well-being of society but this would be a stretch. That the state is an actor in society, with particular institutional interests, compromises any deep democratic notion of accountability.

Each view of the state raises questions about the ability of the government to respond appropriately to the will of the people. To be sure, the fundamental problem is that societies do not have a single or general will but there are conflicting interests at work. It is hard to imagine how any state could be held accountable in such a situation. Liberal regimes attempt to address this by setting seemingly fair procedural mechanisms for deciding state practices and for grievances that arise. But as any observer of even the most democratic regime will explain, while this may bring legitimacy to the rules and the government of a state, it does not ensure substantive accountability.

Internationally, as mentioned, there are arrangements that try to hold states accountable to long-standing rules, norms, and procedures that are valued by a majority of states. But how well do these work? On the whole, it seems that they work well. As Hedley Bull noted a quarter of a century ago, most states obey most international laws most of the time.[14] One could say the same about broader norms and implicit principles of contemporary international life. But it is clear that certain "states" operate outside these restrictions and thus are not themselves accountable to any significant international mechanisms. For example, while the Taliban were in power in Afghanistan they were not recognized by the United Nations General Assembly and exchanged ambassadors with only a few states. The legitimacy of the Afghan state was always in question under such conditions. A similar situation presently exists regarding Taiwan, Tibet, and Burma. Each of these lack membership in the United Nations and possess varying levels of legitimacy in the club of states. The mixed legitimacy of certain states, based on international "standards," suggests that those mechanisms that have evolved over centuries to hold political actors accountable and guard against arbitrary use of power are imperfect at best. One can justifiably ask what accountability really means in such a world. One could further raise such a question in light of U.S. war on Iraq in 2003. Despite widespread opposition to war expressed in the UN Security Council and public sentiment throughout the world, the United States and a small set of allies seemed ultimately unconstrained in their actions. International mechanisms of accountability, then, while present, are often not nearly as effective as suggested by critics of NGOs who implicitly use the state as a point of comparison.

These remarks have to do with the issue of accountability in general. Let us look at the landmines ban campaign and examine how the issue plays itself out in that context. The ICBL is held accountable to various constituencies through its organizational structure and day-to-day practices. The combination of these provides a series of obligations and responsibilities that mimic the accountability mechanisms of states. One can think of these as either "vertical" or "horizontal" forms of accountability.

On the vertical side, the ICBL is accountable to its donors. Like all nonprofit NGOs, the ICBL does not generate its own income but relies on benefactors. In its early years, it depended solely on money received by well-established member NGOs such as Human Rights Watch, Save the Children, and the Lutheran World Federation; foundations such as the Open Society Institute, Merck, and Diana Princess of Wales Fund; and the public at large. In the late 1990s, it began receiving funds from the governments of Canada, Norway, Switzerland, Denmark, and others. While fund-raising is not the same as vote gathering, it requires reaching out to a broad base of people, foundations, and governments, and winning their approval. This remains crucial over the years, as funders can always withdraw support. By virtue that the ICBL receives funds from various member organizations, foundations, governments, and the public throughout the world, there is a strong element of accountability folded into the coalition. The ICBL, like most NGOs, lives or dies based on its ability to satisfy funders.

A second, vertical dimension of accountability has to do with the hierarchical aspect of the coalition. The ICBL has roughly 1,400 members. It is extremely difficult to consult with each one for every decision. While it continuously communicates with members and has held a number of general meetings open to all members, the ICBL uses a thirteen-member Coordination Committee to act as a board of directors to oversee campaign strategy and set general policy. This committee, made up of rotating members, has representatives from each continent and ensures that ICBL operations are consistent with member goals.

While donors and the Coordination Committee provide some vertical accountability, the ICBL is directly responsible to its members and this provides a horizontal form of oversight. As mentioned, individual NGO members are on their own to pursue appropriate local strategies to advance the landmine ban. Members are united simply in terms of ICBL's goal of eliminating landmines. But one should not underestimate the power of this shared concern. According to some observers, the ICBL has been successful because it has kept the lines of communication open between members and has worked to be responsive to member concerns.[15] Additionally, the ICBL has worked in partnership with nonmember NGOs such as the International Committee of the Red Cross (which played a significant role in the campaign) and international organizations such as the United Nations.[16] These partnerships depend on the ICBL communicating and finding common ground with others outside the coalition itself. This adds an additional element of accountability.

A second horizontal type of accountability is simply the transnational dimension of the coalition and its partners. States are accountable to their people and to the international organizations of which they are a part, especially the United Nations. (It is worth noting, however, that most of the organizations that states respect are, in fact, creations of states themselves. The United Nations, for example, while it enters into partnerships and relies on NGOs, is a state-based organization. States are the only formal, decision-making members.) NGOs are different in this regard. Instead of being responsive simply to people within a given territory or to organizations made up of other states, NGOs are responsive to publics throughout the world. Put differently, NGOs are "sovereignty-free" actors that need not work on behalf of the interests of a territorially situated public.[17] This, of course, does not mean that they are somehow accountable to everyone throughout the world but it does increase the geographical scope of their constituency. In this regard, NGOs can be seen ironically as more accountable to global citizenry than states.

All of this is not to claim that NGOs have answered the criticisms about accountability. The issue of legitimacy is, as mentioned, an age-old challenge and few political actors have successfully embodied democratic ideals of accountability. However, many NGOs in general, and the ICBL in particular, have elements of their organizational structure and processes that effect mechanisms of responsibility and obligation to others. The ICBL is not on its own to do what it pleases. It must listen carefully to the concerns of donors, states, various international organizations, and its vast membership, and this forms an imperfect but active type of accountability. NGOs are not states. This robs them of one set of accountability mechanisms. However, other mechanisms exist and NGOs such as the ICBL have learned about and thrive on incorporating them.

Global civil society stands as a realm that performs many functions. One is to be a space in which NGOs can hold states and other actors accountable for their activities. Global civil society is sufficiently autonomous from the state-system to provide some normative and organizational independence. Over the years, NGOs have used this autonomy productively to monitor, question, and challenge state activities. Critics rightfully ask, however, about the status of NGOs themselves and point out insufficiencies in terms of how responsive and representative NGOs are vis-à-vis the world's publics. A study of the ICBL, however, cautions against quick generalizations. It suggests that NGOs may be differently accountable than states but, accountable to a degree, nonetheless. Global *civil* society, then, is not simply a place where anyone with a fax machine and Internet access can shape world affairs; it also has mechanisms of accountability that work to hold actors within it subject to public oversight and pressure.

Global Civil Life or Society?

Some observers associate civil society with private life. The term *civil society* arose partly to describe individual freedom from the state and has always maintained a sense of distinction from that which is officially public. The liberal state was founded on the notion that people find pleasure in different ways and that the meaning of human experience differs among individuals. As a result, it is not the state's job to promote one way of life over another but rather only to establish laws and collective norms that enable people to pursue life as they see fit. Civil society, for many, then, refers to the realm in which people conduct their lives separate from the immediate regulatory mechanisms of the state. There is nothing particularly public about this realm. Thus, while the associations that emerge within civil society may be sociologically or anthropologically interesting, they may, in fact, be politically irrelevant.

A similar understanding exists among some observers of global civil society. Global civil society, for some, refers simply to a realm in which individuals can work with others across state boundaries to meet their needs and pursue their interests independent of the state-system. To the degree that churches, clubs, and other nongovernmental actors concern themselves with people's personal lives, their transnational scope adds little by way of sociality. They represent the cross-boundary extension of private life rather than the cultivation of transnational communal ties. For those who emphasize the private dimension, global civil *society* is a misnomer; there is nothing particularly social about it.

Notwithstanding the importance of freedom from the state at the domestic level and the activities of nonpolitical actors at the global one, civil society is not the same thing as private life. In the private realm, individuals pursue their interests as they understand them, with the consequences having, basically, personal ramifications. Civil society is different in that many actors within it deliberately work to influence public affairs. They aim to influence the way people think and act with regard to public issues. Likewise, global civil society is not simply a transboundary sphere of private intercourse or a place to fulfill one's personal interests. Rather, it is a political space where actors work to shape public affairs in multiple countries. It is a space where NGOs attempt to change laws, codes of conduct, corporate behavior, and so forth throughout the world.

The landmines campaign can shed light on the character of global civil *society*. Many critics of global civil society claim that, if the realm is not simply about private affairs, at best it has to do with low rather than high politics. That is, many point out that while NGOs engage in numerous activities, their efforts are relevant only for the most marginal issues. Yes, NGOs influence policies and public sentiment about human rights, environmental protection, poverty, and so forth but when it comes to the core of world politics—international security—NGOs drop out of the picture. The landmines campaign provides a different understanding.

NGOs have always concerned themselves with security issues. Antiwar groups were among the first and most prominent NGOs on the world stage, and NGOs concerned with arms control have been among the most conspicuous since the beginning of the nuclear age. Groups such as War Resisters International, Pax Christi International, and European Nuclear Disarmament are examples of such NGOs. These organizations have had thousands of members through the years, relatively large budgets, and organized events across state boundaries. The idea that international security is beyond the substantive focus of NGOs is simply wrongheaded.

More to the point is the ambiguous influence of such NGOs. While many organizations work for a more peaceful world, it is difficult to gauge their effectiveness. A number of studies demonstrate that NGOs such as European Nuclear Disarmament had an affect on European governments in their decisions about deploying U.S. intermediate nuclear forces.[18] Other studies go so far as to claim that groups such as the Nuclear Freeze

Campaign (later SANE/FREEZE) played a central role in "softening" the former Soviet Union to the West—by creating a peace-loving image for Western publics—and thus ushering in the end of the Cold War.[19] The evidence in both cases, however, is suggestive but not definitive. Given the complexities of tracing influence in such issues, it has been difficult to point out a direct causal relationship between the efforts of NGOs and states' security policy.

The landmines case provides a more powerful illustration of NGO influence. For decades, landmines were seen as legitimate, conventional weapons, indistinguishable from basic firearms, artillery shells, and air-delivered bombs. States used them widely and folded them into their military doctrines. Landmines were used in both offensive and defensive strategies—to channel enemy troop movements, disrupt supply lines, overcome battlefield deficiencies, and protect already-held territory. Most states had little reason to question landmines as a weapon; indeed, they saw landmines as having genuine military utility and thus directly serving their security interests.

Given the commonplace acceptance of landmines by states, it is not surprising that the critique of landmines emerged outside of governments. As mentioned, humanitarian NGOs and peace groups joined forces in the early 1990s to push for a ban. Their reasoning was based on a combination of factors. First, landmines fail to distinguish soldiers from civilians, and thus have an indiscriminate character that is at odds with long traditions of international law that call for protecting civilians from combat. Although estimates are unreliable, many scholars claim that close to 26,000 people are either killed or maimed by landmines each year. This works out to roughly five hundred per week.[20] The vast majority of these people—by some estimates 80–90 percent—are civilians.[21]

Second, landmines raise significant challenges for peacekeeping forces and postwar reconstruction and development. In the former Yugoslavia, where an estimated three million landmines lay in Bosnia alone,[22] 42 UN peacekeepers were killed and 315 injured in the aftermath of the conflict.[23] This has made peacekeeping a difficult task and has dampened enthusiasm for peacekeeping in general. Furthermore, in postwar settings such as Cambodia, Afghanistan, and Angola, landmines litter the landscape such that civilians and combatants have trouble returning home and significant stretches of land are off limits to food production and development. This has heightened the challenge of, and diminished enthusiasm for, postwar reconstruction and development.

Third, landmines represent humanitarian tragedies. Because of their design, landmines seek to maim their victims more than kill them. The logic is that a severely wounded soldier is more of a drain on the enemy than a dead one. Landmine victims often require amputations, blood transfusions, and long hospital stays.[24] By almost any standard, weapons aimed at misery and dismemberment but not death, especially those that victimize civilians more than soldiers, raise serious humanitarian questions.

Fourth, landmines can be considered illegal according to existing international law. The 1949 Geneva Convention stipulates that belligerents must weigh military utility against humanitarian costs when considering the use of a particular weapon. Use of landmines have a mixed record of military utility. A 1996 report by the International Committee of the Red Cross found that, in twenty-six conflicts since 1940, landmines had little affect in minor skirmishes and never influenced the course of a battle.[25] To be sure, other data suggest that landmines can be used effectively for circumscribed battlefield purposes, such as protecting strategic locations, channeling enemy forces, and denying certain positions to the enemy.[26] In either case, given that 80–90 percent of victims are civilians, serious questions can be raised about the proportionality between military utility and humanitarian costs.

All of these reasons share a humanitarian sensibility and NGOs consistently emphasized this in their work. Given the mixed record of military utility, NGOs steered clear of arguing that landmines were militarily unnecessary. Rather, they pushed the moral argument. Mines should be abolished because they are an affront to humane sensibilities not because they are militarily ineffective.[27]

NGOs used various strategies to put the moral issue on the international agenda. Once a ban on landmines caught widespread attention, NGOs worked to become partners in information gathering for states, international organizations, and the public. Moreover, they took an active role in designing many of the negotiating terms of the Ottawa Treaty. They were able to do this because they positioned themselves as experts on knowledge about landmines, the status of landmines vis-à-vis international law, and the process of demining. This was not very difficult because the issue area was wide open for such expertise. For instance, before ICBL's work in the early 1990s, there was only one U.S. military manual regarding international humanitarian law and landmines.[28]

A number of chapters in this book explain the character of these partnerships and trace the influence of NGOs in putting the issue on the agenda and translating concern into international policy. It is unnecessary to rehash those descriptions here. What is crucial, however, is to underline how central NGOs have been from the beginning, in terms of formulating a critique of landmines; packaging this critique in language that would win widespread support from the public, governments, and economic actors; and becoming full partners in crafting the Ottawa Treaty. As noted above, there would be no landmines ban, no story to tell, without the work of NGOs.

That the ICBL and other NGOs initiated and facilitated the ban demonstrates that NGOs can influence security policy. Military doctrine is not immune from public scrutiny but is an object of NGO influence. This goes against much conventional wisdom and many conventional understandings of global civil society. Security is arguably the most important domain of the state. National security policy, as Richard Price notes, is "where the state ought to be the most autonomous from society at large and able to set its sights on military imperatives relatively independent of societal pressures."[29] Moreover, the rise of NGO influence is often correlated with the emergence of nonsecurity issues on the international agenda and thus global civil society is often taken to be most relevant when it comes to issues of environmental protection, human rights abuses, poverty alleviation, and public health. The landmines campaign problematizes these assumptions. It demonstrates that NGOs can penetrate the inner sanctum of states; they can participate in the high politics of international security. The landmines ban case, then, represents the political dimension of NGOs' work and this helps justify analytically the idea of global civil *society*.

Conclusion

Students of international relations have developed the concept of global civil society to analyze the political significance of transboundary, nonstate relations. The term refers to the intersocietal dimension of global life driven partly by innovations in communication and transportation technologies. Over the past few decades, NGOs have emerged that organize themselves and coordinate action across state boundaries in the interest of advancing particular political agendas.

As research on global civil society has developed, so have criticisms. Scholars question the heuristic utility of the term by questioning just how "global," "civil," or "societal" such a realm really is. This chapter uses the landmines campaign to test those criticisms. It studies the work of the ICBL and other NGOs to see how much the campaign genuinely operated across the entire world (with input from multiple sources of political action and insight), how accountable the campaign was to outside scrutiny, and how significant the campaign's work was. The evidence suggests that the campaign was not simply Western, nor were participating NGOs completely on their own to pursue objectives without any mechanisms of accountability, nor was the campaign aimed at a marginal issue. To put it positively, the chapter finds that there are strong global, civil, and societal dimensions to the campaign. To be sure, this does not relieve the campaign of due criticism nor does it prove that all NGOs operating in the world today—whatever their political stripes—are like those working to ban landmines. Many NGOs are parochial, use their power in an arbitrary fashion, and focus on political issues that are extremely marginal to states. Nonetheless, it is important to recognize the global, civic, and societal character of the landmines ban campaign. It represents a strong case for taking seriously the claims of theorists of global civil society.

Notes

1. Richard Matthew, "Excavating Violence: The Transnational Politics of the Mine Ban Movement" (paper presented at the International Studies Association annual meeting, Chicago, Illinois, February 2001, 13).

2. Ibid., 12.

3. John Boli and George Thomas, "INGOs and the Organization of World Culture," in *Constructing World Culture: International Nongovernmental Organizations* since 1875 (Stanford, CA: Stanford University Press, 1999).

4. Kenneth Rutherford, "The Evolving Arms Control Agenda: Implications of the Role of NGOs in Banning Landmines," *World Politics* 53, no. 1 (2000): 74–114. See also Rutherford's chapter in this volume.

5. See www.icbl.org (May 30, 2001); and www.icbl.org/news/2001/111.php.

6. See www.icbl.org/index_frames.html?country/afghanistan/.

7. Richard Matthew, *Dichotomy of Power: Nation versus State in International Relations* (Lanham, MD: Rowman and Littlefield, 2002).

8. Matthew, "Excavating Violence."

9. P. J. Simmons, "Learning to Live with NGOs," *Foreign Policy* (Fall 1998): 82–96.

10. Ralph Miliband, *The State in Capitalist Society* (New York: Basic Books, 1969).

11. See Robert Dahl, *Polyarchy: Participation and Opposition* (New Haven, CT: Yale University Press, 1972); and Robert Dahl, *Democracy and Its Critics* (New Haven, CT: Yale University Press, 1989).

12. For this criticism and others, see Elmer Eric Schattschneider, *The Semisovereign People: A Realist's View of Democracy in America* (New York: Holt, Rinehart and Winston, 1960).

13. See, for example, Peter Evans, Dietrich Rueschemeyer, and Theda Skocpol, eds., *Bringing the State Back In* (New York: Cambridge University Press, 1985).

14. Hedley Bull, *The Anarchical Society: A Study of Order in World Politics* (New York: Columbia University Press, 1977).

15. Rutherford, "The Evolving Arms Control Agenda"; Richard Price, "Reversing the Gun Sights: Transnational Civil Society Targets Land Mines," *International Organization* 52, no. 3 (1998): 613–644.

16. Ramesh Thakur and William Maley, "The Ottawa Convention on Landmines: A Landmark Humanitarian Treaty in Arms Control?" *Global Governance* 5, no. 3 (1999): 273–302.

17. James Rosenau, *Turbulence in World Politics* (Princeton, NJ: Princeton University Press, 1990), 36.

18. Thomas Rochon, *Mobilizing for Peace: The Antinuclear Movements in Western Europe* (Princeton, NJ: Princeton University Press, 1988).

19. Dan Deudney and G. John Ikenberry, "The International Sources of Soviet Change," *International Security* 16, no. 3 (Winter 1991/1992): 74–118.

20. Price, "Reversing the Gun Sights," 618.

21. Thakur and Maley, "The Ottawa Convention on Landmines," 4.

22. Price, "Reversing the Gun Sights," 618.

23. Thakur and Maley, "The Ottawa Convention on Landmines," 5.

24. Rutherford, "The Evolving Arms Control Agenda," 9.

25. Cited in Thakur and Maley, "The Ottawa Convention on Landmines," 5.

26. Rutherford, "The Evolving Arms Control Agenda," 11.

27. Ibid., 7.

28. Ibid., 4.

29. Price, "Reversing the Gun Sights," 613.

20

Human Security and the Mine Ban Movement II: Conclusions

Richard A. Matthew

W HEN THE EDITORS DECIDED TO ASSEMBLE A VOLUME ON THE MINE BAN movement, we had three objectives in mind. First, we wanted a volume inspired by the concept of participatory research. Second, we wanted to make a theoretical contribution to the academic literature on global civil society and transnational activism. And third, we wanted to offer practical lessons and insights to the nongovernmental organization (NGO) community.

Participatory Research

When we designed the volume, we did so inspired by our conviction that the most authentic account of the mine ban movement would emerge from bringing together the diverse perspectives and experiences of practitioners and observers who had been involved at every stage of the process. Thus,

This chapter includes adaptations of several paragraphs originally written by the author for another article: Richard Matthew and Ken Rutherford, "The Evolutionary Dynamics of the Movement to Ban Landmines," *Alternatives* 28, no. 1 (2003): 29–56.

we sought out those who had founded and directed the International Campaign to Ban Landmines (ICBL); those who had joined the coalition from both developed and developing countries; those who have been affected by the Mine Ban Treaty (MBT)—especially deminers and survivors; celebrities interested in supporting this humanitarian cause; journalists and scholars who had studied the behavior of the ICBL as an important example of transnational politics; officials representing countries that support the MBT as well as countries that do not; individuals skeptical of the goals or actions of the ICBL; and military specialists familiar with the use and value of antipersonnel landmines (APLs) in battlefield situations. Through their various contributions we hoped to put together a comprehensive volume that would tell an engaging story and serve as a valuable resource for scholars, activists, and government officials interested in the landmine issue or in any global challenge. We believe we have achieved this objective. We feel that the voices included in this volume are experienced, thoughtful, varied, and authentic. We are pleased with the story that has been told.

To satisfy questions that were raised by the very thoughtful and encouraging external reviewers of this manuscript, we asked several of our nonacademic contributors to deepen the analytical character of their chapters by reflecting on some of the general implications of their observations and comments. While it is not reasonable to expect practitioners to draw on academic literature and weigh in on academic debates, as scholars we are pleased with the analytical contributions of the practitioner chapters. Of course, they are most important for the perspectives and information they introduce to academics, who often lack direct experience with the phenomenon they want to explore and understand. As for the academic contributors, we invited them to read through the practitioner chapters prior to revising their work.

While there are challenges in bringing people with very different backgrounds, motivations, and interests together to tell a single story, we feel that integrating diverse perspectives has given this volume a unity that is evident and a message that is valuable for both scholars and practitioners.

The Contribution to Scholarship

Insofar as our second, scholarly, objective is concerned, two themes are prominent in many of the contributions that will be of interest to researchers and educators. First, in this case, the nonstate realm proved highly successful in generating power to affect political outcomes in innovative and effective ways. It did not seek to take control of traditional sources of state power such as taxation and military force (as transnational criminal organizations often do), or to work primarily through state mechanisms such as the judicial process or the United Nations (as many environmental and human rights organizations do). Rather, it generated power by flooding global media with unsettling statistics and images, and by using the Internet and other technologies to build an extensive, transnational coalition that could not be dismissed, discounted, or, ultimately, denied.[1] This network placed such tremendous pressure on states that eventually a small group of them accepted that its demands could not be ignored. They agreed to work with nonstate actors (NSAs) to achieve a bold set of humanitarian goals, even though this pushed these states outside conventional negotiating structures and introduced tensions into their relationships with the major powers of the world, which steadfastly refused to cooperate.

The speed with which this occurred is among the mine ban movement's most remarkable features. To begin with, the impetus to ban APLs arose only a decade ago when NSAs, engaged in a variety of development and other activities in mine-infested countries, determined that the long-term human costs of APLs outweighed by orders of magnitude any military value they might have, and resolved to act together to have them banned. Throughout the 1990s, many states responded to NSA pressure by trying to work through existing arms control processes. When this strategy floundered and grassroots activism continued to mobilize support and push for a comprehensive mine ban, a small group of states agreed to design and pursue a novel approach. Working hand in glove with the ICBL, a coalition of over one thousand NGOs, these states prepared a binding multilateral treaty outside conventional state-centric fora. In less than two years, the treaty was negotiated, signed, ratified, and became law. The ICBL's story demonstrates that state behavior can be affected in a clear and decisive manner—even when the major powers of the world oppose the changes being advocated, as was the case here.[2]

A second and more innovative theme that emerges in many of the chapters in this volume concerns the evolutionary dynamics of the mine ban movement, and, by extension, of the nonstate realm of world politics. State-based fora for negotiating changes to the status quo are often slow and cumbersome. Discussions focused on supplementing human rights with a protocol or treaty on indigenous peoples have crawled along for two decades; attempts to strengthen environmental regimes, such as the Framework Convention on Climate Change, proceed at a snail's pace;[3] the goal of unifying trade and the environment under a common governance structure seems as distant today as it was in Rio de Janeiro in 1992; and efforts to expand limits or prohibitions on military weapons through existing channels proved, at least in the case of APLs, so unproductive that a critical mass of states turned away from the process in frustration.[4] One obvious problem is that these official mechanisms are readily infiltrated and disabled by other political agendas, as was demonstrated clearly in the United Nations Security Council during the Cold War.

In contrast, nonstate actors have designed negotiating systems that are far better synchronized with the voluminous information, high speed, and participatory character of the technologies that today shape social life and enable global civil society. They are able to generate policies, or policy recommendations, through negotiations that are quick, fair, and inclusive. Most important, the high-tech discursive settings in which they operate allow policy positions to evolve quickly as new information and perspectives arise. The ICBL not only helped develop an alternative sociopolitical structure within which states could act, it also developed a dynamic network that would both keep this structure from calcifying and influence social behavior in its own right.

The contributors to this volume show not only how quickly the mine ban movement emerged but also how rapidly it is accommodating new information and needs. From its early focus on the humanitarian costs of APLs and its early goal of creating a mine-free world a mere ten years ago, it has moved toward also assessing costs in social and ecological terms and in focusing demining efforts on those areas where they will have the greatest impact in reducing human insecurity and expanding livelihood opportunities. These changes have been generated through the frank discussion, diffuse information exchanges, backroom hardball, and constant feedback that characterize transnational politics. As new ideas and needs have arisen, they have been transmitted to those states willing to work with the nonstate arena, keeping the mine ban movement forward-looking and responsive to the needs of real individuals and communities.

In other words, following its incredible success, the ICBL did not take a vacation. Throughout the last years of the 1990s, it worked tirelessly to pressure states into ratifying the treaty they had signed. Consider, for example, a typical month in the life of the movement, as reported by the New Zealand Campaign Against Landmines:

November 1 [1998]:   Seminar in Bhubaneswar, Orissa, India.

1:   Toronto, Canada. Benefit Concert to raise funds for mine action organized by "consort caritatis," organization of musicians.

2:   Bangkok, Thailand. Premiere of "Life After Land Mines—Survivor Stories" (video by Karen Landmine survivors) and discussion following.

2–7:   Nairobi, Kenya. Workshop on Care and Rehabilitation of Landmine Victims, organized by IPPNW-Kenya.

5–6:   Geneva, Switzerland. Planning Meeting for the Hague Appeal for Justice and Peace.

8–14:   UN International Week of Science & Peace.

10–15:   APEC meeting in Kuala Lumpur, Malaysia.

20:   Universal Children's Day.

20:   Peshawar, Pakistan. Conference on Landmines and Children of the Universe, coinciding with Universal Children's Day, hosted by the Pakistan Campaign to Ban Landmines.

28–29:   Tokyo, Japan. "Ottawa: What Should We Do Next?" The Third NGO Tokyo Conference on Anti-Personnel Landmines hosted by the Organizing Committee of the NGO Tokyo Conference on APL, Association to Said Refugees, Japan (AAR).[5]

This activity continues today, and is likely to continue for many more years. As Wapner argues in chapter 19, we are seeing a global civil society emerge.

The conclusions we are suggesting here speak to a very dynamic literature in the field of international relations. For example, in his landmark study, *Turbulence in World Politics*, James N. Rosenau develops three themes:

> One involves the present era as a historical breakpoint. The second concerns a bifurcation of macro global structures into what is called "the two worlds of world politics" [state and nonstate]. The third focuses on the micro level and the hypothesis that the analytical and emotional skills of adults in every country are increasing.[6]

After developing each theme in detail, Rosenau concludes his study with a description of four scenarios of the future. Put simply, these are (1) states and NSAs merge into a global society with shared norms; (2) states regain the upper hand insofar as the distribution of power is concerned resulting in a "restored state-system"; (3) NSAs become predominant producing a "pluralist" world; or (4) the struggle between states and NSAs continues, a condition Rosenau terms "enduring bifurcation."[7]

Rosenau's theory expands considerably on characteristic functions of NGOs that have been widely acknowledged in the academic literature:

- bringing a neglected issue to the attention of the public and its officials;
- using diverse strategies to build support for a policy position and pressure officials to act on it;

- participating in the design, implementation, monitoring, and enforcement of the policy.

According to Rosenau, as the nonstate world gains experience and expertise providing these services, it may be consolidating a permanent and powerful feature of the global political landscape—commanding loyalty, developing long-term institutions, filling gaps left by states, and reshaping the very structure and character of the international system.

Contributors to this volume clearly demonstrate that, at least based on the experience of this case, the transnational networks of global civil society are dynamic and evolutionary in ways that are probably unprecedented insofar as neglected issues are concerned. As they gain momentum they acquire new perspectives, insights, and knowledge, and in order to remain inclusive and successful, they are compelled to find ways to integrate these into their programs. The politics of the nonstate world is open, fluid, and adaptive.

One explanation for this may be that NSAs do not tend to be bound by constitutions that define their degrees of freedom. Indeed, as some choose to bind themselves to a particular perspective or issue, others are established to extend the overall movement in new directions. This diacritical feature of transnational politics is not shared by states. Of course, this unbounded quality has a downside: constitutions are the basis of a certain understanding of legitimacy; they define political and social roles; they ensure continuity; and they protect against emotionally charged proposals having the day. Insofar as Rosenau's "two worlds of world politics" are concerned, the bifurcation may not simply reflect the fact that some things are better handled by transnational communities while others are better handled by sovereign states. It may also reflect a tension between the desire for the deontological security provided by unbreachable processes, and the desire for the rapid innovations and accomplishments enabled when freedom is given full reign. Ultimately, it is exceedingly difficult in many areas of human endeavor to assess and compare the costs and benefits of acting in accordance with strict rules that have been designed to attain certain objectives, and innovating freely in order to achieve certain ends. NSAs provide opportunities to experiment and focus on consequences that may offset the concerns they inevitably raise about their accountability and legitimacy.

This suggests to us that the case of the mine ban movement is compatible with more than one of the scenarios outlined by Rosenau in the conclusion to *Turbulence in World Politics.*[8] It could be read as an example of the increasing dominance of the nonstate realm. This issue was placed on the global agenda due to the insistence of NGOs. In addition to defining the problems, NGOs defined a solution and engineered it, and now work to refurbish and monitor it. Alternatively, the case could be construed as one in which the state and nonstate realms collaborated to develop and act on shared norms. This was not, one might say, solely the work of the ICBL, but rather a joint venture between the ICBL and countries such as Austria, Canada, France, Germany, and Norway. Or, finally, one might argue that this case is best evaluated in a more general context of a bifurcated world in which state and nonstate actors variously work together or apart, with high levels of consensus or in angry disagreement.

Insofar as the nonstate realm itself is concerned, this case is of great interest because it demonstrates the extent to which transnational politics can grow and change through processes that are extensive, sensitive, and participatory. But it also suggests that one of the great political challenges facing the world today may be to find ways to preserve the accountability and legitimacy that come from constitutionally bound sovereign states, while at the same time benefit from the freedom, creativity, and effectiveness of nonstate ways of generating and utilizing power to influence social behavior and effect social ends.

The Contribution to Activism

Chapter 18 by Stephen Goose and Jody Williams summarizes the practical lessons of the mine ban movement so well that it would be redundant to repeat them here.

Next Steps

Three issues emerge from this volume that might form the basis of an agenda for the future. First, it would be useful to adopt a participatory methodology as the basis for other case studies in transnational politics. This would allow scholars to make comparisons and refine and improve existing theories about global civil society and global governance.

Second, lurking in the background of this issue are valid concerns about the accountability of power that is being generated outside state structures and hence outside the constraints of constitutions and the reach of many monitoring, enforcement, and adjudication systems. It is wonderful that the ICBL was able to mobilize so quickly and act so freely. At the same time, we must be aware that transnational coalitions that are not aimed at addressing global humanitarian challenges—the world's terrorist networks, criminal cartels, and pornographer castes—may follow similar pathways to escape the control of states. Further attention to the general political problem of making sure that power is accountable is desperately needed.

Finally, the contributors of this volume make it clear that much work remains to be done in this arena. The progress has been impressive and substantial, but there are still communities that live in fear, land that is not yet safe, victims who need assistance, and states that have decided to keep APLs active in their arsenals.

This last point deserves some amplification. During the 1990s, a persuasive set of moral, legal, economic, and military arguments emerged condemning the use of APLs. Today, a new challenge is taking shape, grounded in large measure in the post–9/11 effort to combat global terrorism. It seems reasonable to predict that the weak argument made throughout the 1990s—that APLs are required to defend South Korea from an invasion from North Korea—will cede to a new argument that APLs are of great and irreplaceable utility in situations involving special operations forces confronting irregular enemies such as Al Qaeda. APLs allow a lone soldier probing hostile terrain to quickly establish a defensive perimeter—and who would want to deprive this type of warrior the ability to defend himself or herself as well as humanly possible? In fact, high-tension nets, sticky foam, and surveillance systems are among the available technologies that can provide security in this type of situation without leaving a legacy of violence for civilians.[9] The general point here is that as technology changes, the security landscape changes, and hence arguments against the use of APLs will have to be responsive to nonsignatory states that revise the justification for their position.

As this volume makes clear, the ICBL—and perhaps all of transnational politics—is a process, not an assignment. We hope we have opened some windows into this process.

Notes

1. For a useful discussion of the relations between states and nonstate actors, see Paul Wapner, *Environmental Activism and World Civic Politics* (Albany: State University of New York Press, 1996).

2. For an excellent overview and analysis, see Maxwell A. Cameron, Robert J. Lawson, and Brian W. Tomlin, eds., *To Walk without Fear: The Global Movement to Ban Landmines* (Oxford: Oxford University Press, 1998). See also Richard A. Matthew and Ken Rutherford, "Banning Landmines in the American Century," *International Journal on World Peace* 16, no. 2 (June 1999): 23–36.

3. This is in comparison to the speed at which scientists have generated data about climate change and presented arguments for increasingly aggressive action to control greenhouse gas emissions.

4. For a discussion of several such cases, see Kenneth Rutherford, Stefan Brem, and Richard Matthew, eds., *Reframing the Agenda: The Impact of NGO and Middle Power Cooperation in International Security Policy* (Westport, CT: Praeger, 2003).

5. Available at http://www.protel.co.nz/calm/News_Oct98.html.

6. James N. Rosenau, *Turbulence in World Politics: A Theory of Change and Continuity* (Princeton, NJ: Princeton University Press, 1990), 5.

7. Ibid., 447.

8. Ibid., chap. 16.

9. For a discussion, see Richard A. Matthew and Ted Gaulin, "Time to Sign the Mine Ban Treaty," *Issues in Science and Technology* 21, no. 3 (Spring 2003): 69–73.

Contributors

The Honorable Lloyd Axworthy is director and chief executive officer of the Liu Institute for Global Issues at the University of British Columbia. Canada's foreign minister from 1995 to 2000, Axworthy's political career spanned twenty-seven years, during six of which he served in the Manitoba Legislative Assembly and twenty-one in the Federal Parliament. In the foreign affairs portfolio, Axworthy became internationally known for his advancement of the human security concept, in particular, the Ottawa Treaty—a landmark global treaty banning antipersonnel landmines.

Kerry Brinkert is manager of the Ottawa Convention's Implementation Support Unit at the Geneva International Centre for Humanitarian Demining (GICHD). Prior to taking up his post at the GICHD, Brinkert was section head of research and policy development with the Mine Action Team at Canada's Department of Foreign Affairs and International Trade.

Paul Chamberlain is a doctoral candidate in the Department of International Relations at the London School of Economics.

Stacy Bernard Davis is the director for NGO outreach and policy in the Bureau of Political-Military Affair's Office of Weapons Removal and Abatement. She joined the Department of State in 1990 as a presidential management intern and has served in a variety of positions in the Bureau of Political-Military Affairs.

Carlos dos Santos is former ambassador to the United Nations from the Republic of Mozambique and currently serves as adviser to the president of Mozambique.

Glenna L. Fak holds a master's degree in international affairs and administration, with an emphasis on landmine advocacy and research, at Southwest Missouri State University.

Michael J. Flynn, a writer based in Geneva, Switzerland, was formerly the associate editor of the *Bulletin of the Atomic Scientists.*

Leah Fraser is a Ph.D. candidate in the Department of Political Science at the University of California–Irvine and a project coordinator with the Global Environmental Change and Human Security project office at the University of California–Irvine.

Ted Gaulin is a former officer in the U.S. Army and is currently a Ph.D. student in the Department of Political Science at the University of California–Irvine.

Stephen Goose is executive director for the Arms Division of Human Rights Watch and chair of the International Campaign to Ban Landmines (ICBL) Treaty Working Group. He has served as the head of delegation for the ICBL at diplomatic meetings since 1998.

Kevin Hamilton is with the Department of Foreign Affairs and International Trade, Canada. From January 2000 to October 2001, Hamilton was program coordinator for research and policy development with the Mine Action Team of Canada's Department of Foreign Affairs and International Trade (DFAIT). He is currently political analyst for the western Balkans at DFAIT's Southeast Europe Division in Ottawa.

Nay Htun is professor and executive director for Asia and the Pacific at the University of Peace in New York and San Jose, Costa Rica. A native of Myanmar (Burma), he recently retired as UN assistant secretary-general and deputy executive director of the UN Development Programme (UNDP). Prior to joining UNDP, Htun was deputy executive director of the United Nations Environmental Programme.

Colin King left the British army as a major after fourteen years, having served as a bomb disposal officer in a number of operational theaters. He now undertakes demining and other explosive ordnance disposal work as director of an independent consultancy company and government analyst.

Patrick Leahy, a United States Senator (D–VT), has been the leading U.S. officeholder in the international campaign against the production, export, and use of antipersonnel landmines. In 1992, Leahy wrote the first law by any government to ban the export of these weapons. He led efforts in Congress to aid mine victims by creating a special fund in the foreign aid budget. He was instrumental in establishing programs to support humanitarian demining, and played a key role in pushing for an international treaty banning antipersonnel mines.

David Long is associate professor of international affairs at Carleton University.

Richard A. Matthew is associate professor of international and environmental politics in the Schools of Social Ecology and Social Science at the University of California–Irvine (UCI). He is director of the Center for Unconventional Security Affairs at UCI as well as the director of the Global Environmental Change and Human Security project office.

Lady Heather Mills McCartney is a prominent international advocate for people with disabilities around the world and an international fashion model. She is director and founder of Heather Mills Trust, and has a particular concern for the disastrous and indiscriminate effects of minefields on local communities. Heather is determined to ensure that survivor assistance is recognized as a vital component of demining campaigns

Sir Paul McCartney is an internationally renowned musician and humanitarian.

Bryan McDonald is a Ph.D. candidate in the School of Social Ecology at the University of California–Irvine (UCI). He is assistant director of the Center for Unconventional Security Affairs at UCI as well as a project coordinator with the Global Environmental Change and Human Security project office at UCI.

Claudio Torres Nachón is an international environmental lawyer. He is Landmine Monitor researcher for Mexico and Belize and is the contact for the Environmental Aspects of Landmines Subcommittee of the International Campaign to Ban Landmines. Torres is president of the Veracruz State Environmental Protection Council and president of the Centro de Derecho Ambiental e Integración Economica del Sur, A.C. He has lectured in various universities in Mexico and abroad.

Her Majesty Queen Noor is an internationally renowned humanitarian interested in supporting national, regional, and international projects in the fields of integrated community development, education, culture, children's welfare, family health, women, and enterprise development. Queen

Noor has assumed an advocacy role in the international fight to ban antipersonnel mines.

J. Antonio Ohe is a master sergeant in the California Army National Guard in the field of weapons of mass destruction (nuclear, biological, and chemical warfare) and a graduate student in urban and regional planning at the University of California–Irvine. He is a member of the Global Environmental Change and Human Security project office at the University of California–Irvine.

Donald F. "Pat" Patierno is executive director, Bureau of Public Affairs, U.S. Department of State. He is the former director of the Office of Humanitarian Demining Programs, U.S. Department of State.

Kenneth R. Rutherford is an assistant professor of political science at Southwest Missouri State University. He is cofounder of the Landmine Survivors Network, a member of the coordinating committee of the International Campaign to Ban Landmines, and a corecipient of the 1997 Nobel Peace Prize. He lost both his legs to a landmine while conducting humanitarian work in Somalia.

Oren J. Schlein is currently a program specialist with the Mine Action Team, Bureau for Crisis Prevention and Recovery, United Nations Development Programme. He is the former executive director of Adopt-A-Minefield, a program of the United Nations Association of the USA, a New York-based nonprofit organization.

Paul Wapner is associate professor and director of the Environmental Policy Program in the School of International Service at American University. He is the author of *Environmental Activism and World Civic Politics* (winner of the 1996 Harold and Margaret Sprout Award) and coeditor (with Edwin Ruiz) of *Principled World Politics: The Challenge of Normative International Relations*.

Jody Williams is corecipient of the 1997 Nobel Peace Prize. The founding coordinator of the International Campaign to Ban Landmines, she currently serves as an international ambassador for the ICBL (ICBL). Williams is also Distinguished Visiting Professor for Global Justice Issues at the Graduate School of Social Work at the University of Houston.

Raquel Willerman is the advocacy and education associate for Landmine Survivors Network, a Washington, DC, based nongovernmental organization that helps landmine survivors and other people with disabilities reclaim their human rights.

Index

SUNY series in Global Politics
James N. Rosenau, Editor

Life After the Soviet Union: The Newly Independent Republics of the Transcaucasus and Central Asia—Nozar Alaolmolki

Theories of International Cooperation and the Primacy of Anarchy: Explaining U.S. International Monetary Policy-Making After Bretton Woods—Jennifer Sterling-Folker

Information Technologies and Global Politics: The Changing Scope of Power and Governance—James N. Rosenau and J. P. Singh (eds.)

Technology, Democracy, and Development: International Conflict and Cooperation in the Information Age—Juliann Emmons Allison (ed.)

The Arab–Israeli Conflict Transformed: Fifty Years of Interstate and Ethnic Crises—Hemda Ben-Yehuda and Shmuel Sandler

Systems of Violence: The Political Economy of War and Peace in Colombia—Nazih Richani

Debating the Global Financial Architecture—Leslie Elliot Armijo

Political Space: Frontiers of Change and Governance in a Globalizing World—Yale Ferguson and R. J. Barry Jones (eds.)

Crisis Theory and World Order: Heideggerian Reflections—Norman K. Swazo

Political Identity and Social Change: The Remaking of the South African Social Order—Jamie Frueh

Social Construction and the Logic of Money: Financial Predominance and International Economic Leadership—J. Samuel Barkin

What Moves Man: The Realist Theory of International Relations and Its Judgment of Human Nature—Annette Freyberg-Inan

Democratizing Global Politics: Discourse Norms, International Regimes, and Political Community—Rodger A. Payne and Nayef H. Samhat

Collective Preventative Diplomacy: A Study of International Management—Barry H. Steiner

International Relations Under Risk: Framing State Choice—Jeffrey D. Berejikian

Globalization and the Environment: Greening Global Political Economy— Gabriela Kutting

Imperialism and Nationalism in the Discipline of International Relations— David Long and Brian C. Schmidt (eds.)

Printed in the United States
39608LVS00002BA/130-138